Middle Passages

and the Healing Place of History

Middle Passages and the Healing Place of History

Migration and Identity in Black Women's Literature

Edited by
ELIZABETH BROWN-GUILLORY

THE OHIO STATE UNIVERSITY PRESS
Columbus

Copyright © 2006 by The Ohio State University.
All rights reserved.

Library of Congress Cataloging-in-Publication Data

Middle passages and the healing place of history : migration and identity in Black women's literature / edited by Elizabeth Brown-Guillory.
  p. cm.
Includes bibliographical references and index.
ISBN-13: 978-0-8142-1038-3 (cloth : alk. paper)
ISBN-13: 978-0-8142-9116-0 (CD-ROM)
1. Commonwealth literature (English)—Women authors—History and criticism. 2. Commonwealth literature (English)—Black authors—History and criticism. 3. Women and literature—English-speaking countries—History—20th century. 4. Identity (Psychology) in literature. 5. Emigration and immigration in literature. 6. Women in literature. I. Brown-Guillory, Elizabeth.
PR9080.5.M54 2006
820.9'9287'09171241—dc22
              2006021305

Paper (ISBN: 978-0-8142-5712-8)
Cover design by James Baumann
Text design and typesetting by Jennifer Shoffey Forsythe
Type set in Adobe Minion

TO

Lucius M. Guillory,
my husband and champion

Lucia Elizabeth Guillory,
my daughter, one of the miracles of my life

Marjorie Savoie Brown,
my mother, who watches over me from the heavens

Viola Duplechian LaDay,
my great aunt, who loves me special

Camilla Savoie Joseph, Cora Mae Domingeaux, and Essie Marzette,
my surrogate mothers

Leo Brown, Sr., and J. C. Carter,
my father and my uncle, who loves me like a father

Lelia Batiste, Oakley Ann Brown, Theresa Wilson, John Brown, Roy Brown, Leo Brown, Jr., and Ronnie Brown
my beloved siblings

Drs. Monte Piliawsky, Ted Estess, William F. Monroe, and Violet Harrington Bryan,
my dear friends, who have supported me on this and other labors of love

[CONTENTS]

Acknowledgments	ix
Contributors	xi

Introduction: On Their Way to Becoming Whole
Elizabeth Brown-Guillory — 1

1. Conflicting Identities in the Women of Ama Ata Aidoo's Drama and Fiction
   Violet Harrington Bryan — 15

2. Coming to Voice: Navigating the Interstices in Plays by Winsome Pinnock
   DeLinda Marzette — 32

3. Migration, Transformation, and Identity Formation in Buchi Emecheta's *In the Ditch* and *Kehinde*
   Romanus Muoneke — 52

4. Gloria Naylor's North/South Dichotomy and the Reversal of the Middle Passage: Juxtaposed Migrations within *Mama Day*
   Kathryn M. Paterson — 76

5. Reconfiguring Self: A Matter of Place in Selected Novels by Paule Marshall
   Marie Foster Gnage — 96

6. "What a History You Have": Ancestral Memory, Cultural History, Migration Patterns, and the Quest for Autonomy in the Fiction of Jamaica Kincaid
   Julia De Foor Jay — 117

7. "Tee," "Cyn-Cyn," "Cynthia," "Dou-dou": Remembering and Forgetting the "True-True Name" in Merle Hodge's *Crick Crack, Monkey*
   Joyce Zonana — 139

8. Place and Displacement in Djanet Sears's *Harlem Duet* and *The Adventures of a Black Girl in Search of God*
   Elizabeth Brown-Guillory — 155

9. Recovering the Past: Transatlantic Migration, Hybrid Identities, and Healing in Tess Onwueme's *The Missing Face*
   Juluette Bartlett-Pack   171

Notes   183
Works Cited   185
Index   199

[ACKNOWLEDGMENTS]

I am thankful to Heather Lee Miller for meeting with me at the Modern Language Association convention and for encouraging me to submit the manuscript. When Heather left The Ohio State University Press for a position elsewhere, she turned the essay collection over to Eugene O'Connor, who was warm and encouraging and helped to minimize the tensions related to transitions.

I am especially grateful to the scholars who contributed to this volume. I am thankful for their interest, enthusiasm, and their sustained cooperation as we moved through the various phases of this project. I am humbled by the team effort we expended to produce this volume.

I am immensely grateful to Sarah West Rhodes, currently working on a master's degree in Library and Information Sciences at the University of North Texas, for her invaluable services on this and several other scholarly and creative projects since 2000. I chose to mentor Sarah during her undergraduate education at the University of Houston, and now she reads my work with a solid critical eye.

The University of Houston has generously supported my scholarship and creative writing, and for that I am very grateful. While working on this project, I received a University of Houston Small Grant, an English Department Martha Gano Houstoun Research Grant, and a Women's Studies Grant to support my research at the University of Toronto and at the Schomburg Center for Research on Black Culture in New York City. Also, I wrote and edited portions of the manuscript while I was on sabbatical in the spring of 2005.

I would like to acknowledge my former chair, John McNamara, and my current chair, Wyman Herendeen, for their involvement in and support of my creative and scholarly work. I cherish my relationships with my colleagues and friends in the UH English Department, and I value deeply their continued support.

Finally, I wish to thank my husband, Lucius M. Guillory, and daughter, Lucia Elizabeth Guillory, for allowing me take on fresh challenges academically and personally. They cheer me on and reinforce for me what it means to be in the trenches with those whom we love.

[CONTRIBUTORS]

Juluette Bartlett-Pack is Assistant Professor of English at DeVry University in Houston, Texas, and at the University of Phoenix–Houston. Her articles have appeared in several collections of essays, including *Nigeria in the Twentieth Century* (2002), *Urbanization and African Cultures* (2005), and *Yoruba Creativity: Fiction, Language, Life and Culture* (2005). Several of her articles are forthcoming in *Writing African American Women* and in *African Health and Illness*. She is completing a book-length manuscript on the works of Nigerian playwright and novelist, Tess Onwueme.

Elizabeth Brown-Guillory is Professor of English at the University of Houston, where she is a four-time winner of teaching excellence awards. Her books include *Their Place on the Stage: Black Women Playwrights in America*, *Wines in the Wilderness: Plays by African-American Women from the Harlem Renaissance to the Present*, and *Women of Color: Mother-Daughter Relationships in 20th-Century Literature*. She has had twelve plays produced in Washington D.C., New York City, Los Angeles, Denver, New Orleans, Houston, Cleveland, and Chicago. Ten of her plays have been published in *Black Drama: 1850 to Present*.

Violet Harrington Bryan is Professor of English and Chair of the African American Studies program at Xavier University of Louisiana. She is the author of *The Myth of New Orleans in Literature: Dialogues of Race and Gender* (University of Tennessee Press, 1993) and has contributed articles on African American and Louisiana writers to the *Encyclopedia of American Poetry* (Greenwood, 2005), *Creole: The History and Legacy of Louisiana's Free People of Color* (LSU Press, 2000), and *Literary New Orleans in the Modern World* (LSU Press, 1998) as well as in journals such as *WarpLand: A Journal of Black Literature and Ideas*, the *Xavier Review*, and the *CLA Journal*.

M. Marie Foster Gnage is President of West Virginia University at Parkersburg. She has taught writing and topics in American literature at Alcorn State University, Florida A&M University, Farleigh Dickinson University, as well at colleges and universities where she has served in administrative roles: Broward Community College, Central Florida Community College, Pima College, and Raritan Valley Community College. She has published *A Bibliography of Southern Black Creative Writers, 1829–1953* (Greenwood Press, 1988) and a number of articles on African American women writers in edited collections and scholarly journals, including *SAGE* and the *MAWA Journal*.

Julia De Foor Jay is Professor of English and Director of the Honors Program at San Jacinto College Central, where she won an outstanding teaching award in 1998. She teaches both on-campus and online courses in literature and composition. The author of articles on Ntozake Shange, Beth Henley, Cherrie Moraga, and Maria Fornes, she is focusing her research on language and self-definition in the works of American women playwrights. She has published essays in *Women of Color: Mother-Daughter Relationships in 20th-Century Literature* and in the *Journal of Intercultural Disciplines*. She also acts in Houston-area theaters.

DeLinda Marzette is Assistant Professor of African American Literature at Prairie View A&M University in Prairie View, Texas. She has taught composition at the University of Houston and contemporary Africana literature at Texas Southern University. She is revising for publication her dissertation, *Africana Women Playwrights Performing Diaspora, Staging Healing: Africa, Britain, the Caribbean, and the United States,* which examines the manner in which Africana women writers negotiate issues of displacement and hybridity.

Romanus Muoneke is Associate Professor of English at the University of St. Thomas, Houston. He has taught English at Texas Southern University and at Prairie View A&M University as well as in Nigeria and Ireland (Dublin). His area of concentration is postcolonial literature and African literature. He is the author of *Art, Rebellion and Redemption: A Reading of the Novels of Chinua Achebe* (1994). He has presented numerous papers at conventions held by the Modern Language Association, the African Literature Association, and the College Language Association.

Kathryn M. Paterson is a Ph.D. student in creative writing and literature at the University of Houston, where she has worked with such writers as Dan Stern and Edward Albee. A recipient of the UH Barthelme Fellowship in fiction writing for her story "Assembly of Saints," she is currently working on a full-length play, several academic articles, and her dissertation. In addition to her academic work, she teaches undergraduate- and graduate-level classes at the University of Houston–Clear Lake and serves as mentor and teacher to felony prisoners in a Texas state prison.

Joyce Zonana recently accepted a position as Associate Professor of English at Borough of Manhattan Community College, after fifteen years at the University of New Orleans. Her much-reprinted essay, "The Sultan and the Slave: Feminist Orientalism and the Structure of Jane Eyre," won the Florence Howe Award for Feminist Criticism. Her scholarly articles and personal essays—on Victorian literature, feminist theory, and postcolonial studies—have appeared in *Signs, Tulsa Studies in Women's Literature, Hudson Review, Meridians,* and *Jewish Women's Literary Annual.* She has recently completed a memoir, *Dream Homes,* chronicling her experiences as an Egyptian Jewish immigrant in the United States.

[INTRODUCTION]

On Their Way to Becoming Whole

Elizabeth Brown-Guillory

Since the early to mid-1980s, interest in women writers of color has become increasingly strong, and the publication of critical texts examining women writers from Africa and the African diaspora has not adequately met the demand from scholars in feminist studies, African studies, African American studies, diaspora studies, American literature, American studies, and postcolonial studies. With the inclusion in this volume of scholarship on works by black women from England, Canada, and the Caribbean, the dialogue surrounding migration and identity formation extends beyond the already existing corpus of scholarship that has tended to focus largely on black women writers in the United States and, occasionally, in Africa. One of my motivations for making this collection available was to attempt to fill a void, one that begs for critical texts that explore the burgeoning field of black women writers from Africa and the African diaspora.

This volume grew out of interest expressed by academics in the United States and abroad. Key leadership in the South Central Modern Language Association (SCMLA), the Modern Language Association (MLA), and the College Language Association (CLA) has encouraged me over the years to organize panels around the works of black women writers. The SCMLA special sessions on women writers of color were a hugely successful draw, opening the dialogue to capacity crowds consistently for six years. In 1993, SCMLA approved the "Women of Color" session as a permanent offering of the organization. "Women of Color" continues to serve as a popular session, particularly among junior faculty in the academy who are eager for scholarship that brings together an array of critical approaches to explore race, class, and gender issues impacting identity formation in texts by black writers in various parts of the world. Since the mid-1990s MLA and CLA, both national associations committed to inclusiveness, have taken the lead in encouraging panel proposals on women writers of color for annual conventions. Since

2002, I have organized several MLA and CLA sessions around migration and black women's identity formation, a topic that drew a respectable number of scholars competing for slots on the panels. It became clear to me that there was sufficient interest and need for a volume that might extend the existing excellent critical studies on migration and black female identity.

This volume engages several single-authored texts that treat migration and black women's identity formation: *Moorings and Metaphors* (1991) by Karla F. C. Holloway, who established cultural moorings as the motivation for migration; *Black Women, Writing and Identity: Migrations of the Subject* (1994) by Carole Boyce Davies, who concentrated on migration and opened the discussion as a major field of study; *The Difference Place Makes* (2003) by Angeletta K. M. Gourdine, who offers a plausible definition of diaspora consciousness and explores the importance of place in black women's identity; and *Black Subjects* (2004) by Arlene Keizer, who reexamines slavery as a vehicle for interpreting identity crises in recent black literature. *Middle Passages and the Healing Place of History* is unique in that the essays in the collection offer new insights and approaches to the topic of migration and the politics of black women's identity as well as uncover and engage broader research agendas within the field of black women's writings across the African diaspora. Of particular significance is that this volume—in addition to coalescing these writers' migratory narratives—introduces lesser-known writers and recontextualizes established writers. No other collection, to my knowledge, brings together a multiplicity of critical approaches to literature, including fiction and drama, to as diverse a group of women writers as represented in this volume. In term of depth and breadth, Martin Japtok's volume *Postcolonial Perspectives on Women Writers from Africa, the Caribbean, and the U.S.* (Africa World Press, 2003) comes closest to the objective of this project; however, his volume does not embrace black women writers from England and Canada, nor does it include several emerging writers from a variety of African countries.

I became increasingly aware of the need for a more inclusive volume on black women writers when I traveled to the Sorbonne in Paris in 2000, the University of Bristol in England in 2002, the University of Toronto in 2004, and the Freie Universität Berlin in 2006. In each of these locations, I met with graduate students and faculty alike who complained about the dearth of research available on so vital a group of writers living within their respective countries. On one occasion, someone in a session at a conference where I was making a presentation on black women playwrights asked quite blatantly, "Why haven't you included black women writers from London in your research?" The passion with which she spoke served as an impetus for me to begin the journey of excavating texts by black British women playwrights. My research at the University of Bristol introduced me to nearly twenty black women playwrights currently writing in Great Britain. Additionally, discussions I had with academics in Beijing, China, in 2001 circled back to a need for scholarship on black women writers. Shortly after my research in Asia, Professor Hongeal Sohn of Taegu University in South Korea secured permission to translate and reissue my book, *Their Place on the Stage: Black Women Playwrights in America*. These engagements with academic and nonacademic readers of black women's texts ultimately served as the driving force for initiating my journey to bring this project to fruition. During the 2003 annual meeting of CLA in Washington, D.C., I announced a national call for papers for a volume on migration and identity in black women's literature.

Several unifying threads weave their way through the essays in this volume, the most important of which is the theme of "women on their way to becoming whole." In nearly every essay, the female characters struggle against multiple yokes of oppression, giving voice to what it means to be black, female, poor, old, and alone. Despite debilitating barriers, these women triumph as they migrate to physical, emotional, spiritual, and social spaces of survivability. The movement away from home engenders ambivalence and fuels feelings of alienation, loss, and separation. Characters in several of the studies experience a longing for the mother(land), which leaves them conflicted; there is no possibility of returning "home" without reconciling that the reclamation of self depends upon an acceptance of competing identities. Hybridity—the mutability of identity—echoes loudly as one resolution in these narratives of separation and loss. Healing rituals also serve as a unifying link in the works of black women writers; these rituals empower women to resist the systems of oppression that are both internal and external to the community. The rituals generally involve water and motion and are intricately connected to reenactments of the Middle Passage and subsequent voluntary and involuntary migrations. The women often race to bodies of water where they bear up each other, riding the waves of disappointment, disenfranchisement, dislocation, and disconnection. The bonds that the women develop become the bridge that allows them to survive destabilized terrain. This volume attempts to answer the questions that emerge from these themes of migration and black women's identity formation: Who are these women? How do they self-identify? What critical methodology allows for such a grouping of women writers from seemingly disparate cultures? Ultimately, the volume coalesces around black women's identity formation and the role that displacement—the common denominator—continues to play in the lives of black women in various parts of the world. The essays examine the journeys taken by women who refuse to accept fragmentation as their inheritance.

While considering an organizational structure for the volume, I discovered that certain topics, which are an outgrowth of the unifying themes, surfaced in connection with specific locales and seemingly provided a sense of the organic whole. These tentative topics—"Black Atlantic Writers: Transgressing Boundaries," "African Writers: Tradition versus Modernity," "African American Writers: Passages and Explorations," and "Caribbean Writers: Longing for Motherland"—invariably proved to be reductive to the essay groupings. I came to recognize that to signal distinction in this collection I needed more critical rubrics that would allow the essays to be grouped relatively free of artificial constraints. In a collection designed to explore border crossings, it seemed counterproductive to try to harness these essays in rubrics that did not coherently and cohesively illuminate this volume's unique contributions. The writers included in the studies have themselves participated in sometimes multiple border crossing, and their narratives replicate the displacement engendered by their own experiences. For example, Buchi Emecheta, born in Nigeria, now lives in England. Tess Onwueme, also born in Nigeria, now lives in the United States. Djanet Sears was born in England but lives in Canada. Paule Marshall, whose roots are in the Caribbean, is recognized as a U.S. writer. Does one define a writer by her current locale or by her place of origin? One point is certain: both the past and the present—like the theme of tradition versus modernity—merge in the selected writers' migration narratives. Also adding to the conundrum was the fact of spillage—themes that applied to one or more groups of writers often applied just as much to other writers listed under a different subtitle. The process of determining rubrics crystallized for me the justification for bringing these groups of women together in one volume: they are sisters, spiritually and emotionally, and in that undeniable relationship it is almost impossible to divide them into separate groups. The ties that bind them outweigh the specific cultural and/or geographical differences. Once I reached that epiphany, I finally understood why I really wanted to publish this volume. I wanted a book that validated what I feel about black women around the world: we acknowledge that we share a common ground, we are not easily divided, and we stand upon each other's shoulders dispensing healing balms. While some critics might point a wagging finger and hurl the dirty word "essentialism," I believe that our history and herstory commingle; the trauma that ensued when Africans were loaded onto ships in chains continues to haunt black women, and men too, wherever they find themselves in this present moment in the diaspora. If in black women's texts reenactments of the Middle Passage are the call, then the healing rituals are the response. I resolved then to abandon artificial groupings and organize the volume around one essential rubric: *Middle Passages and the Healing Place of History*. All of the nine essays coalesce around this one telling rubric.

The women writers that were selected for this volume were chosen because their texts stage displacement and healing—two of the most important issues in the larger research agendas within the field of black women's writings in Africa and the African diaspora. The individual essays congeal around culturally specific experiences of blacks in select African countries, England, the Caribbean, the United States, and Canada. I decided to arrange the essays in a pattern that is reminiscent of the triangular slave trade, which suggests the international and interactive character of American commerce more than describes a specific route. Given the writers' preoccupations with displacement narratives, it seems only fitting that the organizational structure of the volume perform its own reenactment of the Middle Passage and the concomitant sense of loss. While it was impossible for the slave ships to make stops in all of the dispersal sites in the Americas during each voyage, our imaginary ship crosses multiple borders—sometimes making reverse migrations—in this volume. As we journey through the collection of essays, the first stop is Africa, the site of the original rupture, with a study of identity dilemmas by Ghanaian writer Ama Ata Aidoo. Departing West Africa, we sail to England, where we read narratives of loss and reclamation by Winsome Pinnock, who has roots in the Caribbean, and Nigerian-born Buchi Emecheta. The voyage continues from England to the United States, where Gloria Naylor's displacement narrative includes cultural metaphors of Africa. The border crossings continue to the Caribbean, where herstories by Paule Marshall, Jamaica Kincaid, and Merle Hodge delineate the struggles for freedom during a postcolonial era. The narratives' movements back and forth among the United States, the Caribbean, England, and France underscore the destabilization associated with postcolonialism. The ship, picking up steam, then sails into Canada, where playwright Djanet Sears tells of displaced blacks who fled the United States searching for the haven that, in many cases, never materialized. Finally, the voyage concludes back in Africa, where Nigerian playwright Tess Onwueme writes about the missing faces of blacks who were kidnapped from Africa and the ultimate journey to return to the African continent to heal the wounds—the chasm—initiated by the Middle Passage. *Middle Passages and the Healing Place of History: Migration and Identity in Black Women's Literature* is a voyage, in a symbolic sense, that acknowledges the Middle Passage as the tropological site of identity disintegration and attempts to illuminate the various types of struggles black women have encountered on their personal journeys to becoming whole.

The contributors included in this volume represent both established and emerging scholars, most of whom have presented versions of their papers at SCMLA, MLA, CLA, and other national and international conferences. Because I want this book to be accessible to diverse intellectual, ethnic, and economic groups, I have taken care to discourage esoteric scholarship. The scholarship within the essays is both substantial—the essayists have done their research well—and highly readable. I am hopeful that this volume—with its coverage of multiple authors and texts—will be especially useful in introductory courses on black women's literature, of which there is a proliferation in the past two decades, as well as in graduate courses that focus on black women's writings as an evolving genre. The contributors apply an array of theories, including Africanism, postmodernism, modernism, psychoanalysis, postcolonialism, feminism, womanism, negofeminism, and historicism. I offer the following brief summaries of the essays to provide a sense of the breadth of this volume but, more importantly, to entice readers to join the voyage, to participate in the reenactments of the Middle Passage, and to remain on board to witness the healing that reverberates in black women's texts.

Violet Harrington Bryan's "Conflicting Identities in the Women of Ama Ata Aidoo's Drama and Fiction" is an exploration of the lives of women seeking to define themselves on their own terms, both in Ghana and in their migrations abroad. Ghanaian author Ama Ata Aidoo chronicles the dilemmas facing women during neocolonial Ghana—ruled by President Kwame Nkrumah immediately after establishing its independence from England in 1957. Bryan argues that Aidoo, a product of the matrilineal Fanti people of Ghana, constructs complex representations of women in indigenous and modern African societies. She cites critic Maggi Phillips's research on psychic schisms and sites of ritual healing in modern African literature, applying this critique to Aidoo's writing. Aidoo's reliance upon the dilemma tale convention facilitates her probing of maternal subjectivity, one of the central themes not only in Aidoo's work but also in African women's literature in general.

Bryan argues adroitly that Ghanaian women negotiate spaces for themselves in a myriad of roles in Aidoo's drama and fiction, including *The Dilemma of a Ghost; Anowa; No Sweetness Here; Our Sister Killjoy: Reflections from a Black-Eyed Squint;* and *Changes: A Love Story.* Her work explores the longing for home and the painful recognition of the impossibility of returning. The heroines often migrate from rural to urban areas, from Africa to Europe or America, and back again—attempting to reconstitute themselves and to renegotiate space that will accommodate their hybridized identities. The space that Aidoo illumines is one in which multiple, competing identities collide as they experience the ever-changing, fluctuating dynamics associated with displacement and gender restrictions. Bryan offers a much-needed close reading of the texts, revealing Aidoo's emphasis on transition and movement and the many roles that self-exile plays in the formation of Ghanaian women's identities.

DeLinda Marzette's "Coming to Voice: Navigating the Interstices in Plays by Winsome Pinnock" explores the negotiation that takes place within the fragmented interior space of ruptured identity. She argues that the works of Winsome Pinnock, a black British female playwright who has roots in the Caribbean, function as a performance of diaspora. Marzette illustrates a parallel between Pinnock's own ritualistic return home via the creative process and the migrations of her fictional characters. She returns home metaphorically through the creation of characters, embracing the ideology that home is not an empirical impossibility. Pinnock foregrounds movements of exile and return to homeland in *Talking in Tongues*, *A Hero's Welcome*, and *Leave Taking*. She structures her plays around the coordinates of homeland, displacement, and metaphorical return. Her plays—with dual settings that move physically and/or metaphorically between London and the Caribbean—investigate the global dilemma of black identity erosion as manifested by characters suffering from alienation, fragmentation, displacement, and disconnectedness.

Marzette's essay aptly situates black women within Britain's hegemonic codes, particularly when migration continually subverts and reconfigures fixed notions of black identity. Citing postcolonial critics Stuart Hall, Homi Bhabha, and James Procter, Marzette adroitly explains that Pinnock's primary characters attempt to embrace hybridity, to reconcile home with their place of exile. Marzette argues cogently that Pinnock's drama functions as ritual migration, with each performance serving as a mode of journeying home and satisfying a need to belong. Pinnock's women transgress boundaries to claim sanctuary, passage, and nurturance in the interstitial spaces characterized by conflict and ambivalence. Successful navigation of hybridity in Pinnock's plays necessarily involves black women creating and maintaining transformative bonds that traverse generations, geographies, histories, class, and culture.

Romanus Muoneke's "Migration, Transformation, and Identity Formation in Buchi Emecheta's *In the Ditch* and *Kehinde*" examines issues of separation and loss among migrants who traverse foreign lands to flee outmoded, indigenous customs or the hardships engendered by ruthless colonial rule. Buchi Emecheta, a prominent African novelist living in London, fictionalizes her personal experiences to explore the various ways in which migration impacts individual identity in *Kehinde* and *In the Ditch*. Muoneke's essay explores the migrant's disorientation as a result of movements, transformations, and self-reconstruction that must occur during the quest for a useable identity. The transformation generally involves the migrant accepting life-giving elements from both tradition and modernity, which results in a hybridized identity.

Muoneke aptly cites Homi Bhabha and Frantz Fanon in the development of his thesis—the struggle to overcome obstacles in the country of destination leads to a transformation of the individual and ultimately to a search for a new identity that involves multiple forms of negotiation. He argues deftly that Emecheta besets Ada, the central character of *In the Ditch*, with numerous trials in London—abandonment by her husband, threats of eviction from her greedy and unsympathetic landlord, and many other ordeals in a welfare complex—to illustrate the trauma associated with displacement and the determination with which the heroine seeks to redefine herself. Likewise, Emecheta portrays Kehinde, in the novel of the same title, as a woman who, after migrating to London with her husband, is later compelled to return to Nigeria, where she struggles against the demands of patriarchal norms. Kehinde returns eventually to London where she reinvents herself. The essay includes a full discussion of liberation strategies employed by women committed to self-rehabilitation.

Kathryn M. Paterson's "Gloria Naylor's North/South Dichotomy and the Reversal of the Middle Passage: Juxtaposed Migrations within *Mama Day*" explores the connections among history, genealogy, and African American identity. The essay examines the juxtaposition of the migrations and subsequent displacement of Cocoa Day and George Andrews in *Mama Day*. Paterson argues skillfully that in Cocoa's journeys back and forth between North and South, Naylor destabilizes the myth of the free and cosmopolitan North, as represented by Manhattan Island and New York City. Cocoa longs for home when she is in New York, but recognizes the impossibility of returning permanently; as a resolution to Cocoa's conflicted self, Naylor offers hybridity. Paterson presents an intriguing treatment of George's migration to the South from New York, arguing that Naylor metaphorically reverses the journey of the Middle Passage. When George relinquishes his dependence on the dominant American culture, he aligns himself with the African roots of Willow Springs and reclaims his own heritage, as he is physically and spiritually grafted into the genealogy of the island.

Paterson theorizes that Cocoa's and George's various migrations stimulate marginalization within each other, and instead of paralyzing that subaltern within the self and inhibiting integration, Naylor enables full integration by imbuing spirituality into their relationship and allowing the two characters to participate in a dialogue that transcends not only time and space but also death. Paterson approaches *Mama Day* as a text that highlights conflicting modernities; both Cocoa and George are challenged to negotiate spaces of inbetweenness—their African American ancestry and the dominant American culture. Paterson argues that in developing Cocoa and George as fractured, splintered characters, Naylor replicates the initial rupture caused by the Middle Passage. She offers a careful examination of the text to illustrate the various ways in which healing is possible, including reintegration of fragmented selves into a collective, authentic whole. Characteristic of the texts examined in this volume, women take center stage as healers, and in *Mama Day,* Naylor empowers Cocoa's living and dead female relatives with the gift of healing.

Marie Foster Gnage's "Reconfiguring Self: A Matter of Place in Selected Novels by Paule Marshall" is an examination of place—setting, social status, and psychological point in life—and its role in the transformation of women's lives in Paule Marshall's *The Chosen Place, The Timeless People; Praisesong for the Widow; Daughters;* and *The Fisher King.* In each work, "place" is a crucial factor in women's transformation. Gnage examines closely the transformative nature of movement as Marshall's female characters migrate between the Caribbean islands and the United States, England, or France. Products of brutish imperialism, the women in Marshall's novels traffic to new sites, searching for better opportunities and attempting escape from racism and sexism. The characters cross waters in somewhat of a formulaic pattern on their way to becoming whole. Marshall's displaced characters endure tumultuous unrest—experiencing a sense of dislocation as they attempt to embrace their pasts and associated demons—while adjusting to new environs that are, in some cases, as oppressive as those left behind. In all four novels, Marshall's characters experience identity crises because they discount their painful childhood memories rather than seek to integrate their old and new worlds, past and present. Marshall also suggests that the women are fragmented because of a disconnection to their spiritual source: Africa. They must return to Africa, literally or figuratively, as part of their journey to selfhood. Gnage's essay delves into what is lost and what is retained as Marshall's characters attempt to create a space for shifting identities.

Arguing that migration leads to self-discovery, cultural discovery, and historical reference, Gnage cites Carol Boyce Davies and Abena Busia in her study of place and displacement in Marshall's novels. The psychological "place" that each character enters as she journeys toward reconfiguration necessitates a mentor, a spiritual guide, opiates, memories, rituals, and rites of passage—a process generally overseen by a community of women. Marshall presents these characters reaching out to help other women find a safe space—physically and psychologically—one that is conducive to reconfiguration.

Julia De Foor Jay's "'What a History You Have': Ancestral Memory, Cultural History, Migration Patterns, and the Quest for Autonomy in the Fiction of Jamaica Kincaid" examines the plight of Dominican and Antiguan women in colonial and postcolonial societies, as well as their brave struggles to rise above the past and create new, sovereign selves. Kincaid's stories reflect her own heritage and journey for self-determination and a creative, more independent lifestyle. Jay argues capably that the distant past—grounded in the annihilation of the Carib Indians, the involuntary migration of African slaves, the colonization by Spanish, French, and British aristocracy, and the ensuing tradition of abuse, disease, poverty, and corruption—engenders in the women either intense anger or profound despair. Kincaid pays close attention to ancestors who articulate stories that heal; grandmothers function as transmitters of cultural knowledge and are initiators of ritual and ceremony. The women who are in the process of evolving into wholeness, Annie John in *Annie John*, Lucy in *Lucy*, and Xuela in *The Autobiography of My Mother*, in particular, are nearly incapacitated by a history of powerlessness attributable to imperial greed, racism, and sexism. Each heroine, armed with rage and self-determination, challenges old memories and present realities.

Jay's central thesis is that each of Kincaid's heroines despairs of realizing her ambitions—dreams of freedom from place, family, ancestral memories, and powerlessness. For the women, independence from place, Dominica and Antigua, is crucial, for these island dreamlands represent tyranny. Freedom from family, particularly the mother, represents a movement toward a keener, more independent, hybrid identity. Jay concludes that in attempting to counter ancestral memories of colonial marginalization, the women participate in healing rituals that allow them to transgress boundaries and move into a space that offers renewal. A community of women, including Obeahs and surrogate mothers, employ transformative and curative powers to facilitate regeneration in young females suffering from displacement. Jay proffers that the women in most of Kincaid's stories prosper, precisely because of their ties to a community of women.

Joyce Zonana's "'Tee,' 'Cyn-Cyn,' 'Cynthia,' 'Dou-dou': Remembering and Forgetting the 'True-True Name' in Merle Hodge's *Crick Crack, Monkey*" examines Trinidadian writer Merle Hodge's 1970 novel, *Crick Crack, Monkey*, which concludes with her young heroine's movement to the "Mother Country." Zonana insightfully explores the internal turmoil that besieges the narrator, who is torn between the dreams and ambitions of her working-class, dark-skinned "Tantie" and her middle-class, light-skinned "Aunt." Caught between worlds, the narrator eventually longs to be transported to England. Zonana argues that the plot offers no real resolution to the narrator's struggle for a stable identity, but instead tenders ambivalence as a way of life. The adult narrator moves back and forth between her Caribbean motherland with its African oral traditions and values originating before the Middle Passage and her European-inflected, literate modernity. When Tee lives among her "poor relations," she experiences unselfconscious selfhood, which morphs into self-loathing during her stay with Aunt Beatrice, who demands imitation of colonial standards.

Zonana's essay interrogates the novel's evocations of the European "Mother Country," the African motherland, and the Caribbean mother('s) land. She argues that the novel demonstrates the impossibility of a return to the African past—what Edouard Glissant calls "reversion." Yet, because imitation of the white colonial masters inflicts what Glissant calls "insidious violence," the narrator must fashion a hybrid identity, grounded in the present-day realities of the Caribbean. Tee learns that knowledge equals white colonial power equals black marginalization. To survive self-division and self-contempt, the heroine has to accept the shifting nature of black female identity. Through its focus on language and naming, Hodge's novel enacts what such an identity might be; "Tee" is never at ease with her proper name, and "Cynthia" seems finally to accept "Cyntie" as a functional hybrid that will hopefully unite her conflicted self.

My contribution to the volume, "Place and Displacement in Djanet Sears's *Harlem Duet* and *The Adventures of a Black Girl in Search of God*," examines African Canadian women's identity formation as linked to physical, psychological, or social movement. I argue that the plays reveal the nuances of the struggle that black Canadian women endure as they attempt to negotiate destabilizing terrain. Sears's plays reenact the rupture or fissure caused by European colonization of African countries, the Middle Passage, slavery, and urbanization, all of which served to disenfranchise and dislocate blacks. I attempt to underscore the history and cultural practices in Sears's plays that inhibit or advance the transformation of women's lives in Canada.

"Place and Displacement . . ." explores the ways in which Sears's female characters resist negative aspects of both the old and new worlds and struggle to embrace life-giving elements of both. Sears's heroines live amidst contradictions; they navigate in a society that views them simultaneously as valuable and valueless. This study explores strategies for survival among black Canadian women; these characters are able to reconcile contradictions, adapt to ambivalence, and become community builders in an increasingly individualistic, modern society. Sears's plays disrupt assumptions about the Canadian black experience and the idealized experiences of blacks fleeing oppressive conditions of slavery and the Reconstruction era. Citing Leslie

Catherine Sanders, George Elliott Clarke, Renaldo Walcott, and Joseph Mensah, I interrogate erasure and acts of reclamation in Sears's plays. One of the key points of this study is that it offers insights about the connections among race, place, and identity. In Sears's plays—one set in Harlem and another set near Toronto—the heroines resist racist and sexist constraints and form deep, meaningful relationships with women as they struggle to heal old family wounds.

Juliette Bartlett-Pack's "Recovering the Past: Transatlantic Migration, Hybrid Identities, and Healing in Tess Onwueme's *The Missing Face*" argues that Nigerian playwright Tess Onwueme dramatizes late-twentieth-century voluntary crossings and migrations between Africa and America, foregrounding issues of place and displacement. A transplant in America, Onwueme critiques present-day African and African American values, which continue to be influenced by the overwhelming sense of displacement inflicted upon blacks by colonial rule and the Atlantic slave trade. Onwueme portrays the effects of alienation and disenfranchisement on a modern African American woman who immigrates to Nigeria in search of family roots and lost identity, a journey she undertakes after a Nigerian man who had come to America for education and better opportunity abandons her. Bartlett-Pack applies an Africana feminist critique—one that privileges home, family, and community over Western feminism that tends to valorize individual choice to the detriment of imagined community traditions and values—to Onwueme's plays. As a postcolonial writer who interrogates the ramifications of the colonial experience on her characters, Onwueme portrays the clash between Africans and African Americans and demonstrates that continuing conflicts between the two groups are inextricably linked to the initial forced migration. Citing Frantz Fanon and Albert Memmi, Bartlett-Pack examines conflicts that are manifested in feelings of alienation, instability, and assumed superiority. She concludes the essay with an assessment of Onwueme's view that an engagement with one's distant past is not only possible but also necessary for a usable identity in the present.

I view this volume as a recovery project, an act of reclamation, because the contributors participated in rescuing several of these texts and/or the writers from [near] obscurity. This book needed to be written now because the intellectual constituency of several disciplines are earnestly seeking texts that will support teaching and enhance their research. Additionally, and perhaps more importantly, this collection is timely because it underscores the changes, the renegotiations, taking place in world politics and, consequently, literary and cultural productions. Emerging voices are insisting on being heard. The once-rigid literary canon is shifting increasingly toward inclusiveness, a fact suggesting that the global village has arrived, bringing difference. This volume not only recognizes the proliferation of difference in our contemporary world, but it also directs us to study, understand, and embrace it. Without this collection, we can continue to assume that there is an inconsequential body of literature and critical theory regarding black women writers across the globe. However, this collection invites artists, scholars, and the general public to open their ears, eyes, and hearts to texts—specifically by black women writers—that offer healing strategies for the world community.

Should there to be a second volume, one may expect essays on texts by black women from Central and South America, particularly Brazil, whose black population is exceeded only by Nigeria, West Africa. Before Britain's trafficking in slaves began, Portugal had transported approximately 4.5 million Africans to Brazil between 1440 and 1640. Space must be made for critical studies of the works of Brazilians of African descent. Several scholars are now working on translating from Portuguese to English a number of novels and plays by black women from Brazil. When these texts become available, I suspect that a study of these works will enhance our understanding of the African diaspora and its relation to and impact upon world communities. There are millions of blacks in South and Central America who share similar experiences—namely, psychic distress associated with displacement—with their counterparts in different parts of the world. If we can read black women's literature as healing balm, we can begin to transform our individual and collective circumstances. Like the displaced and dispossessed black women in the texts selected for this volume, we can and must cast aside shackles on our way to becoming whole.

[CHAPTER 1]

Conflicting Identities in the Women of Ama Ata Aidoo's Drama and Fiction

Violet Harrington Bryan

In all of her writing—drama, short stories, poetry, and fiction—Ghanaian author Ama Ata Aidoo writes about the lives of women engaged in quests of self-exploration in Ghana and in their migrations abroad. She uses the *heteroglossia* of the many voices of the community as observers and participants confronting the dilemmas of neocolonial Ghana, or Ghana after Kwame Nkrumah, its first president after independence in 1957. Ama Ata Aidoo, product of the matrilineal Fanti people of Ghana, has always recognized the complexity of the woman's role in traditional African societies, as well as in colonialism and neocolonialism. In her drama and fiction—including *The Dilemma of a Ghost* (1965), *Anowa* (1970), *No Sweetness Here* (1970), *Our Sister Killjoy* (1977), and *Changes: A Love Story* (1991)—Ghanaian women continue to negotiate spaces for themselves as mothers, wives, workers, and nationalists. They often migrate from village to city, from Africa to Europe or America, and back again. In attempting to reclaim their identity, they must often migrate from home to what Gloria Anzaldua calls "borderlands," places where "people of different races, sexualities, classes, genders occupy the same territory . . . places where multiple identities collide and/or renegotiate space" (qtd. in Davies, *Black Women, Writing and Identity,* 66). Aidoo's writings emphasize transition and movement, and in women's migrations and self-exile, their reclamation of identity.

Ama Ata Aidoo began writing drama as an undergraduate at the University of Ghana, where she participated in the university writers' workshop founded by Efua Sutherland. Like Sutherland, who believed in the importance of theatre as an instrument of social change and also as a way of preserving the folklore, music, mime, and dance of the people, Aidoo also views her plays as an important expression of Ghana's cultural life. In her plays *The Dilemma of a Ghost* (1965) and *Anowa* (1970), we see Ghana at a crossroads between traditional rural society and urbanization. With the changing roles of men and women, Ghana needed to hear voices speaking out, often arguing, about the women's role in the survival of the national culture.

With independence, many African theaters experienced a turning point that "coincided not only with the rise of a new generation of literary talent," says Karen C. Chapman, "but also with a new sense of practical, shared enterprise—a sense of collective identity that . . . was able to explore itself freely and be explored" (7–8). Ama Ata Aidoo participated in this new adventure in Ghanaian theater. Her first play, *The Dilemma of a Ghost*, which she wrote as an undergraduate at the University of Ghana, was first performed in 1964 and published in 1965. In the play she enters into themes of African recognition of the diaspora and slavery, the conflicted identities of the African American wife, Eulalie, and her husband, Ato, the "been-to," a pejorative term in African literature used to describe someone who has traveled to America or Europe to receive an education and becomes so enamored of the West that he forgets or denigrates his own community traditions. Her second play, *Anowa*, published in 1970, is based on the same African legend as Flora Nwapa's *Efuru*—that of the lake goddess worshipped by barren women. Aidoo explores the themes of self-exile, woman's identity, motherhood, and the African involvement in the slave trade. She uses the dilemma tale convention in most of her literature to raise issues with which the characters contend. The dilemma tale, a genre that is ubiquitous in African folklore, ends with some form of irresolution and makes it essential that the audience take responsibility for making a decision about the drama's outcome (Odamtten 18–20).

Aidoo often uses a protean storyteller—"The Bird of the Wayside," which appears by that name in *The Dilemma of a Ghost* and *Our Sister Killjoy*, "The-Mouth-that-Eats-Salt-and-Pepper" in *Anowa*, the squinting Sister Killjoy in the novel by that name, and Ama and Aba in *Changes*—to comment on the action and the social/political context of the narratives. The narrator also serves as a chorus that gives the reader a second, even third, reading of the drama. *The Dilemma of a Ghost* opens with a prologue presented by "the Bird of the Wayside." The Bird is associated with strangers or wayfarers; in the prologue she does not define herself except to say that she is a shadow, "an asthmatic old hag," "a pair of women chatting" (*Dilemma* 33). What we will hear is a story of the Odumna clan, not everything, "for the mouth must not tell everything. Sometimes the eye can see / And the ear should hear" (*Dilemma* 33). It is the story of an old family, many of whom have become rich and left the village, but this is the story of one who had become a scholar in the "white man's land" and has returned. The community watches and comments as the protagonists—Ato, the young scholar, and Eulalie, his African American wife from Harlem, also very recently a student—come to the stage. The two village women, who come on stage bearing water pots on their heads as they have just come from the river, become a part of the chorus. They discuss the theme of motherhood, which will be prominent, as the young African American woman, Eulalie, searches for her identity in the village of Ato's youth. They also point toward Ato's mother, Maami Esi Kom, who has had to continue the Odumna clan without the help of her son. Hopefully, he will bring new wealth and prosperity to the family after all of his learning. Up to this point Esi Kom has depended only on her brothers and brothers-in-law to hold up the estate.

The grandmother (Nana) also awaits the coming of Ato. She plays a pivotal role in the play and in the community. The grandmother in a matriarchal African society, and particularly among the Fanti, the group to which Ama Ata Aidoo belongs, is honored because she is "believed to be closest to the ancestors, who were important because they could assume god-like status" (Hill-Lubin 37). Ato goes to speak to Nana before he goes to speak to his mother. She is thinking about the ghosts of the ancestors when he comes. When the family members come (Ato's mother, Esi Kom, his sister and uncles), they have fun calling Ato the "master scholar" and trying to bring up the delicate subject of marriage. When Ato admits to his family that he is already married, to a woman named Eulalie, not a Fanti name, Nana asks what she can say to the ancestors: "The daughter of slaves, who come from the white man's land. / Someone should advise me on how to tell my story. . . . / My Royal Dead / That one of their stock / Has gone away and brought to their sacred precincts / *The wayfarer* (my italics)" (*Dilemma* 50).

Maureen Eke describes Eulalie as a wayfarer, but also a sojourner, and in some ways the Yoruba *abiku* spirit, who is "migrating between two worlds, the past (dead) and the present (living). . . . For Ato's people, she represents the ghost from their past come to haunt them in the present" (61). Naana Banyiwa Horne argues that in *The Dilemma of a Ghost*, "Motherhood is situated at the cusp of limitation and transcendence" (308). Mothering is both at the crux of maternal agency and subjectivity in Aidoo's works and in much of African culture. For example, the chorus of the two village women, who represent the community, comment on Esi Kom's childbearing. It has not been profitable, says the second woman, who has a house full of children herself. It has brought her only unhappiness. Esi's daughter Monka will seem never to marry well, and her son, who went away to study, has come back with a "black-white" wife, when he could have married a well-respected member of the community, the daughter of Yaw Mensa. Esi Kom was all ready to pay the bride-price. Even so, the second woman of the chorus, who has no children, prays to Eternal Mother Nature, Queen Mother of childbirth, for her own chance of childbirth (*Dilemma* 52–53).

To Ato's family the most unforgivable thing about the marriage of Eulalie and Ato is that the two are using birth control and plan to have children only when they are ready. Eulalie herself doubts whether this decision to put off childbirth is a wise one. "Ato, isn't it time we started a family?" (58) Eulalie asks when she, in fear, hears funeral drums one evening. However, Ato, playing his role of patriarchal subject, advises Eulalie to stick to their plan and have children only when they are ready (58–59). When the family thinks that Eulalie has a problem with infertility, they come to wash her stomach, heal it, and make her fertile again. The washing will drive away all evil spirits and bring her the ancestors' blessing. Eulalie does not truly understand, but Ato does. He says, "They [the family] would say we are displeasing the spirits of our dead ancestors and the Almighty God for controlling birth" (80–83). When Ato finally tells his mother the truth that his wife is not barren but using birth control, Esi Kom replies, "Why did you not tell us that you and your wife are gods and you can create your own children when you want them?" (91).

At the end of the play, the two women of the chorus envision Ato as a ghost at his door. Earlier Ato had heard the children outside his door playing a traditional ring game and singing the song of "the ghost at the junction":

"Shall I go
To Cape Coast,
Or to Elmina
I don't know,
I can't tell.
I don't know,
I can't tell." (*Dilemma* 93)

Ato is distressed by the song, which he loved to sing as a child. He wonders if he had been dreaming, but the voices come back to him when Eulalie returns after running off and is taken by Esi Kom, her mother-in-law, into the ancestral home. Esi welcomes her in, she who has no mother, but whose mother's ghost probably watches over her as she goes through her adventures in her husband's home. The voices of the children seem to remind Ato again at the end of the play that he is lost and the ghosts of his ancestors are watching him until he comes again into the fold, the community of his people, living and dead.

The dilemma of Ato and Eulalie is a continuing theme of Aidoo. Angeletta Gourdine calls the dilemma of the play "the reconciling of historical dissonance" ("Slavery in the Diaspora Consciousness" 31). Eulalie, a child of the diaspora, does not have an ancestral memory of the past in Africa, and the people of Ato's village have not easily accepted this "black-white woman," who, in her guise as a free-spending modern American, squanders her husband's money on machines she does not need and expresses disdain for the foods, hospitality, and religious traditions of her husband's family. The clash of cultures that Eulalie brings about is the result of the rupture caused by the African past—the Middle Passage, slavery, and racism that Eulalie and her ancestors faced in the United States—and alternatively, the historical amnesia that the people of Ghana and the rest of Africa assume to ameliorate the tragedy and guilt of the past and the oppressive conditions of the present. Eulalie assumes several divergent identities during the play. Her marriage and migration to Africa have been daring. She is a child of Harlem and in the scene when she speaks to the ghost of her mother, she tells her how well she has done in marrying her "Native Boy" and that the country is much better than she would have thought. Her mother counsels her to keep on moving to the top: "'Lalie, you must not stop. Chicken, you must make it to the top. . . . You'll be swank enough to look a white trash in the eye and tell him to go to hell" (*Dilemma* 55). Aidoo's near-caricature of the African American girl from Harlem is somewhat of a mimicry. Her drinking, smoking, and other actions, including throwing away the snails that the mother brought them as a delicacy, and her insults to Ato about his village of "stupid, narrow-minded savages," finally lead to her husband's slap and return insult, "How much does the American Negro know?" (87). Eulalie neither transcends the limitations of her upbringing nor counters the latent patriarchy of her husband's society.

Although Esi Kom accepts Eulalie in the end, she is the ghost of the past, which the people of Ato's village are not willing to face. No one wants to hear about the complicity of Africans in the Atlantic slave trade, although the historical slave ports of Elmina and Cape Coast mentioned in the children's ring game refer to that part of African history. In a similar vein, Eulalie's negotiation of a space for herself in the diaspora gives her a sense of connection with the center of African womanhood and motherhood. However, as Trinh T. Minh-Ha points out, "The center itself is marginal. . . . Wherever she goes she is asked to show her identity papers. What side does she speak up for? Where does she belong (politically, economically)? Where does she place her loyalty (sexually, ethnically, professionally)?" (216). Eulalie is welcomed into the Odumna household at the end of the play, but does this mean she is ready to give birth to a first child? And will she continue to remind Ato's people of slavery and its part in Africa's tortured past? How secure is her identity in the space she has negotiated?

Aidoo, like her mentor Nkrumah, seems to believe that an African recovery of its past is essential to the continent's move toward a productive future. In her second play, *Anowa* (1970), Aidoo continues to work with this theme of "historical dissonance" (Gourdine, "Slavery," 31). Aidoo uses the legend of Anowa to bring together many of the prevailing ideas about women's identity as mother and wife in African society and to create a character who defies these definitions, demanding partnership with her husband in marriage and voicing her opposition to her husband's business in slavery. Aidoo also chooses a particular historical moment in Ghanaian history—1870—thirty years after the Bond Treaty, which put the Gold Coast more squarely under British rule, to describe the dilemma as the Fanti moved toward materialism and imperialism, particularly the "new wealthy trader class of Ghanaians," notably Kofi Ako, Anowa's husband (Odamtten 71).

Through words of the chorus, which in *Anowa* is composed of the Old Man and Old Woman called "The-Mouth-That-Eats-Salt-and-Pepper," the reader learns that Anowa is a "strange woman" and "a child of several incarnations" (*Anowa* 7). At many times during the play, characters, including Anowa's mother and father, allude to her other-worldliness. Her father thinks that the mother should have apprenticed her to a priestess, "to quiet her down" (11); she is really a prophet, "and a prophet with a locked mouth is neither a prophet nor a man" (13). The women of the community, including her own mother Badua and the Old Woman of the Mouth-That-Eats-Salt-and-Pepper, criticize Anowa without pity. Anowa does things that no other woman has ever been able to do successfully. First, she chooses her own husband without consideration of her mother's wishes. Then she disagrees with her husband, Kofi Ako, openly when he decides to make money by trading slaves. While her husband makes millions and becomes the richest man on the Guinea coast, Anowa revolts, never buying new clothes or jewelry, not even shoes, dressing just as poorly as she did when they walked miles from one trade post to the other to run their trading business in the early years of marriage. The community, who criticized the couple so much in their early years, then observes them with amazement. The father Osam and mother Badua discuss the progression of the marriage:

> BADUA: Yes, for someone whose soul is wandering, our daughter is prospering. Have you heard from the blowing winds how their trade with the white man is growing? And how they are buying men and women?

OSAM: Yes, and also how unhappy she is about those slaves, and how they quarrel from morning to night. . . .
BADUA: Which woman in the land would not wish to be in her place?
OSAM: Anowa is not every woman.
BADUA: *Tchlaa!* And who does she think she is? A goddess? (33)

As her husband's wealth increases, Anowa weakens physically and looks within to find her own identity. She sees herself as a wandering soul and a wayfarer. "To call someone a wayfarer," she says, "is a painless way of saying he does not belong. That he has no home, no family, no village, no stool of his own; has no feast days, no holidays, no state, no territory" (37). She has chosen exile instead of the gender constrictions of her village of Yebi. But her husband's "Big House" is also gender-restrictive. The highway, where she and her husband built their trade business together, is the only place where she has been free to negotiate her own space. As Carole Davies puts it: "Anowa's preferred space is that shifting site of transition and movement. Anowa's borderlands are the intersections of gender and class, colonial and neo-colonial relationships, masculinity and femininity, freedom and constraint" (*Black Women, Writing and Identity* 67).

Phase Two of *Anowa* is titled "On the Highway." In the early days of the marriage, Anowa plays an equal role with Kofi Ako in establishing their trading business. They work and sweat together. In the first scene the audience sees Kofi Ako exhausted from carrying monkey and other skins that they will soon trade. Anowa is also carrying skins and is even shivering from her own exhaustion. They have traveled about 270 miles toward the coast with thirty more miles to go. In their exhaustion, Anowa suggests that Kofi Ako take on another wife, who could help them in their efforts. He says that he is not interested in another wife, although he needs her help desperately (she is, in effect, the brains and the brawn behind the business), but he thinks that it would be good to acquire some men to help them in the business.

ANOWA: We were two when we left Yebi. We have been together all this time and at the end of these two years, we may not be able to say yet that we are the richest people in the world but we certainly are not starving.
KOFI AKO: And so?
ANOWA: Ah, is there any need then to go behaving as though we are richer than we are?
KOFI AKO: What do you want to say? I am not buying these men to come and carry me. They are coming to help us in our work.
ANOWA: We do not need them.

> KOFI AKO: If you don't, I do. Besides you are only talking like a woman.
> ANOWA: And please, how does a woman talk? I had as much a mouth in the idea of beginning this trade as you had. And as much head!
> KOFI AKO: And I am getting tired now. . . . What is wrong with buying one or two people to help us? They are cheap. . . . You know, Anowa, sometimes, you are too different. . . . I know. I could not have started without you, but after all, we all know you are a woman and I am the man. (*Anowa* 29–30)

Anowa recognizes that her husband's entry into the slave trade is a way of promoting his business as well as making money in its own right, but it also ends their highway years of "liminal" space. Anowa and Kofi Ako meet in what Homi Bhabha calls a "liminal," "hybrid," or "third" space, where they are able to negotiate their differences in gender, class, and cultural traditions. Bhabha describes this location as a space that "makes it possible to begin envisaging national, anti-nationalist, histories of the 'people.' It is in this space that we will find those words with which we can speak of Ourselves and Others. And by exploring this hybridity, this 'Third Space,' we may elude the politics of polarity and emerge as the others of our selves" ("Cultural Diversity and Cultural Differences" 209). Anowa and Kofi Ako are both in effect exiles from their homelands and for a while are willing to accept their strengths and weaknesses as individuals independent of their social constructions. Kofi Ako is not ashamed to say that Anowa is superior to him in strength and wisdom. "You ought to have been born a man," he says. She is not restricted by her culture at this time either and suggests that her husband should marry another woman. "At least she could help us" (*Anowa* 24). However, almost immediate with his idea of partaking of the new capitalist culture brought about by the Bond Treaty, Kofi Ako begins to criticize Anowa and claim his superior male status. He announces to Anowa, as she sleeps, "Anowa, I shall be the new husband and you the new wife" (27). He also insists that the reason she cannot see herself in the future is because she has no children. "Women who have children can always see themselves in the future" (36). Later we find that the true reason for the couple's inability to have children is Kofi Ako's impotence brought about by his obsession with acquiring wealth. The liminal space of the highway, which allows the couple the liberty to define themselves as they see fit, ends with their reentry into society and their life with slaves at the Big House at Oguaa (Phase Three of the play).

Anowa knows that Kofi Ako's participation in the slave trade and willingness to use humans as material for his own gain is wrong. She sees in his actions a return to the behavior of African ancestors in slavery; she is the priestess and must uncover the truths of Africa's past. The sinfulness of slavery had been made more real to her by the story that her grandmother told her about the Atlantic slave trade when she was a child and the terrible dream she had that night and will always remember. In her despair she tells her dream to the slave women in Kofi Ako's "big house at Oguaa": "I dreamt that I was a big, big woman. And from my insides were huge holes out of which poured men, women and children. And the sea was boiling hot and steaming. And as it boiled, it threw out many, many giant lobsters boiled lobsters, each of whom as it fell turned into a man or woman, but keeping its lobster head and claws. And they rushed to where I sat and seized the men and women as they poured out of me, and they tore them apart, and dashed them to the ground and stamped upon them" (*Anowa* 46).

The dream of the forced migration of Africans to the Americas during the Atlantic slave trade works on several levels. Maggi Phillips discusses the "manifold dimensions" of dream activity in modern African literature (90). Phillips describes dream activity in Africa as "the site of ritual psychic healing; dreamselves travel out of bodies, and sorcerers, gods, goddesses, spirits, and the dead physically enter the dreamers' presence; finally, dreaming transgresses chaos and contacts the highest sacred authority"(90). In Anowa's dream, she becomes Africa herself and feels the multitudes of African men, women, and children, violently taken away from her by the white men. The psychic schism that she feels because of her knowledge of the complicity of Africans in the slave trade is not healed by her telling of the story, but she does share the dream with everyone in the "Big House," in hopes that the acknowledgment of the past will be liberating to herself as well as to all the others who listen.

When she acknowledges to everyone that her husband is the problem for their infertility, that he has been emasculated by his greed in acquiring slaves, and when he hears her, Kofi Ako walks off and shoots himself (the audience hears the gunshot offstage). Then, in a very melodramatic way, Anowa addresses the furniture and the painting of Queen Victoria to tell them that she is leaving as well. The Old Woman of the Chorus runs in to tell the audience that Kofi Ako has shot himself and Anowa has drowned herself—that it was all Anowa's fault: "Anowa ate Kofi Ako up." She has "behaved as though she were a heroine in the story" (*Anowa* 63–64).

In both plays, *The Dilemma of a Ghost* and *Anowa*, the heroines (perhaps anti-heroine, Eulalie) and Anowa (reworked mythological subject) are restlessly searching for their identities. Their identities are unclear, partly because of their complicated existences somewhere between traditional and modern society, but also because of Aidoo's changing alternatives for African womanhood. Eulalie, flawed character that she is, still attempts to declare independence from traditional African society in her decision, along with her husband, to use birth control, until she takes her mother-in-law's hand and walks into the communal existence of the village. The dilemma tales are left with these questions: Is this a healing move or a submission? Even if Anowa's suicide is an act of resistance to a restrictive society that she cannot accept as a part of her lived experience, does her death reflect triumph or defeat? As Opoku-Agyemang writes: "The disappointment of *Anowa* lies in its silence over the alternative avenues of growth for the intelligent, independent woman" (21). Both plays end as dilemma tales, posing questions about women's attempts to establish their subjectivities.

In Aidoo's book of short stories, *No Sweetness Here* (1970), urban as well as village women are renegotiating their space in neocolonialism, a time when many held on to the patriarchal restrictions of African societies, while, on the other hand, women are moving to the city to take advantage of new job opportunities and progressive attitudes. In the city many of them are accepting the Western ideals of beauty, wearing wigs and Western dress; some are becoming prostitutes.

As with her use of orature in drama, Aidoo bases many of her stories on dialogues between characters, as in the story "Something to Talk about on the Way to the Funeral." The story is told by two women who are walking to the funeral of their old friend and neighbor, Aunti Araba. They describe the development of their neighbor's character and her difficulties in finding her way in the society despite her various strengths. The narrator addresses Adwoa as "my sister," conversing with her often in their "nation language." For example, Adwoa says she has just had time to pick up her *akatado* (outer garment) before coming. Reminding the reader that the story takes place during the neocolonial period, she points out that her husband was not able to attend because he was not able to leave his government work, but would come with her to the next *Akwanbo* (village festival).

A typical community person in African society, Aunti Araba is talented, but sacrifices herself to her community and her family. Her voice had always been "delicate"; Aidoo describes her voice as she does Africa on Sissie's return in the novel *Our Sister Killjoy,* and Sissie describes Africa as a place "that felt like fresh honey on the tongue" (*Our Sister Killjoy* 133). She says that Aunti Araba's voice had a "thin sweetness that clung like *asawa* berry on the tongue" (*No Sweetness Here* 114). The Bosoe dance group would sing a "bread song" at the funeral, for they had turned one of Aunti Araba's bread songs into a Bosoe song. She had baked wonderful bread and sold it in the market, although her ovenside became a marketplace in itself. However, despite her strengths, Aunti Araba had had many troubles in her personal life; the origin of them all could be attributed to her "lawyer-or-doctor-or-something-like-that" ("a big man") (*No Sweetness Here* 115). She had a child (who later became "the scholar Ato") with the "lawyer-or-doctor-or-something-like that," who was already married: he was "the lady's husband" (husband of a woman of a higher class). Because of Aunti Araba's pregnancy, her mother treated her very badly, and after the baby's birth she moved away from her parents' home and started to earn money by baking delicious and delicate breads. They would have sold better to the city people than those in the village. "Our people in the villages might buy *tatare* and *epitsi*, yes, but not the others" (117). She finally started baking ordinary bread and married the ordinary laborer, Egya Nyaako. She worked harder than ever to give her son, Ato, a good education, but before he was six, her son was fighting her, and later his natural father, the "lawyer-or-doctor-or-something-like that," claimed him.

When her son Ato's girlfriend from the village, Mansa, got pregnant, as Aunti Araba had in her youth, Mansa and Aunti Araba became close friends and Aunti Araba taught her breadmaking. Nevertheless, Ato refused to marry Mansa because he had also impregnated another girl, of higher class. After the rejection, Mansa left for the city. It was rumored that she became a prostitute, but Aidoo ends the tale by showing that Aunti Araba had passed on her strength to the young woman. In the city Mansa made a living by baking bread with machines. But Aunti Araba became sick. About three months earlier, she had come "to squat by her ancestral hearth" (125).

When the two friends arrive at the funeral, they wonder if Aunti Araba's son, Ato, would come to the funeral. Would his "lady-wife" come? Would the rejected Mansa come?

> "Hmmmn ... it is their own cassava! But do you think Mansa will come and wait for Aunti Araba?"
> "My sister, if you have come, do you think Mansa will not?" (126)

In the eleven stories of *No Sweetness Here* the women face societal problems—adapting to European criteria of beauty ("Everything Counts"); moving to cities to work, sometimes taking up prostitution or other demeaning jobs ("In the Cutting of a Drink," and "The Message"); surviving to take care of children and grandchildren in the rural areas, while the men go away to join the army or work in the city ("For Whom Things Did Not Change"); negotiating with the continuation of polygamy in neocolonial Ghana ("No Sweetness Here"). In the many voices of women in the city and rural areas, Aidoo uses the ancient art of storytelling and verbal performance to portray the varied lives of Ghanaian women. She uses her dilemma tales to raise questions about womanhood and society that remain unresolved. In the neocolonial period, the African woman is left to define herself under changing conditions.

After publishing her two plays, the collection of short stories (*No Sweetness Here*), and several years of lecturing and traveling, Aidoo published her first novel, *Our Sister Killjoy: Reflections from a Black-Eyed Squint* (1977). Odamtten categorizes *Our Sister Killjoy,* as well as her earlier *No Sweetness Here,* as a *nutinyawo,* or collection of prose-poetry narrative performances, ending with a final meditation, "A Love Letter" (119). Traveling from Africa to Europe and back again, Sissie, the protagonist, undergoes a "journey from innocence to experience as she leaves Ghana to sojourn in both Germany and England, and as she returns to Ghana" (Ivory 250). Her observations of Europe are a learning and maturation process, which inevitably open her eyes from the youthful state of *a Black-Eyed Squint,* and teach her to see sociopolitical and racial truths that determine so much of her experience. She begins to see around the "ticky-tackies we have / saddled and surrounded ourselves with, / blocked our views, / cluttered our brains" (*Our Sister Killjoy* 5).

Upon receiving a scholarship from the government to study abroad, Sissie, one of the young people chosen to represent Africa, leaves her home in rural Ghana, travels to Accra, then to Lagos, Nigeria, to meet a plane from Johannesburg, South Africa, that would take her on to Europe. The narrator remarks that most planes were not allowed to stop at Accra because planes from Johannesburg, South Africa, "and other Afrikaaner cities formed a backbone to their African business" (*Our Sister Killjoy* 10). Before leaving on the plane, Sissie is invited to the ambassador's house, where she is unfortunate enough to meet Sammy, an obsequious African, who tells her how lucky she is to be chosen for this trip to Europe: "she derides his role-playing as a Sambo," notes Ivory (253). Sammy is a type that she will meet often on her journey. Later, being asked to leave the front seat with the Europeans from South Africa to sit at the back of the plane with "her friends" (other black Africans) confirms her beginning racial awakenings.

Leaving Africa and crossing the Mediterranean into Europe, Sissie says to herself, "Good night Africa. Good morning Europe" (*Our Sister Killjoy* 11). But the dawn that she expected turns out to be a false promise, tempting like the plums that the young German housewife, Marija, offers her on her first stop in Bavaria, Germany. "Plums," the title of this section of the book, are completely new to Sissie, and she loves them for their traits similar to her, their "Youthfulness / Peace of mind / Feeling free: / Knowing you are a rare article, / Being / Loved" (40). These poetic words of the narrator express the warm feeling of the young Sissie as youth and freshness in a cold, sterile environment, which she looks upon very skeptically, tempt her. Marija, the young wife, in her loneliness, with only her young son, Little Adolf, and her absent husband, Big Adolf, is just as happy to learn something of the world outside of her narrow experience; Ghana, which she confuses with Canada, is worlds away. The dream life ends, however, when Marija tries overtly to start a lesbian relationship with Sissie. Her feelings for Marija have not been completely one-sided, but, as Gourdine says, "Sissie sees her desires as not only a potential source of shame for herself and her family, but also as further evidence of Europeans' negative influences on the African psyche" (*The Difference Place Makes* 96). Both Sissie's private and public selves are involved. Relieved that the time in Bavaria has come to an end, Sissie says goodbye to the lonely Marija, whose ancestry, Sissie reminds herself, includes the slaveholders, colonizers, and imperialists of Europe.

Sissie's next stop is London, where she sees nothing but "been-to's," Africans who have given up their original intentions of returning home because of their infatuation with, and false dreams of acceptance by, London society. All the Africans she meets declare themselves to be students. To Sissie, London seems to say to the many black "students," "Tell us / Boy / How / We can make you / Weak / Weaker than you've already / Been" (*Our Sister Killjoy* 87). Blacks were poor and poorly clothed. If and when they went back home as "been-to's," the ghosts of their former selves, they "lied" about the wonders of living overseas. One of the major topics of conversation in London was of the dying white man who had received the heart of a young black man who had died on the beach. "His heart had been removed from his chest and put in the Dying White Man's Chest" (95). The African intellectual friend that she meets—Kunle—thinks that the event was one of "the beauties of Science" and the hope of future race relations. Kunle, who has stayed in England for seven years, finally returns home to help his family, but showing off as a "been-to," he hires a chauffeur to drive him to work and unfortunately dies in an accident when the chauffeur is going eighty miles per hour. The double irony is that his insurance does not cover an accident caused by such an irresponsible chauffeur, and his family in Ghana will receive no money.

On Sissie's return flight to Ghana, she writes a letter to her male friend in London. Aidoo's orature is complex here, for while she is writing, she imagines her friend's responses. The boyfriend explains that he has reached the top of his profession in London. "And, anyway, all this preaching at us to come home.... What is there? Apart from stupid and corrupt civilian regimes, coups, and even more stupid and corrupt military regimes? (127).

The doctor friend/researcher will stay in the sophisticated place where he has made his name and enjoys the facilities of the best hospitals and laboratories. Sissie returns home to her "Africa . . . that felt like fresh honey on the tongue: a mixture of complete sweetness and smoky roughage. . . . Crazy old continent" (133).

Although Sissie never mails the letter, she is able to carry on her dialogue about the things that mean the most to her—"the importance of language, . . . group survival and . . . reconstructing the future. . . . It [the letter] celebrates Sissy's strength as a woman but mourns what she has lost as a result of her newly defined womanhood" (Chetin 157). Chetin sees Aidoo's decision to end her book with a letter that she does not even send as a new type of closure "that wants to leave behind, to exclude all those who do not share her African female-centered consciousness, a consciousness turned in on itself as a means of resisting attempts to appropriate an image of African womanhood for needs other than the writer's own" (149). The image of the African woman that Sissie personifies is a woman whose identification of her own voice leads to her acceptance of her African home and rejection of migration or "exile." Her travels, in fact, reinforce her developing voice. She puts the restoration of home—nationhood—above romance.

Romance, however, is of crucial importance to Aidoo's next novel—*Changes: A Love Story* (1991). What is particularly surprising in this novel is that the modern career woman, Esi Sekyi, not only divorces her first husband but later starts a relationship that leads to her becoming the second wife in a polygamous affair. Tuzyline Jita Allan, in her Afterword to *Changes,* notes that "the love plot is a common feature in Aidoo's work" (178), but critics generally subordinate the love plots "to 'the loftier' issues of cultural conflict, communal authority, and cultural disintegration" (178). However, in her works Aidoo always couples the personal and the political. A comprehensive reading of her works must encompass both realms.

Esi, a career woman of postcolonial Accra, Ghana, definitely put her career as analyst in the Department of Urban Statistics well above any duties she owed as a wife. As a matter of fact, she and her husband, Oko, have had many battles that affect them and their only child Ogyaanowa long before the morning that Oko commits what Esi calls "marital rape," a term that would not have been validated in any African society. Esi settles on divorce, in spite of the fact that her husband's folks call her a "semi-barren witch and told her that they thought their son and brother was well rid of her, thank God" (*Changes* 70). Esi's mother and grandmother think of her as a fool for considering divorce from a good husband, "her own husband" (95). The grandmother answers Esi's question about love: "Love? . . . Love? . . . Love is not safe, my lady Silk, love is dangerous. It is deceitfully sweet like the wine from a fresh palm tree at dawn.... Ah, my lady, the last man any woman should think of marrying is the man she loves" (42).

Becoming the second wife of the man that she loved, Ali Kondey, who is good-looking but married to his teacher-training school sweetheart with three children, is not all that Esi hoped for, particularly when he starts to stay away for long periods of time, first to visit his other family and three years later to spend time with his new secretary. The life of the modern urban African woman is difficult. There are still customs that she must follow, even in Ali Kondey's negotiation of a second marriage with the elders of her family and with his own. One of the main things required by both families is that he secures his first wife Fusena's acceptance of the arrangement. "In the village, or rather in a traditional situation, it was not possible for a man to consider taking a second wife without the first wife's consent. In fact, it was the wife who gave the new woman a thorough check-over right at the beginning of the affair. And her stamp of approval was a definite requirement if anything was to become of the new relationship" (97). Changes do not occur without nodding to the past and tradition. However, marriage conventions and power relations were changing dramatically in the urban areas. As the two community persons, Ama and Aba of the chorus, note, in modern times it was not just the power of the second wife's father (his wealth, connections, land, etc.) that led to a man's decision to marry again:

> ABA: We must not forget that these days it could be the woman herself who could have such power.
> AMA: Indeed it is not necessary for her to be anybody's daughter if she has the power of beauty, of youth, political, financial.... Nor should we forget high education, a degree or two.
> ABA: A government job with side benefits.... One of the largest pay packets!
> (102)

Such is the case with Esi. She brings her own power, education, and financial package to the marriage.

Odamtten views *Changes* as a continuation of ideas and techniques that Aidoo uses in her earlier works. He calls the novel "a new tail to an old tale" (the title of his chapter 6). "Echoes of her [Aidoo's] other works reverberate through these pages and in her characters' words and actions, so that we are almost taken in by the Bird of the Wayside's performance.... We are allowed to forget neither the personal in the political nor the political in the personal decisions of each of the characters" (Odamtten 162–63). Esi has changed from Aunti Araba of the short story "For Whom Things Have Not Changed," who gives all to her son, loses her son to his natural father when she and her husband divorce, and, finally, is rewarded by a large community funeral that her son might not take the time to attend. Esi has gained in self-assertion and awareness and does not lose her life because of a son's callousness. She has changed from Anowa and is able to confront her husband and face the hostilities and questioning of the community. Moreover, Esi has laid claim to her body and her identity and has written her own narrative of the modern African woman and her acceptance of ancient traditions.

Nevertheless, the end of *Changes* shows that Aidoo's novel is still a dilemma tale, and the answers to all major problems are not resolved. Esi will not divorce her second husband; she will remain his second wife, although it has become evident to her that he is a womanizer, for she has trained herself to embrace material things and job advancement and to accept the inadequacy of his love. Many questions remain: "So what fashion of loving was she ever going to consider adequate? She comforted herself that maybe her bone-blood-flesh self, not her unseen soul, would get answers to some of the big questions she was asking of life. Yes, maybe, 'one day, one day' as the Highlife singer had sung on an unusually warm and not-so-dark night" (*Changes* 166). We see Aidoo's vision of West African womanhood as growing and changing through all her works. The question at the end of her tales remains, "What to do?" A collective of audience, author, and characters will have to decide.

During the neocolonial period in which Ama Ata Aidoo writes her narrative-performances, she explores the many roles that African women play, both public and private. In their quests to establish their identity, both African and diasporic, they often find themselves as wayfarers—dislocated from their roots but also from themselves. Eulalie, of *The Dilemma of a Ghost*, is wayfarer, sojourner, and orphan, in search of her source, the motherland, but confused by the popular Western conceptions of Africa, which she has to transcend before being able to accept or be accepted by her ancestors. Ato, Ama Ata Aidoo's earliest "been-to," is lost as well, for he has adopted Western ways, although the West has not accepted him, nor his village, now that he has changed.

The willingness to remember its past history in the Atlantic slave trade and its complicity in it, as well as to recognize the diaspora of African descendants all over the world, is, as Nkrumah believed, important to Africa's restoration. Recovery of the past and ancestral memory is a recurring theme in Aidoo's literature. Anowa puts herself into self-exile, partly to get away from the gender restrictions of her society, but that migration away from her home takes her into another part of her history, which has always horrified her—the slave trade, which her husband has become implicated in, even during the 1870s. The quest for materialism, in terms of the selling of human flesh, still holds. "The reconciling of historical dissonance" (Gourdine, "Slavery," 31) is not achieved in *Anowa,* nor is Anowa able to attain black female subjectivity. Our Sister Killjoy/Sissie and Esi of *Changes* are also in search of clarity about their identity and the roles they must play for themselves and for Ghanaian society. The issues are raised, although they remain dilemmas for the characters and the audience.

[CHAPTER 2]

Coming to Voice
Navigating the Interstices in Plays by Winsome Pinnock

DeLinda Marzette

> ENID: . . . But this white man country, a black woman less than nuttin'. . . .
> Give me something to save them.
> MAI: . . . Maybe you can save them you'self.
> —Winsome Pinnock, *Leave Taking*

Jamaican-born British scholar Stuart Hall simply but aptly affirms, "[M]ost black experience is a diaspora experience" (273). As a result, black writers at some level engage diasporic issues and impacts in their writings. The experience of diaspora and migration as it relates to black identity can be complex. On the one hand, it fosters a black aesthetic that is rich and diverse by exploding homogenous, one-dimensional notions of blackness; therefore, the literatures of black diaspora are inherently polyphonic, vibrant. On the other hand, a profound sense of alienation, marginalization, and fragmentation often subsists. This is increasingly problematized when one considers the Middle Passage and colonization in that peoples of African descent can be thrice removed from their land of original roots. This dilemma is compounded for ensuing generations of African descent. Africa as "home" becomes largely theoretical, increasingly remote, indistinct, and inaccessible. The migrant is displaced, alienated—sufficiently estranged from both old and new worlds—not quite fitting into either. When considering the deculturalizing and alienating effects of colonization and its configuration within diaspora experience, Jamaica Kincaid—from the perspective of the colonized—convincingly recounts the unfortunate fallout. Kincaid candidly testifies, ". . . what I see is the millions of people, of whom I am just one, made orphans: no motherland, no fatherland, no gods . . . and worst of all and most painful of all—with no tongue" (*A Small Place* 31). Though Kincaid is painting a portrait of postcolonial Antigua, a similar scene surfaces on countless diasporic landscapes, whether in the Caribbean, Britain, Africa, or the Americas. The global dilemma of black identity erosion (alienation, fragmentation, displacement, disconnectedness) and its fast ties to racism and systematic white rule permeate the thematic content, tone, and structure of diasporic literatures. This diasporic stylistic is illustrated in the works of black British playwright Winsome Pinnock, particularly *Talking in Tongues* (1991), *A Hero's Welcome* (1993), and *Leave Taking* (1989).

To better understand the cultural and racial milieu of Britain, one must bear in mind its history of colonization, migration, and black settlement. Britain is the destination site of a series of diasporas; today there are numerous people of color—Africans, African Caribbeans, Hindus, and Muslim Sindhis—who inhabit Great Britain since British colonization of the Indian subcontinent, the Caribbean Islands, and Africa. Long before British colonization, historian Paul Edwards argues there is clear evidence of an early African presence in the British Isles since the Romano-British period (9). Yet, the largest influx of black migration occurred circa 1947 and was largely composed of African Caribbeans seeking better opportunities abroad. Unfortunately, the following decades proved progressively precarious for black Brits who made up a small minority throughout the United Kingdom. In *On being Black in Britain* Chris Mullard contends that blacks were dubiously welcomed in the 1950s, discriminated against throughout the 1960s, and found "Britain's xenophobia had reached a new peak" by the 1970s (174). From Mullard's perspective, a "polarization process" continues to propel governmental, industrial, and social systems in Britain and is exemplified by "obvious hostility towards blacks" and a permeating "acquiescence" regarding white racism (175). Against such a blanch backdrop, black writers of all genres came forward depicting the dynamic life experiences of being black in Britain.

Meenakshi Ponnuswami claims black performers can be traced in British broadcast media as early as the 1930s but cites 1956 as the year of a distinct black British theatrical emergence with male playwrights such as Caryl Phillips (The Caribbean/Britain), Wole Soyinka (Nigeria), and Derek Walcott (The Caribbean) at the helm (217). Soon a growing cadre of black women writers in Britain began cultivating rich, dynamic, literary voices that, in concert, resisted the pervading sense of intolerance toward difference in the United Kingdom. Now we can map a noteworthy legacy of writings by black British women such as Jacqueline Rudet, Maria Oshodi, Buchi Emecheta, Zindika Kamauesi, Beryl Gilroy, Grace Nicols, Amryl Johnson, Merle Collins, and Joan Riley. Many of these women migrated during the 1950s to 1970s from various regions in Africa and the Caribbean—Nigeria, Guyana, Trinidad, Grenada, Jamaica—to train, to work, to study, or to seek exile. Still, some, particularly the younger writers such as Winsome Pinnock and Amryl

Johnson, were born in London or arrived at a very young age with migrating parents, yet these women writers still embrace Afro-Caribbean heritage. All these women writers uniquely occupy a diasporic space that allows them to share experiences from a hybridized perspective.

Pratibha Parmar maintains that because black British women are part of many diasporas, it intrinsically informs and shapes their historical memory and subjectivity; moreover, their cultural identities and perspectives are rich and complex—not static (293). Where do black women configure within Britain's hegemonic codes, particularly when migration continually reshapes any static notions of black identity and cultural perspectives? Furthermore, in what ways do Africana women writers convey their subjective diasporic histories and experiences? Commenting on the unique position of contemporary black British women writers, Lauretta Ngcobo reveals: "[I]n Britain today, Blackwomen are caught between white prejudice, class prejudice, male power and the burden of history. Being at the centre of Black life, we are in daily confrontation with various situations and we respond in our writings to our experiences—social, political and economic. We write about life as we live it" (3). Black British women write their narratives on their own terms, from the distinctive vantage point of femaleness and blackness, which engages the contemporary postcolonial black condition in England and the numerous intertwining issues affecting and complicating the lives of people of color in general and women of color in particular. While simultaneously interrogating the intersection of race, class, and gender issues, women writers of color also expose the problematic effects of migration as it relates to identity. One indelible effect is a suspended, often irreconcilable, state of psychic discord related to migration, dislocation, and (un)belonging. This hybrid space of interstices is a key concern that consistently emerges in the contemporary plays by black women writers of diasporic heritage.

A black British female playwright with roots in the Caribbean, Winsome Pinnock is the product of a diasporic heritage, and many of her plays can easily be described as "diaspora-ization" in writing, to cite Stuart Hall's term (273). More interestingly and specifically, Pinnock performs diaspora. Performing diaspora, in my context, is not only to report migration as historically authentic and veritable, but also to make migrating passages home through the creative and performance acts. "Homing desire" and "movements of exile and return" to homeland are carried out via artistic invention and theatrical performance (Brah 180; Davies, *Black Women, Writing and Identity,* 2). It becomes a negotiatory act or praxis—another creative mode of traversing diasporic gaps and negotiating the strangelands of "entredeux" (Cixous 9). The majority of Pinnock's published plays, including *Talking in Tongues* (1995), *A Hero's Welcome* (1993), and *Leave Taking* (1989), engage migration in a central way. Features of Homi Bhabha's "diasporic aesthetic" and Stuart Hall's "diaspora-ization" are palpable (Bhabha, *How Newness Enters the World*, 301; Hall 273). The plays have dual settings that move—physically and/or metaphorically—between London and the Caribbean. Embracing an ideology of return, Pinnock charts and navigates her own ritualistic return home within her writing and creative process, imaginatively performing diaspora. Episodes of migration, arrival, and return occur through the art of dramatic invention and ensuing performances. Seemingly, Pinnock and her primary characters attempt to negotiate hybridity and wrest a sense of reconciliation with strangeland and homeland. In this way, Pinnock's drama is much more than historical narrative; it is ritual migration, a way of ritually returning home. With each performance, a return home is navigated; the play becomes a performance of passage, a mode of journeying home, of conjuring a sense of homeland and belonging. What also becomes unmistakable in Pinnock's works is that black women create and maintain transformative bonds—across generations, across geographies, across histories, across class, and across cultures—that provide sanctuary, passage, and support in the interstitial spaces of hybridity, conflict, and flux.

Theorists and cultural scholars are continually examining migration as it relates to identity. Frantz Fanon, Albert Memmi, Homi Bhabha, and Kenneth Ramchand have written extensively on the severe alienation that results from colonization and migration. Their research reveals the indelible imprint colonizing conquests have left on the sociopsychic terrain of the colonized. Frantz Fanon's *Black Skin, White Masks* and Albert Memmi's *The Colonizer and the Colonized*—both eminent studies on the psychological effects of colonization—emphasize that the colonizer (oppressor) as well as the colonized (oppressed) are adversely affected. Martinican psychiatrist and writer Fanon argues in his chapter "The Fact of Blackness" that people of African descent in particular—perhaps more so than other colonized groups that are less phenotypically tabooed—internalize an insidious inferiority and uncertainty that virtually ensures alienation. "That this self-division is a direct result of colonialist subjugation," Fanon maintains, "is beyond question" (*Black Skin, White Masks* 17). In this way, the alienation and fragmentation associated with diasporic dislocation—colonizing, self-imposed, or otherwise—has compound, ambiguous, and unsettling results both internally and externally. Kenneth Ramchand suggests this embedded anxiety is a kind of alienation within alienation (231). Likewise, Bhabha's perceptive theories related to the location of cultural hybridity or inbetweenness, which he terms "life at the interstices," is quite fitting when analyzing literatures of the diaspora ("How Newness" 301). Bhabha maintains that such interstitial cultures create literature with a characteristic ethos, a "diasporic aesthetic," which broadly corresponds with Stuart Hall's notion of "diaspora-ization" (Bhabha 301; Hall 273). Clearly, these seminal scholars provide fertile ground for approaching postcolonial literatures of diaspora. Granted, they do not always shed considerable light on the myriad experiences of black women and the unique position they occupy within a postcolonial, patriarchal framework.

There is, however, a burgeoning discourse by contemporary women writers that especially considers the patterns identifiable in works by women of color as they relate to migration and identity. Carole Boyce Davies's scholarship on migrating identities and black women's work, Isabel Hoving's rich concepts surrounding the tropes of exile, journey, and moisture inherent in Caribbean migrant women's writings, and Gabriele Griffin's informative research on the recurring motif of estrangement in plays by British women of color lend keen insight into the unique issues surrounding migration and black female identity (Davies, *Black Women* 2; Hoving 17, 58; Griffin, "Constitutive Subjectivities," 386). Each engages tenets directly associated with negotiating alienation, fragmentation, and migration in a feminine context. These women writers provide intriguing departure points for mapping plays in the works of Winsome Pinnock.

Recalling her own diasporic path in *Black Women, Writing and Identity,* Carole Boyce Davies suggests diasporic migrations form communities and identities that are dynamic but remain inscribed with a circuit that revolves around departure, arrival, and homecoming. Remembering her mother's migration, Davies candidly intimates: "My mother belongs to a generation of women who migrated in search of opportunity. . . . She is also a member of a number of overlapping communities which, with each departure, are instantly hurled into a movement of exile and return" (2). Movements of exile and return can occur in the physical realm or in memory, fantasy, and desire. They are episodic homecomings that share a rootedness in the past, while a certain unrecoverability simultaneously exists. Migrants cannot simply or wholly return to their homeland; it is desirable but often impossible to reify in a tangible, emotive, or immediate way. If a physical homecoming occurs, the migrant often finds herself oddly ill-fitted—a foreigner at home. Lauretta Ngcobo, relating the ambiguous identities of the black British community, admits, "It is a desperately lonely existence. . . . [A]n arrival in a [British] community that will not accept them . . . parallels the way we no longer belong even to our so-called homes in the Caribbean and Africa, after the long years away. . . . [T]he great majority . . . feel sufficiently estranged" (10). Migrant yearnings for home(land) coupled with the complications associated with accessing (a sense of) home (abroad) is problematic. Hence, a sense of rupture, estrangement, and attempts at recovery often configure within the thematic conflicts of diasporic literatures.

Employing and expanding upon Avtar Brah's notion of diasporic space charted in *Cartographies of Diaspora,* and applying Hélène Cixous's intimate account of entredeux described in *Rootprints,* Gabriele Griffin, in "The Diasporic Space in Black British Women's Theatre," eloquently speaks to a motif in plays by black British women that revolves around estrangement. Griffin insightfully observes: "the representation of migration as a movement which places the individual into an estranged relation both to her country of origin and to the place to which she migrates, result[s] in a longing for the homeland on one hand and a recognition of the impossibility of return on the other. Caught in this entredeux, the characters . . . negotiate complex and ambivalent long-ings across generations as they interrogate their own . . . life choices" (1). One can note the sense of ambivalent longings in Pinnock's plays. Geographical and mental settings regularly move from England and the United Kingdom to the Caribbean and vice versa within the plot sequence. These vacillating movements externally reflect the interior or psychological migrations that are not as easily mapped. Ngcobo also recognizes that often black British writings can be thematically "cyclical" and/or internally irresolute: "people are caught up in a whirl of events without resolution" (10). Such structural shifts and cycles in Pinnock's drama move the reader/audience through a kind of virtual migration—relocating us, displacing us, mimicking migrant destabilization. Performing diaspora, Pinnock is our agent of passage; we imaginatively participate in migration and its concomitant alienation. This psychic movement provides an intimate and immediate sense of journeying and return for the audience. Similarly, in at least two of the plays I examine, *Talking in Tongues* and *A Hero's Welcome,* Pinnock seems to represent the ambivalence and alienation associated with displacement through injuries to the feet, which function as a metaphor for violent rupture, hindered mobility, and inability of passage. Just as significant, Pinnock utilizes women as agents of passage through these injurious sites. Female bonds are the stabilizing sites of such passages, and Pinnock regularly relies on woman-to-woman ties to heal, encourage agency, and promote empowerment.

Pinnock's *Talking in Tongues* brings to light the contours of relationships, old and new. This play examines the blurred lines between black and white, wife and husband, and gender and identity. But the transformative bonds between women of color are particularly imperative. On the threshold of a new year, old friends inadvertently unearth intimacies about one another, namely complicated lives with fading loyalties, professional disillusionment, and personal infidelities.

Talking in Tongues, which has been called a performance of social miscegenation, fulfills a contemporary, postcolonial moment.¹ We enter the scene at an already established, culturally hybrid site—multiethnic London. Jeff (white) and Bentley (black), also known as "the two-tone twins," have been friends since college. Likewise, Leela, Claudette, and Curly reminisce about teenage parties. Blacks and whites are intricately interwoven professionally, socially, and sexually, but the racist fallout remains problematic especially as it relates to interracial ties of friendship, sex, and desire. By the fifth scene of the first act, we are aware of two adulterous, interracial affairs, but these relationships are far from equal in power distribution and loyalty. Through Pinnock's critique, we are forced to explore the intricacies underlying interracial desire as well as the ensuing fissure it can cause in black unions. The motivation surrounding interracial desire is a phenomenon that African American filmmaker Spike Lee coins "jungle fever."² From a psychoanalytical perspective, Fanon hyperbolically argues that because the blackest part of the black man's soul desires whiteness, "by loving me, she [a white woman] proves I am worthy of white love. I am loved like a white man. . . . When my restless hands caress those white breasts they grasp white civilization and dignity and make them mine" (*Black Skin* 63). Similarly, Grier and Cobbs maintain, "for the black man, the white woman represents the socially identified female ideal and . . . she has been identified as precisely the individual to whom access is barred by every social institution" (91). Usually in the context of vehement debate, the subject of interracial unions is still somewhat taboo even in contemporary discourse on black identity and sexual politics.

In *Talking in Tongues*, Claudette and Leela experience rupture and displacement in the midst of interracial desire. Claudette proclaims, "My foot. . . . He trod on my toe. He's crushed it. It's hanging off on its cord . . . trust me to get caught in the stampede. . . . It's always the same when a white woman comes into the room. . . . I'm flat on my back with footmarks all over me" (175). The rupture metaphorically signaled by Claudette's foot injury is directly related to oppression, displacement, and immobility. Carole Boyce Davies points to the importance of freedom and mobility for women of color when she asserts that "[i]ssues of movement, freedom" are directly related to women's "circumscribed or flattened identities" (*Black Women* 3). Though Claudette and Leela are not so physically bound, the notion of injurious immobility and debasement is plain; it represents marginalization at a very intimate and fundamental level. The evocative image of Claudette's flattening or trampling by men, black men in particular, as well as Leela's abandonment by her black husband for a white woman, brings to the fore the unpopular sentiment that black women are at a proverbial bottom, objects of undesirability or worse, invisible. Again, Claudette remarks:

While he's dancing with me he's looking over my shoulder at her. I might as well be a burst blow-up doll he's dragging around.... What is it with our men?... What do they feel when they're holding her? Have you watched their faces when they're holding a white woman? They look as though they're in a seventh heaven. Makes you feel like the invisible woman.... [y]ou [can't] escape from it. She's everywhere you go ... and once she's done ... they're both off without a backward glance ... and he doesn't want to be reminded of the detritus he left behind on his way to the top. (176)

Talking in Tongues frankly reveals in voice through Claudette and in action by Bentley the perspective that some black men prefer white women to black women. This preference seems to be significant in that it is the location of Claudette's psychic injury, which suggests a larger fissure that exists between black female and male relationships. Claudette is injured, immobilized, powerless and left with only anger and hostility regarding her demotion. The black woman in this context occupies a space of outsidership; she is debased and displaced—beyond the boundaries of preference and desire. Just as significant is the concomitant status of invisibility this displacement fosters and perpetuates.

Interestingly, Claudette and Leela are not the only females in Pinnock's plays who are somehow objects of abandonment by black men. In *Leave Taking*, Mai's son is mysteriously in absentia. Enid's husband has abandoned her, and his untimely leave-taking forces her to raise their two daughters alone with limited financial resources. Even in *A Hero's Welcome*, the bonds between black females and males are precarious at best. Time and again, the bonds between women repeatedly emerge as the saving grace for Pinnock's women characters. From the fragile space of outsidership, of alienation and rejection, Leela journeys from London to the Caribbean. Leela's respite is established through the agency and sanctuary of other women, which culminates at the shores of the Caribbean.

The entire second act of *Talking in Tongues* shifts from London to Jamaica, which is pivotal because it charts the site of Leela's climactic transformation at the gully. Within the plot sequence, Pinnock seems to employ what Meenakshi Ponnuswami refers to as an "invocation of diasporic histories" indicative of diasporic writing practice (225). Returning home, either physically or metaphorically, provides empowerment and healing for Pinnock's women characters. And, more often than not, successful migrations—ones of (re)membering and reconciliation—are made by, through, and alongside other women. Leela, assisted by a cross section of women, journeys through struggle and pain. Surely, Leela's passage cannot be made without the key roles of female bonds, which develop into a feminine collective of voice and support.

The evocative character, Sugar, emerges in the second act and is an essential element of the transformation and healing that takes place for Leela. Sugar has blended connotations; it evokes and echoes certain herstories. Sugar, as substance, recalls the commodity associated with the Caribbean's history of plantation slavery and colonization; in this paradoxical sense, sugar connotes bitterness. At the same time—perhaps more immediately—sugar suggests sweetness; more specifically, it is an agent of sweetness. Considering both contexts, Sugar—the feminine figure—blends generations of women and (her)stories. Metaphorically, Sugar is the sweet substance that materializes between women across generations, across histories of oppression and survival. In the play's prologue, Sugar recounts girlhood memories surrounding the "mystery of womanness" (174). She retells the story of Jamaican women at the gully—where no man could tread—doing the real work of journey and restoration.

> Them used to say them was going down a gully fe go wash clothes. . . . Sometimes them man would try to follow back a dem, but they would only reach so far before something bad happen . . . no man ever find them. . . . You couldn't move when you hear them singing. Then all of a sudden the silent woman [Dum-Dum] . . . was shouting—a woman I never hear say a word in my life—was shouting to the sky loud loud and saying words very fast in a language must be not spoken for a million years, a language that go back before race. . . . I always wonder what madness them release when they shout out like that. (174)

Dum-Dum—suggesting muteness and ignorance—comes to voice at this site. The entire scene is one of empowerment, healing, and transformation. One "mystery of womanness" that Sugar discovers is that women supply sweet respite, comfort, and support for one another often without men (174). What is also significant is the site of passage at the river—a feminized place of agency work.

Many feminist scholars have focused on the spaces and places of women's work. Vèvè Clark points out, "for centuries women have gathered around the well, or water spigot where these sanctioned areas of communitas allowed them space and time to express the unspoken in their private lives" (251). "Communitas," Clark reasons, are safe sites of "discreet discourse" where women "reform their anger into rites of passage" (250). Coupling this passage with its link to dramatic performance, Clark contends: "Theater has remained a primal site for catharsis. . . . [It] is the quintessential medium for shedding light, literally, on the unspeakable. . . . [T]heater requires that we name the violence publicly, inviting others to witness the display as a form of healing. . . . [W]e learn that theater as a genre offers a unique place for women to transgress publicly against personal, collective, and symbolic violence" (248–51). This phenomenon is illustrated throughout Pinnock's dramatic performance. It is at the river that the women talk in tongues, the site where women can speak the unspeakable and make passage from silenced rupture to voice. As the audience we not only witness women's work of coming to voice and healing, but we also participate in the migratory journey and transformation as Pinnock creates a performance of diaspora on the stage.

Furthermore, the Jamaican women at the gully illustrate and perform the spatial recurrence in migrant women's writings that Isabel Hoving calls the "trope of moisture" (59). Hoving insists that sites of moisture frequently represent the "liquid nature of the Black feminine . . . the threshold, the frontier . . . [the] intermediary areas between lost past, lost tongue, and alienated presence, wherein a new tongue is growing" (59). Hoving observes: "This spatial figuration functions even more strongly as a woman's image, as it separates and links an inside—a home of sorts, traditionally a woman's domain—and an outside . . . from the threshold, while never really leaving it, it undertakes its very specific journey and it negotiates the world by spreading, growing, and flowing" (58). Water as imagined in literature is linked to the feminine and, emblematically, evokes images of cleansing and purgation as well as fluidity, fertility, and growth. Hoving's notion of moisture coincides with Pinnock's scene at the gully in that at the water's edge a "new tongue" thrives (59). It is at the water's edge that these women negotiate their worlds; the water's edge is a threshold towards spiritual growth, where black women make journeys toward healing and wholeness.

The play's climax is located at the water's edge. Coming to terms with her pain, Leela confides to Sugar, "I'm angry. . . . I hate the world that tries to stifle me. . . . I want to lash out" (223). It is at the water's edge that Leela talks in tongues like her feminine forebearers, and it is where Sugar bears Leela up—literally and emotionally—"and rocks her from side to side like a baby" (223). Leela makes a significant journey with the cross-generational, cross-cultural support of Sugar. Like her foremothers, Leela comes to voice and makes passage through pain and finds restoration and rest.

The significance of women coming to voice is emphatically confirmed in bell hooks's seminal work, *Talking Back*. Historically, hooks declares that the most significant and meaningful verbal performances and exchanges took place between and among black women: "The sharing of speech and recognition—took place not between mother and child or mother and male figure but among black women. . . . The intimacy and intensity of their speech—the satisfaction they received. . . . It was in this world of woman speech, loud talk, angry words, women with tongues quick and sharp, tender sweet tongues, touching our world with their words, that made speech my birthright—and the right to voice" (6). *Talking in Tongues* seems to recall a tradition that is characteristically feminine in origin, expression, and maintenance. When one considers Bhabha's notion of "life at the interstices" as well as feminized spaces of sanctuary, I suggest that Pinnock utilizes tongues as a primordial language or utterance that negotiates interstitial spaces for her women characters. Many believe that speaking in unknown tongues is a very spiritual act; St. Paul states to speak in an unknown tongue is to speak mysteries to God for inner exhortation and edification.[3] In this light, another "mystery of womanness" that Sugar alludes to is the mysterious ability to access the supernatural (174). In this way, the episode of women talking in tongues is an utterance of healing as well as coming to voice. In *The Healing,* Gayl Jones asserts that chant fills the space between speaking and song.[4] Perhaps talking in tongues can also be viewed as a linguistic mode of expressing the interstices, of somehow speaking the unspeakable and negotiating hybrid spaces of complexity. Coming to voice from the interstices not only supersedes silence but also suggests renewed possibilities and growth, movement from brokenness to healing.

With innovative skill, Pinnock also shows up what occurs and takes shape in between: in between belonging and unbelonging, in between pain and reconciliation, in between hurt and healing, even in between fe/male identity—as in the case with Irma. Haitian-born writer Myriam Chancy, in the prologue to her book *Searching for Safe Spaces,* speaks intimately regarding her own interstitiality further problematized by her blackness and femaleness. Chancy openly admits: "Somehow the road home is always longer and harder than one expects. . . . I continuously attempt to ease myself in a life of 'in-between' . . . with the knowledge that existing in this way is counter to the norms established for survival in a mainstream where power is determined primarily by sex and race. . . . For Afro-Caribbean emigrant women . . . such forced denial often produces a sense of acute alienation" (xi). Pinnock not only considers the alienation and the spaces in between, but she highlights this space. And more than any other device of intervention, it is the agency women provide for one another—mother to daughter, sister to sister, woman-friend to woman-friend—that enables women to traverse and navigate "life at the interstices" (Bhabha, "How Newness," 301).

Irma is a marked example of Pinnock's treatment of interstitiality, the spaces of inbetweenness, the spaces of hybridity and flux. Stuart Hall notes that contemporary black British artists iconoclastically express diasporic experience through hybridized representations: "The new politics of representation [by black British artists] has to do with an awareness of the black experience as a diaspora experience, and the consequences which this carries for the process of unsettling, recombination, hybridization and "cut-and-mix"—in short, the process of diaspora-ization" (273). Hall's notion of "diaspora-ization" is apparent in Pinnock's treatment of Irma. Irma, a black hermaphrodite born in Britain, is the hybrid embodiment of "life in the interstices" (Bhabha 301). S/he is the physical representation of inbetweenness (male and female) in much the same way talking in tongues functions linguistically as the utterance of the interstices. Not surprisingly, when considering Pinnock's reliance on woman-to-woman empowerment, Irma receives unconditional love, acceptance, and direction from her mother. When faced with Irma's dualized gender, her mother supports Irma's hybridity and uniqueness—deeming Irma "perfect" (93). Moreover, her mother saves Irma from surgical genital mutilation. Irma reflects on her birth in Britain thirty years prior: "[T]he doctors told my mother that she had to make a choice, or I would be plagued by severe mental confusion and distress for the rest of my life. . . . However . . . she had already become attached to me and found me perfect the way I was. So even while the surgeon was sharpening his knives mother had wrapped me in an old shawl, woven by her own grandmother, and taken me home" (93). Wrapped in the protective cross-weave of generations of women, Irma, like Sugar, is in touch with the sweet, transformative strength of female bonds. These female bonds are more than passive sentimentality, but a force that encourages solidarity across difference, a way of constructively (re)shaping hybrid spaces. As a result of this awareness, figures like Sugar, Irma, and Mai emerge as strong, self-assured, whole characters that cultivate and maintain a tradition of feminine collective support. While transgressing a conventionally taboo boundary, Pinnock deconstructs either/or boundaries. She not only acknowledges difference, but she pushes the limits by privileging difference. Pinnock reveals a positive, encouraging attitude toward difference, toward an aspect of hybridity that is largely unexpressed within most black communities and much of the conventional Africana literary canon.

Through both occurrences—women talking in tongues and Irma's body politic—Pinnock represents the unspeakable space of interstitiality while underscoring the importance of a body of womanly support, a feminine collective of empowerment. Pinnock gives body and voice to the space of irreconcilability. Migration and irreconcilable spaces surrounding "home" are broached from a slightly different yet traceable angle in Pinnock's play *A Hero's Welcome.*

Winsome Pinnock's *A Hero's Welcome,* set circa 1947, is yet another exploration of Caribbean life laced with conflicting ideals surrounding migration and movement. This play highlights Avtar Brah's notion of "homing desire" (180) perhaps more clearly than any of Pinnock's published plays. The primary female characters of the play—Minda, Ishbel, Sis, and Nana—engage migration and/or movement in fundamental ways. Interestingly, the younger generation of women—Minda, Ishbel, and Sis—seem to associate migration and mobility with their ability either to marry or make passage with a man. Perhaps movement is largely a male activity. It seems that an essential aspect of mobility is intricately linked to accessing money and/or a man. When asking Nana for a love potion, the young women note, "If we're not careful we'll never get married . . . these days it's not enough to be able to cook an' keep a house clean . . . a woman has to know certain tricks" (26). "Home" is a precarious and ambiguous site; while it is culturally intimate and familial, it is also a hostile environment due to stark poverty and the lack of educational and employment opportunities.

On the other hand, Nana, the dramatic matriarch of the play, prefers mobility and an exterior existence based on her own terms. When Len, the play's male "hero," tries to designate Nana's boundaries of movement, she resists. Len duplicitously argues, "You free to come an' go as you please. As long as you don't go further than that line I mark out over there." Nana retorts, "You might as well lock me up" (22). Nana refuses to be imprisoned by the stifling boundaries of others; she designates her own boundaries, if any. Nana regularly takes leave in the exterior world of the island rather than accept marginalization to a circumscribed existence. Because Nana feels integral to her island surroundings, she feels entitled to the outer world rather than fearful of it. When Len asks Nana why she leaves and whether she is frightened, Nana cogently responds: "Couldn't cope with the strain a pretending to be a poor helpless old woman. . . . I'm happier out there. . . . Women like me ain't frightened a nothing. In my day us women helped to build the world with our bare hands . . . scratching a living from the soil. . . . I leave because I've got something to run away to" (22–23). Nana is in touch with her genuine self, her full identity. It is clear that Nana has actualized her place in the world—a place she participated in cultivating. The ability and power to traverse her own space, "to walk and walk . . . and smell the soil," (32) is essential to Nana's happiness, individuality, and womanness. She will not be limited nor let her path be blocked or delineated. Nana, like most of Pinnock's matriarchal figures, including Sugar in *Talking in Tongues* and Mai in *Leave Taking*, emanates a vital, strong force. She is a figure of empowerment who embraces tradition, history, and voice.

The younger Minda, Ishbel, and Sis, however, are still finding their paths and laying claim to their dreams. These young women are precariously situated in the economic world; they are "those people," to cite Mrs.

Walker, the play's middle-class black employer (29). In other words, they are victims of poverty and lower-class citizenship. Sis is forced to discontinue her education "a long time ago" to help her mother at home (29). Minda, a second generation domestic worker, cannot afford shoes. She, much more than Ishbel and Sis, demonstrates a concerted effort to find a better space for herself—primarily through sex and manipulation. Even though Minda is perceived as "a nasty girl," she pushes the limits of female sexual objectification and social mores (29). Minda candidly notes, "I'm too poor to be choosy" (28). Minda comments on her desires to escape the island: "Some people think this island is the centre of the universe. Imagine. They don't think that there's anything beyond that horizon. I want more than that ... much more.... I can't stand to think I'd stay here and rot till the day I died. ... First chance I get I'll be off" (34–35). Minda seems too fast, too mobile for the slower island life. Similarly, when Ishbel and Sis sit overlooking the bay and watching a ship pass—they fantasize of a better life. Ishbel cries, "Oh. Take me with you. Please" (48). Minda, Ishbel, and Sis seek a home away from home; their "homing desire" (Brah 180) is aimed abroad. "Homing desire," in Brah's definition, is bipolar opposite of yearning for a return to homeland, but rather the "indigene subject" or "native" hopes for a home abroad (180).

Len, a soldier, represents for many of the younger generation the triumphant villager who escaped small island life during his military tour of duty. Conversely, Len disputes such illusions about migration: "That's what's wrong with this place. Everybody wants to go somewhere else. Everybody running away without knowing that everything they want they can find here, right on this island ... they leaving the island because they got the promise of a life of luxury an' glamour somewhere else. Is just illusion.... Our place is here ... to stay an' build a better world" (36). Ironically, Len's migration abroad causes him to yearn for and to appreciate his homeland. Conversely, when he returns it is as if "homing desires" (Brah 180) have somehow crisscrossed; many of Len's companions, particularly Minda, Ishbel, and Stanley, actively seek and/or ultimately migrate away from the island. This ambiguous relation to homeland summons up Brah's concept of "diaspora space," which she maintains can consist of entanglements of dispersion as well as staying put (181). This is particularly true as it relates to Minda, who oscillates back and forth regarding homeland. On one hand, she "hates [the] stinking 'rarted island," (38) but then decides to marry Len and stay. In so doing, she admits a sense of feeling settled and safe (45). Soon after, Minda is discontent with the "sit-down-in-one-place-type" of island life and when Len will not take her to England, she runs abroad with Stanley (45). Minda, virtually the anti-hero of *A Hero's Welcome*, thrives on movement to feel alive and safe, not stability and groundedness.

Brah further contends that for the migrant, home is largely an imagined community: "this home is a place with which we remain intimate even in moments of intense alienation from it" (4). Minda, Ishbel, and Sis perceive the island as their homeland; yet it is also a site of limited educational and economic opportunities, which makes home alienating and marginalizing. Again, Pinnock metaphorically critiques aspects of female immobility; these young women have limited options for autonomy and advancement. Like the downtrodden Claudette in *Talking in Tongues*, whose immobility is signified by injuries to her foot, Minda, Ishbel, and Sis are also metaphorically hindered. They, too, must trudge forward through alienation and oppression. Their immobility is further underscored by an underlying notion that progressive movement is markedly reduced without a man. They have not yet experienced or accessed the healing balm of the female community like Leela, Sugar, and Nana; or like Sis's mother, who when challenged with foot injury, "heal[s] right up" from Nana's balm (25). Sis proclaims, "she did rub it in. She say it warm her foot and soothe it" (25). Again, the theme of women as sweet balm, as soothing restorative agency, reverberates throughout Pinnock's drama; a cross-generational feminine collective encourages a foundation of support that can carry women forward.

Interestingly, Pinnock evokes a critical time period of migratory movement and resettlement. Her play is set "on an island somewhere in the West Indies in 1947," which was a historical moment of migration in the Caribbean region (*A Hero's Welcome* 21). In 1948 Britain's Nationality Act went into effect, allowing immigration from her colonies and former colonies. Although there had been smaller waves of diasporic migration into Britain, the *SS Empire Windrush* docked at Tilbury with one of the largest groups of West Indians up to that point.[5]

The postwar sentiment toward migration was one of attraction and promotion; Caribbeans were courted by Britain, and we are exposed to this moment of migratory lure historicized in *A Hero's Welcome*. Stanley—Minda's ultimate vehicle off the island—declares, "All over the island them putting up posters: 'Come to England,' 'Come find a job in England,' 'The motherland needs you.' But how am I going to get a place on that boat I ask myself" (44). This particular island sentiment Pinnock reflects is in line with propaganda permeating the Caribbean at that historical moment. Social historian Chris Mullard insists, "West Indians thought they were 'coming home' . . . and all of them had been brought up to believe that England was the 'Mother Country' . . . most West Indians . . . expected to be welcomed in Britain" (41). Alongside the belief that they would be welcomed with open arms were aggrandized expectations of a material success. When coaxing

Minda, Stanley reveals romanticized, unrealistic ideals of wealthy life found abroad: "You'll like England. . . . They got cars as long as rivers, houses that touch the sky" (45). Minda fantasizes about a home abroad, a strange land never visited but nonetheless desired. Stanley, Minda, and Ishbel are characters at home who long for an imagined home across the ocean; seemingly, a lure pulls them from beyond their communal boundaries. They exemplify the ambiguities of migration undergirded by a "homing desire" situated in a location away from homeland (Brah 180). It is interesting that these characters—all of African descent—do not long for an African homeland, but one even further removed—England.

Perhaps Len's final words best portray the diasporic discord embodied in the migrating soul: "You get sick, I tell you. Not only because you can feel the sea moving in your belly but love sick with desire for the place you going to and heartbroken for the place you leave behind" (54). This cogent sentiment of ambiguity rings true throughout *A Hero's Welcome*. What is most troubling about Minda, Ishbel, Sis, and Stanley is that although they manage to maintain an intimate connectedness with homeland, home is fraught with irreconcilability. Sentiments of exodus abound. There is a sense that the small island homeland is in transition, a migratory flux; what was once regarded as site of stability and belonging may dissolve.

Sis seems to make the most development in her cadre of friends. The most bookish of the three young women, Sis comes to terms with the fact that marriage does not necessarily ensure a better life. She maturely reveals to Ishbel, "Everybody's lonely, Ish. . . . I don't think I ever will marry, Ish. Some people never do" (48). Furthermore, Sis makes a contemplative decision to improve her lot through educating herself. Ultimately, Sis is also "going away" (55). She has an opportunity to go away to study, and since she "can't change the world ignorant"—she is leaving (55). Unlike Minda, however, it is clear that Sis is torn by her decision. Griffin emphasizes in her essay "Constitutive Subjectivities" that characters like these are figures of inbetweenness, caught up in Cixous's notion of "entredeux" and "their identities are shaped by this in-between-ness, and not just along two dimensions. Gender, race, class and a certain idea of origin haunt all the characters who do not want to, or cannot, make simple either/or choices" (Griffin, "Constitutive Subjectivities," 9; Cixous 386). In *A Hero's Welcome*, the coordinates of stability—once epitomized by the island homeland—are destabilized. It seems that many of the primary characters are experiencing the kind of inner alienation and estrangement to which Griffin refers (386).

According to Cixous, "entredeux" is tumultuous and violent—often related to "bereavement and loss" (9). She writes, "Thus, we are launched into a space-time whose coordinates are all different . . . we are thrown into strangeness. This being abroad at home is what I call entredeux. Wars cause entredeux in the histories of countries. But the worst war of all is the war where the enemy is on the inside" (9). For Minda in particular, the coordinates of home and stability are in flux. It is as if she is in a suspended state of discord unable to reconcile her image of home with the reality of home. Instead of wresting safety and stability at home, constructing a home-like life with Lem causes Minda anxiety and discontent. Minda occupies a diasporic space that is geographical as well as psychological; it is a hybrid site of destabilization and migration where her sense of home is "rooted and floating . . . simultaneously a place of safety and of terror" (Brah 180). *A Hero's Welcome* is an intimate psychological snapshot of migratory flux, capturing the intricate complexities often overseen by the naked eye. Pinnock exposes a similar migratory dynamic in her play *Leave Taking*, but from the vantage point of displaced migrants unable to integrate wholly into their new world.

Leave Taking traces the lives of a mother, Enid Matthews, and her two daughters, Del and Viv, who have migrated from the Caribbean to London for an improved existence. These women characters are signifiers of migratory displacement; they are topographical migrants in psychological exile, disconnected transplants attempting to reroot. Enid, perhaps more so than her daughters, lays bare a severely splintered psyche; though she migrated to London, she is emotionally and financially burdened by the relatives and homeland she left behind. Enid poignantly states, "Sometime I feel like a cat chasing him own tail. Going round and round and getting nowhere but dizzy" (164). However, she dubiously reminds herself the "Promised Land," England, is the best place for her to raise her daughters (159). Geraldine Cousin, in her book *Women in Dramatic Place and Time*, accurately confirms how significant place configures within Pinnock's drama. Cousin insists that "[p]lace, in a number of its attributes: birthplace, home, making a place for oneself, feeling displaced, and also the problems of survival in an inhospitable place" is primary when considering *Leave Taking* (48). Cousin's sentiment is reminiscent of my notion of Pinnock's diaspora performance process of returning to and/or (re)covering home and the difficulties surrounding the search for belonging. We see such difficulties emerge in *Leave Taking*.

As a case in point, Enid is displaced—fragmented geographically, emotionally, and certainly economically. Likewise, Enid's daughters speak with the clipped dialect and colloquialisms of Britain in addition to conveying contemporary British ideals; however, they do not seem to fit fully into British constructs of identity. These women attempt to exist and operate in a mental and physical space that is often irreconcilable; it is an ambiguously hybrid space which Bhabha refers to as "living in the interstices" ("How Newness" 301). This interstitial or hybrid space can generate an interior tension, which echoes Frantz Fanon's notion of "self-division," W. E. B. DuBois's "double-consciousness" dilemma, as well as Cixous's concept of inner violence at "entredeux" (Fanon, *Black Skin,* 17; Du Bois 45; Cixous 9). Enid's space of alienation in England is compounded by her husband's abandonment. Enid bluntly divulges a historical response that resounds globally in writings by black women from Zora Neale Hurston to Ama Ata Aidoo: ". . . this is white man country, a black woman less than nuttin'" (148).[6] One cannot help but hear echoes of Janie's grandmother in *Their Eyes Were Watching God,* who poignantly confirms, ". . . de white man is de ruler of everything. . . . [he] throw down de load and tell de nigger man tuh pick it up. He pick it up . . . because he have to, but he don't tote it. He hand it to his womenfolks. De nigger woman is de mule uh de world so fur as Ah can see" (14).

Within the framework of this play, Pinnock's leave-taking women figures personify and demonstrate what Isabel Hoving declares is a "trope of exile" in Afro-Caribbean women's writings (49). This trope, according to Hoving, consists of transient and imagined journeys and violent struggles for belonging; Hoving insists that "postcolonial displacement lands migrants in a discourse of struggle" (49). In *Leave Taking,* Pinnock's women make such journeys and experience such struggles. With aim and desire, Enid migrates to the "Promised Land," England, in hopes of an improved existence and better opportunity, but with heart and soul longing for home (159). Her memory and history are inextricably connected to a home that is no longer at hand. However, Mai assists Enid and her daughters, enabling them to negotiate this gap.

Leave Taking speaks to the transgenerational ties between women that can reach beyond migration. The "old-time" Obeah woman Mai, who "can't live without a few fowl" in her backyard and has African figures throughout her small room that "smells of pigs," harks back to a homeland that Enid has lost in the wake of migration (145). Mai's essence evokes Caribbean culture and homeland in a way that is reminiscent of Sugar in *Talking in Tongues.* Actually, Mai is the bridge that links Enid and her daughters to their Afro-Caribbean heritage. Mai encourages what Myriam Chancy would likely regard as a sound uprooting for Enid and her daughters, which Chancy asserts is particularly difficult for black women since patriarchy, racism, as well as sexism limit movement and safe space-finding efforts (xi). For Chancy, "uprooting sound" is linked to feminized "safe places" that invoke "grandmother's hearth" (22, 30). In similar fashion, Mai provides a safe landing site that blends old and new worlds, which allows these women to (re)discover and (re)member the legacies of strength that lie within them. When Enid intimates, "Them father never give me a penny, just kick the womb out a'me an' go him own sweet way . . . this white man country, a black woman less than nuttin'... [g]ive me something to save them" (148), Mai inspiringly responds to Enid by stating, "I can't... maybe you can save them you'self" (148). Mai suggests a remedy that supersedes Obeah magic. Mai has an empowering and transformative effect on these women's lives.

This transformation is especially true for Del, who initially finds Mai ignorant, backward, full of "mumbo jumbo" (142). As the plot unfolds, Mai develops into a matriarchal mentor in Del's life, and there is a sense that the transgenerational bonds between these women will cultivate and grow. Del is pregnant, which has futuristic implications, and she is also learning the ancient rites of Obeah conjure from Mai. It seems that the past and future have somehow linked within Del. Furthermore, Del restores her estranged relationship with her mother through the agency of Mai. Speaking directly to this cross-generational reconciliation, Cousin emphasizes how this (re)membering "brings into conjunction within the present moment four generations of a family in a way that works to undo the linearity of time" (51). Moreover, Mai's small hovel becomes a site of "communitas," a space of "secret discourse" where women make pivotal "rites of passage" and do the work of healing (Clark 251). The women characters of *Leave Taking* discover alternative spaces of possibility—spaces that are nurturing, healing, and dynamic. Echoing Clark's communitas concept, Cousin correspondingly notes that "the secretness of these places and their link with home constructs them also as inner spaces—places of the heart" (51). By the conclusion of *Leave Taking*, we are left with the impression that contrary to circumstances, these women just might "conjure happiness outa' thin air" (149).

The emphasis on diasporic impacts and the concomitant hybrid space of interim that follows seems to motivate, if not haunt, Pinnock's characters and abides just beneath the surface of her dramatic conflict. As depicted, her diasporic characters are often marked nodes of duality, hybrid sites of "entredeux"—simultaneously at home and abroad at once (Cixous 9). Many of Pinnock's primary characters—usually led (un)consciously by a "homing desire"—are perpetually migrating on many levels (Brah 180). Often Pinnock's characters are displaced and in a metaphoric exile geographically and/or psychologically. The result is an irreconcilable tension or episodic discord that occurs first from migratory displacement and fragmentation, and second from an attempt to secure a sense of stability, belonging, and wholeness that is often elusive.

Performing diaspora, Pinnock highlights the complexities surrounding migration and black female identity. Pinnock plots navigations at the convergence of hybridity and difference that locate the impasse of outsidership. Her works also illustrate the diaspora within: the fragmented interior space of ruptured identity and belonging, the hybrid, exilic psyche. Such spaces are multilayered, transitory spaces in flux; hence, vacillating episodes surrounding home(land) and (un)belonging recur. Sayyid, referring to the cultural phenomenon of modern diaspora, writes that ethnic minority groups reside and act in "host countries" yet maintain "strong sentimental and material links to their country of origin—their homeland" (37). Furthermore, speaking to the articulation and narration of displacement and longing, Sayyid poetically adds, "the homeland acts as a horizon for the community, when a people are displaced but continue to narrate their identity in terms of that displacement . . . narratives that are organized around the co-ordinates of a homeland, a displacement, and a horizon of return either as a redemptive gesture or an empirical impossibility" (38). In the same way, Pinnock shapes her plays around the coordinates of homeland, displacement, (un)settlement, and metaphorical return. Seemingly, Pinnock's playwriting is her "redemptive gesture," her mode of "returning" to a homeland that is, in many ways, irretrievable or problematic in the physical realm (Sayyid 38). Her writings evoke migratory passages and embrace an "ideology of return" (Brah 180). Pinnock metaphorically returns home through her characters and through her creation, embracing and transporting ideal elements of homeland. In this way, she ritually performs diasporic homecomings with each playwriting endeavor; furthermore, the migratory pattern reverberates with each subsequent live performance, lending voice and body to the faint echoes of an estranged homeland. Most importantly, configured within the coordinates of homeland—in the spaces of interstices and alienation—Pinnock regularly relies upon female links and support during migration and its concomitant challenges. Ultimately, female bonds of support provide safe passage toward stabilization and wholeness.

[CHAPTER 3]

Migration, Transformation, and Identity Formation in Buchi Emecheta's *In the Ditch* and *Kehinde*

Romanus Muoneke

People who have experienced migration know that at some point in their lives they want to tell their own story, if only for others to learn from their experiences or to understand how far they have come to get to where they are. Buchi Emecheta is one of the few who have had the opportunity to share their stories with the public. She experienced migration firsthand and knows that immigrants go through all forms of transformation to reach their goal. Immigration brings about tremendous changes in people's lives, and in the course of these changes, some people pass through hell to achieve success, while some others are simply crushed. Many are lucky to reconstruct their lives in the process and become better persons. But there are others who cannot cope with the rigorous transformation involved and end up either totally destroyed or forced back to their point of origination. A close reading of Buchi Emecheta's heroines Adah (*In the Ditch*, 1979) and Kehinde (*Kehinde*, 1994) reveals the impact of migration on female identity formation. We shall see that in migration, the struggle to overcome obstacles in the country of destination leads to a transformation of the individual and ultimately to a search for a new identity that involves multiple forms of negotiation.

Migration occurs when there is a permanent change of residence by a person or a group, although that may not exclude an intention to move back later to the original place. The exact definition of "permanent" should not be a major concern as long as the original intention is to relocate and settle in another place. History is replete with several examples of immigrants from Europe, Asia, and Africa who spent many years in America and later moved back to their country of birth.

Migration may be voluntary or forced. Forced migration, especially if politically initiated, often results in exile. Transatlantic slavery and the expulsion of Ugandan Asians by Idi Amin are forms of migration that fall under this category. But strictly speaking, there is a thin line between forced and unforced migration in the sense that there is always some compulsion behind all migration; in other words, even where there is choice, there is always some compelling reason that makes the individual or group move to another location. To explain the dynamics of migration, sociologists often use the concepts of "push" and "pull." Some migrants are "pushed" by circumstances (e.g., famine, wars, civil disturbances, natural cataclysms) to seek elsewhere to obtain basic means of livelihood, while some others are "pulled" by attraction (e.g., marriage, opportunities for jobs, or desire to live in an ordered and technologically advanced society).

The push and pull factors sometimes combine to initiate migration process. A good example is found in Buchi Emecheta's *The Family* (1990), where hardships linked to unemployment add sweetness to cravings for a kind of paradise fulfilled in the various socioeconomic opportunities that the United Kingdom offers her former colonial subjects in the Caribbean. In this sense, migration serves as a quest for solution to life's problems. Often the quest yields good results for some and thus gives rise to rumors of exaggerated fulfillments in regions of destination. The bridge once established, the mad rush for the gold of life follows. The outcome is often the unexpected, for the emigrants are filled with such high expectations that they hardly ever stop to consider that other forms of hardship also exist in the regions of their destination, for example, racism, strange cultural environment, discrimination based on accent, communication skills, gender, age, and religion. One should, however, not get the impression that migrants are given only a one-sided and often golden image of their destination through letters from friends and relatives and through newspapers and television. In fact, migrants, especially voluntary migrants, are mostly informed of future hardships and problems in their dream countries, but the urge to escape "the dungeon" and the romantic excitement about moving to a better place blind them to the realities awaiting them.[1]

In Emecheta's novels, migration involves male and female characters; however, her concentration is on female migration, which epitomizes her own migration. Her concentration on women in migration should not be viewed as another case of a writer twisting the hand of history, for studies on migration show that in the last half century, the flow of migration, especially into the United States, has been dominated by females (Houston, Kramer, and Barrett 908). Sylvia Pedraza argues that the focus by writers on the achievements of men from Europe to America at the turn of the twentieth century, to the neglect of the women's, was as a result of "the persistence of negative stereotypes which made it appear that women did little worth writing about" (304). Common factors responsible for female migration include job opportunities, especially in the health care industry, socioeconomic conditions, but more emphatically, marriage and family reunification (Pedraza 306). Several women migrate to Europe from poorer countries to seek positions as domestics, seamstresses, and factory workers, but nothing has moved women to migrate to Europe or America as much as marriage. According to Leslie Page Moch, "Marital relations were the impetus for women leaving for Europe to join a spouse or a man to whom they were engaged. Marriage was an explicitly female strategy for the transoceanic migration of thousands of women who left their homes in order to marry men whom they did not know" (11).

One of mankind's most barbaric experiences is the nearly four centuries of forced migration of Africans to Europe and the Americas on slave ships. The rupture caused by slave trade is an ugly legacy that only time can repair. It is interesting to note, however, that from colonial period down to the mid twentieth century, the flow of migration was from Europe to Africa and the West Indies, but in recent times, more especially in the postcolonial era, the reverse has been the case. There are now over two million black immigrants in Britain alone, most of them from the West Indies. Knox attributes this flow of migration to the motherland to poverty and unemployment and to what he calls the "ratchet effect," meaning that the more people migrate from the Caribbean to the motherland, the more others are encouraged to migrate (Knox v). Consequently, "There are some districts in the West Indies today where there are more people away in Britain than there are at home. Those who remain feel left out, and depart to join their family and friends. It is clear that this momentum is likely to be self-perpetuating" (v–vi). There is no doubt, of course, that the despoliation of Africa as a result of slave trade and colonialism is partly to blame for the new transatlantic waves of migration from Africa to Europe and America.

The two novels of Emecheta discussed in this paper are essentially fictional autobiographies that deal with female migration, transformation through marginalization and other oppressive conditions, and the renegotiation of identity. In her nonfictional autobiography, *Head above Water* (1986), she makes it clear that most of her earlier novels, like her children, are too close to her heart; they are "too real," and "they are too me" (1).

A number of African writers have written about migration and identity in various forms, but none experienced migration to the extent Emecheta did. She left her home country, Nigeria, in her early years and settled in

London. Most of her novels are fictionalized accounts of her life experiences. Writing was her powerful tool to share her experiences and to reconstruct her identity, giving meaning to Edward Said's theory in *Culture and Imperialism* concerning the power of the story to achieve emancipation and identity formation (xii–xiii). At nineteen she moved to Britain with her husband and two children in 1962. While in Nigeria, England had represented for her "the kingdom of God, a place we all dreamed of coming to" (Kenyon 46). Moving to the United Kingdom was partly a realization of that dream and partly a fulfillment of a promise she had made to her father that she would one day go there (*Head above Water* 26). But her first encounter with England (via Liverpool) was shockingly disappointing: "I felt like walking into the inside of a grave: I could see nothing but masses of grey, filth, and more grey" (26–27). Yet, not withstanding her disappointment with England, she was resolved "to make it here or perish" (27). However, her marriage collapsed, having deteriorated to the point where her husband had burnt the manuscript to her first novel, *The Bride Price* (1976). Emecheta remained a single parent with five children whom she had to feed and shelter under the most wretched housing conditions.

But she persisted and finally emerged from "the ditch," creaming her efforts by obtaining a degree in sociology. Both while in the ditch and later, she used her writing as a form of therapy to deal with her "woes" and the truth about her life. Concerning her novels, she writes, "I must say that many a time I convinced myself that nobody was going to read them anyway, so I put down the whole truth, my own truths as I saw them" (*Head above Water* 58). As an immigrant, her "woes" were no doubt multiple. She was no stranger to dislocation and disruptions that gravely affected her personality. The "truths" of her life, that is, the extent of the disruption, was "too horrible" and unbelievable, and so she decided to use fiction to deal with them (58).[2]

By using fictitious characters to reenact her experience (including invented additions here and there), Emecheta is able to objectify events, evaluate her actions, and reconstruct or reconnect or renegotiate or define her true identity. The use of the narrative in reconstructing the self or establishing personal identity is of renewed interest to modern scholars in psychology. According to Espin, recent studies by Polkinghorne (1988), Erikson (1975), and McAdams (1990) focus on the following: 1) the idea that a self needs a story for its reconstruction; 2) the need to reconstruct life through the narrative to give it form and order; and 3) the role of the narrative in binding together our lives in time (450). These studies and others have demonstrated the way in which "narratives transform the passing of life into a coherent self" (Espin 450).

Buchi Emecheta's use of metafiction in recreating reality places her in the company of postmodern writers such as John Fowles, Doris Lessing, Margaret Drabble, Toni Morrison, and Margaret Atwood—writers who through their fiction explore the modern dilemma of self and meaning. According to Kolawole, many African women writers have not adopted a "disinterested attitude" in their works. To them, "writing is not a synonym for elusive fiction but a source of self-actualization," which explains why many of their works are biographical (167).

Emecheta is also in company with African women writers like Ama Ata Aidoo, Flora Nwapa, Bessie Head, and Nawal El Saadawi who, as Africans and women, encountered difficulties in order to be published. These women "represent various levels of the quest for self-expression against a background of gender and other related forms of oppression" (Kolawole 168). Their use of biographical forms to initiate changes is a redemptive act that leads to self-definition and self-healing (168).

Emecheta's *In the Ditch* and *Second Class Citizen* (1977) are two closely related novels that present a common protagonist, Adah, who is most representative of the author's experience. According to Emecheta, "'Life in the Ditch' is a documentary novel of the daily happenings of my life when I was living in the place officially known as 'Montagu Tibbles' off Prince of Wales Road in North London. By the time I moved in there, however, the block of flats was known locally as 'Pussy Cat Mansions'" (*Head above Water* 66). *In the Ditch* deals with the multiple life experiences of Adah, a young Nigerian immigrant who undergoes tremendous ordeal in her struggle for survival in London. Abandoned by a lousy and improvident husband, Adah is stuck with five children who need shelter, food, and tender care.

The story begins with a picture of Adah's life in a London slum. She lives in a rat- and roach-infested apartment that she has rented from a Nigerian landlord who creates havoc in her life by charging her double the rent and terrorizing her with his juju antics. The problem with him started when Adah requested that he repair the apartment so as to get rid of the decay and filth. Shouting at her children, switching off the electricity and giving her eviction notices are other methods he used to try to get rid of Adah and her kids. Being black and harnessed with five children and no husband, it would have been almost impossible for any landlord to offer her accommodations if the Nigerian landlord had succeeded in throwing her out. The interesting thing about this landlord is that he is himself an immigrant who had apparently come to England in search of education. Part of the money he collected from rents was used to pay for his studies. His is a case of an immigrant preying on a fellow immigrant, a phenomenon not uncommon among immigrant societies. He does his best to subjugate Adah, but she summons her energy to resist.

After nine months of struggle involving "court-going, letter-writing, and tribunal-visiting" (13), Adah is relocated to the Pussy Cat Mansions, a council flat in a housing project that Mrs. Devlin describes as "a God forsaken place" unsuitable for a hardworking woman with young children (11). Pussy Cat Mansions is likened to a prison yard, with its barbed wire windows, "impersonal bricks," and dark interior (17). Littered with rubbish piled high all over the place, with no central heating, and with wet slimy stairs that some teenagers use as a toilet, and all the rancid stench therewith, it is obvious that the Pussy Cat Mansions is not much of an improvement from her former abode. This lateral movement is by no means redemptive; rather it offers Adah a lateral transition from one oppressive condition to another. Such an experience is common among immigrants as they grope and stumble in suffering, ever hoping that things will improve. It is this fleecy hope that sustains the immigrants' faith and enables them to continue their struggle in the face of overwhelming crises. This is the case with Adah as she goes through her compounding problems. These include the problem of how to keep her job, go to school, and at the same time take care of the children, for already the other tenants are complaining about her children's noises and her leaving them alone too long before and after school. After much consideration, Adah quits her minimum-wage job and goes on the Dole (welfare), a step she loathes to take knowing it offends her African sensibility and pride (33). But she has no alternatives, and the only one open to her—writing African stories—is aborted by constant rejection by publishers.

Life in the Pussy Cat Mansions is purgatorial, a type of baptism by fire. In London, Adah experiences the kind of tough life that she had least expected. The challenges she meets are numerous and overwhelming, and yet she manages to succeed, thanks to her ability to adapt and her unmitigated resolve to overcome all trying circumstances. Just three days after she moves into the Mansions, her next-door neighbor, Mr. Small, comes with anger to complain that her children are disturbing his three-week-old baby boy by the noise they make with their boots. His first statement is enough to upset a proud soul: "Look, I don't mind your colour!" (18). This racial statement is only a preface to an unsavory complaint and warning that follows. Adah may have escaped the ordeals of a tribal, fetish landlord but not the stinging punches of a racist. Yet, to overcome this new monster (racism), she must devise a winning strategy. Should she apologize or return punch for punch? In the prison-like community of the Mansions, an apology is spurned, for it signals weakness and this invites an opponent to suppress the victim (19). Nevertheless, Adah refuses to sink that low and rather apologizes and befriends Mr. Small and his family.

To counter racism one must not trade ignorance with one's opponent: "But how did one become friends with someone who believed himself to be superior, richer and made of a better clay? . . . One of the methods she had found very helpful in securing friendship in England was to pretend to be ignorant. You see if you were black and ignorant you were conforming to what society expected of you. She was determined to try it with the Smalls" (20). In a confrontation with an old Greek lady in the washhouse, however, she is not so successful in containing a racial slur. When this angry old lady speaks spitefully to her, "Why don't you go back to your own bleeding country?" Adah quickly retorts, "You don't look English to me" (110). The other women at the washhouse laugh, while the old woman—herself an immigrant—picks up her clothes and leaves. Adah later regrets the incident. By whatever method Adah uses to contain racial discrimination and prejudice—by friendship or by personal confrontation—one point is clear: she gradually becomes one with the community of the Pussy Cat Mansions.

This integration with the interracial community, and in particular with the women, the oppressed victims of society, helps Adah's transformation from a state of aloneness and helplessness to a state of belonging. Carol Boyce Davies, in her work on black British women writers, states that a central theme in their works is the notion of not ever belonging even as one makes one's home in the Mother Country (*Black Women, Writing and Identity* 105). The theme of unbelonging is clearly present in Emecheta's *In The Ditch*, but as the novel progresses, and as Adah persistently asserts herself, taking advantage of the welfare system at her disposal, the notion of exile yields to the notion of community and hope.

Although the Pussy Cat Mansions still bears the stamp of poverty, it provides warmth and friendship that ease the pains of sorrow: "The little group talked, gossiped and laughed; all were happy. They found joy in communal sorrow. . . . Adah stopped being homesick. She was beginning to feel like a human being again, with a definite role to perform—even though the role was in no other place but the ditch. It was always nice and warm in the ditch. That night she thanked God for her good neighbors" (61). These down-and-outs in the ditch, the so-called wretched of the earth, provide support for each other through friendship that is warm and natural (54). Such friendship and support fulfills William Wordsworth's idea of the advantages of love in the poem "Michael": "There is a comfort in the strength of love; / 'Twill make a thing endurable, which else / Would overset the brain, or break the heart" (276). The natural warmth provided in the Mansions contrasts with the cold, mindless, artificial, and often bureaucratic relationships characteristic of the London sophisticated society. Poverty and rejection reduce multiracial and multicultural groups to a common level in which prejudices and differences are eclipsed. In the Mansions, "differences in culture, colour, backgrounds and God knows what else had all been submerged in the face of greater enemies—poverty and helplessness" (71). Solidarity with the common folks is therefore a major key to Adah's rehabilitation of the self.

With repeated assistance from Carol the Welfare worker, Whoopey and other inmates, and also the influence of such aggressive ones as Peggy (94), Adah gradually but finally regains her self-confidence. Earlier in the novel, her disposition is described as "insecure, uncertain, and afraid" (70–71). Her condition is fully expressed in the often quoted passage: "It is a curse to be an orphan, a double curse to be a black one in a white country, an unforgivable calamity to be a woman with five kids without a husband. Her whole life had been like that of a perpetually unlucky gambler" (71). By the end of the novel she is strong enough to think for herself and make her own decisions independent of other people's feelings, as is evident in her joining with the other Pussy Cat dwellers to revolt against her friend Carol for her pretentious relationship with them (99–100), and in the fact that she now attends meetings and goes to the pub to drink and dance with Whoopey and Carol.

Thus, Adah's spectacular development from a feeling of insecurity and uncertainty to that of confidence is a form of transformation resulting from her ability to create a space that enables her to embrace old ways and new ways, tradition and modernity, her African past and her present reality. This spatial extension calls for a radical dismantling of the identity inscribed on her as an ex-colonial subject and an immigrant. As an African female living in the Pussy Cat Mansions, she is already a marked victim of two forms of "difference" that determine her stereotyped image—racial and sexual. Adah, however, has taken steps to deal with such racial/cultural otherness that separates her from the rest of the community, and she does that through active and scrupulous participation in community affairs. Hence, she is always anxious to act correctly, "to follow her own instincts as a mother and yet to fit in with accepted ideas so that people would not talk" (75). And consequently, when Bubu throws a toy at a boy's head causing him to bleed profusely, she "shook him and boxed his ears" (75). Adah will do what it takes to dislodge the "otherness" even if it calls for negotiating her identity: "She was always frightened that her real self was not good enough for the public. She would gladly play any role expected of her for the sake of peace" (75–56). In *The World, the Text, and the Critic,* Edward Said argues that the exile's survival depends on his or her ability to negotiate alliances and allegiances, even to the extent of assuming the status of a social actor: "On the one hand, the individual mind registers and is very much aware of the collective whole, context, or situation in which it finds itself. On the other hand, precisely because of this awareness—a worldly self-situating, a sensitive response to the dominant culture—that the individual consciousness is not naturally and easily a mere child of the culture, but a historical and social actor in it" (15). In essence, Adah chooses to anchor her identity in a collective communal identity, and since the Mansion community is mostly female, her action further fulfills Rita Felski's feminist theory of integration, which promotes friendship and reconciliation with a female group as a form of an affirmation of self. The advantage is twofold: "On the one hand, this model of female community provides a means of access into society by linking the protagonist to broader social group and thus rendering explicit the political basis of private experience. On the other, it also functions as a barrier against, and a refuge from, the worst effects of a potentially threatening social order by opening up a space for non-exploitative relationships grounded in common goals and interests" (Felski 139).

The Housing Department finally decides to move the Pussy Cat Mansions dwellers to the high-rise buildings popularly known as the city matchboxes. The flats are beautiful, new, peaceful and private, but Adah refuses to live there because of her children and all the danger associated with leaving the children high up there. She is later assigned to a new flat in an affluent district near the famous Regent's Park. This is a wealthy district, home to writers and actors. Adah, with all her ambition to be a writer, knows no better place to live than this. Before finally moving out of the Pussy Cat Mansions, something highly symbolic happens. After her last meeting with Carol, a meeting marked by its tone of reconciliation and gratitude, Adah walks to her flat through the Mansions' cemetery. Reflecting on her life in the ditch, something becomes clear to her: she has to get out of the ditch for good and should never depend on any social officer for her needs. And furthermore, she is determined that she is not going to "lower herself any more for anything. The world had a habit of accepting the way you rated yourself. The last place in which she was going to incarcerate herself was in the ditch" (127). Then as she reads the names of those buried there, she bids them farewell, "Goodbye, ghosts, whoever you are, and sleep well" (127). When she gets home an offer for the new accommodation is already waiting for her. She moves out of the ditch a week later, "to face the world alone, without the cushioning comfort of Mrs. Cox, without the master-minding of Carol. It was a time she became an individual" (127). Thus, having symbolically buried the old self, she is to begin life afresh, with new determination and new personality. It is an important step in Adah's transformation in which, like a Phoenix, she now rises from the ashes of a downgraded self into a new consciousness of empowerment.

A number of modern theorists have used the body image to describe the triumphant reintegration of a displaced subject. Michael Dash in his work on Caribbean literature discusses two prominent colonial/postcolonial writers that used such body images: Aime Cesaire and Frantz Fanon. Cesaire's epic poem, "Cahier," for example, "ends with a triumphant vision of sensory plenitude as the subject is possessed by the lost island-body" (Dash 332). Cesaire's poetry in general is rich with images of dismemberment and reintegration. Similarly, Fanon manipulates corporeal imagery to express the ideal of revolutionary self-assertiveness; for example, he "attempts to rewrite the body of colonized man, creating a new subject from the dismemberment and castration inflicted by the coloniser's destructive gaze" (Dash 333). In Emecheta's *In the Ditch*, the dead bodies buried in the cemetery point to the dismembered self from which Adah has triumphantly emerged in the course of her transformation.

Before we change our focus on the novel *In the Ditch*, we need briefly to examine Emecheta as a protest writer, with particular reference to this novel. Emecheta is an ex-colonial subject now migrated to the metropolitan center from where she is more properly situated to engage the old master on his claims to superiority and excellence. *In the Ditch* is an attempt to unmask the sophisticated claims and pretensions of an imperialist power; it is a fight-back by a subject who uses the instrument of writing to attack the colonial authority, in order to redefine her self-image. Salman Rushdie's famous phrase, "the Empire writes back," now title of a book, implies that postcolonial subjects write back to the metropolitan center, questioning the bases of her authority and claims (Ashcroft, Griffths, and Tiffin, *The Empire Writes Back*, 39).

The first step toward a decolonization of the mind is to destroy the colonial mystique that turgidly hangs over the colonial power. As a colonial subject, Emecheta had perceived England as a paradise or a kingdom of God. But once in England, she gets disillusioned and uses the opportunity to launch her protest against the imperial authority. In her novels she consistently questions what Katherine Fishburn terms "the construction of gender" (52), and also the impact of colonialism on the African mind. Fishburn rightly says that Emecheta's *In the Ditch* "celebrates a plurality of protest" (52). Apart from the need for demythologization of the imperialist's claim to exclusivity, Emecheta has more reasons to protest. As soon as she stepped out of colonial subjugation, thanks to political independence, she stepped back into it in her migratory relocation to the London Council flats where racism is rife, and where the women are marginalized and, indeed, colonized. As Ashcroft, Griffiths, and Tiffin have rightly pointed out, marginalized women in imperialist countries "share with colonized races and peoples an intimate experience of the politics of oppression and repression, and like them they have been forced to articulate their experiences in the language of their oppressors" (*The Empire* 174–75).

The heavy reliance on tradition in the novels of Emecheta is, in a sense, a form of protest, for, according to Ashcroft, Griffiths, and Tiffin, "... the study of national tradition is the first step and most vital stage of the process of rejecting the claims of the center to exclusivity" (*The Empire* 17). "Without ever stating it outright," Fishburn comments, "this novel [*In the Ditch*] shows how even British women living in the ditch can benefit from traditional Igbo values" (60). Adah's appreciation of her African values, though dipped in protest, is indeed the beginning of what Soyinka has characterized as the "process of self-appreciation" (xi). In migration or exile, such old values do contribute to the heroine's survival, more so if she is able to integrate them into her new environment (Fishburn 60–61).

The internal migration, which originates from a private landlord's apartment in a slum and traverses a city ghetto, ending in an affluent district, charts the progress the immigrant makes in the process of integration within the new community. It is as winding as it is multiculturally embracing. This upward movement is indicative of the migrant's successful adaptation and acculturation, in short, the actual transformation that is part of migratory experience. In ritual language, it is a purification process leading to self-redemption. Although Adah's movement within London is winding and upward, migration in this novel is a linear process: the protagonist from Africa explores all available means to sort her life out in a strange and difficult environment with no explicit intention to go back.

A totally different picture of migration is presented in *Kehinde*, where the movement is gyral—from Nigeria to England, back to Nigeria, and then back to England. In the former novel, *In the Ditch*, Adah, despite all her struggle, never wishes to go back to her country of origin, whereas in *Kehinde*, Albert Okolo, accompanied by his wife, goes to England for further studies, but they also plan to return to Nigeria sometime later, which is common with many Nigerians who go abroad for their education. Whereas Adah's problem is predicated on survival, that is, on how to climb out of the ditch made possible by husband abuse, poverty, racism, and the ordeal of single parenthood, all of which lead to a dislocation that has to be repaired for meaningful life to emerge, Kehinde's problem is different and is best summarized in a simple question: where is home?

The novel opens with news about a letter from Albert's sisters asking him to return home to Nigeria and settle down for good. Kehinde is quick to object, pointing out that the invitation to come home excludes her and their children, Bimpe and Joshua. This objection introduces the major conflict in the story, namely, where should be home for the Okolo family after eighteen years of migration to England? Meanwhile, Kehinde and Albert are well established in London: Kehinde is employed in a management position at Barclays Bank, while Albert is done with schooling and now works as a shopkeeper. Their combined income makes it possible for them to own a house in London. The greater part of the income, however, comes from Kehinde, and, indeed, it is right to say that Albert and their two children were at one point totally dependent on Kehinde's income for their school fees and sustenance.

The theme of economic exploitation and eventual betrayal of the female protagonist by the husband is common in Emecheta's novels, and is dominant in *Kehinde*. On the surface, Kehinde and Albert enjoy a perfect relationship in their marriage; Kehinde relates to Albert "as a friend, a compatriot, a confidant" (6). But the unfolding conflict is further defined in the fact that Kehinde is feeling fulfilled in England, whereas Albert is not, for he still longs for the "sunshine, freedom, easy friendship, [and] warmth" with which he associates Nigeria (6). To a fellow migrant worker, Prahbu, a Pakistanian by birth, he confides that he is uncomfortable with his westernized self, for in England he is a "nobody," and life is full of restrictions. This means that he misses the freedom and male dominance that traditional life afforded his father and his counterparts in Nigeria. And again, he does not exert traditional control over his wife: "I'm fed up with just listening to my wife and indulging her" (35). All this prepares us for the unromantic relationship that will characterize their marriage in Nigeria. We get further hints of this future relationship when the narrator reveals that Albert loves his wife "in his own way, but needed room to breathe" (35). Moreover, Kehinde herself knows that "behind the veneer of westernization, the traditional Igbo man was alive and strong, awaiting an opportunity to reclaim his birthright" (35). It is therefore not surprising that Albert should vigorously pursue his sisters' importunity for their emigration.

Albert and Kehinde are both liminal figures who, in Said's notion, are occupying a median state, an in-between space separating two cultures, the colonial and the metropolitan: "The exile therefore exists in a median state, neither completely at one with the new setting nor fully disencumbered of the old, beset with half-involvements and half-detachments, nostalgic and sentimental on one level, an adept mimic or a secret outcast on another" (*Representations of the Intellectual* 49). What matters indeed is not so much the couple's liminal situation as much as the choices they make from it between the two competing cultures. Albert, resisting his dislocation and migration to the metropolis, becomes an exile yearning for the "fresh pots of Egypt" or the homeland. He thus fails to benefit from the insight and strength that liminality offers, for according to Bhabha, the liminal space "prevents identities at either end of it from settling into primordial polarities," and further "opens up the possibility of a cultural hybridity that entertains difference without an assumed or imposed hierarchy" (*The Location of Culture* 4).

On her part, Kehinde has no illusions about going back. Being so fully adapted to her London environment, and though not totally disengaged from her traditional Igbo background, she feels confused and at best reluctant at the prospect of returning to Nigeria. In this cultural hybridity, she might be said to represent an impulse commonly shared by many immigrants, including Buchi Emecheta herself. In an interview with Julie Holmes, Emecheta admits to keeping in touch with her ancestral roots in Africa, and that by her constant visits she is able to maintain her two worlds (*The Voice*, July 1999). Emecheta and her fictional other fulfill Edward Said's concept of "voyage in." The concept relates to the works and experiences of Third World intellectual immigrants who have integrated into the colonizer's metropolis, thus reversing the former trend of the colonizer's intrusion into the colony: "These incursions concern the same areas of experience, culture, history, and tradition hitherto commanded unilaterally by the metropolitan center" (*Culture and Imperialism* 244). The "voyage in" allows Emecheta to discuss and even critique the African as well as the metropolitan culture. Kehinde, her fictional self, uses the voyage hybridity to her advantage: she is able to judge the two cultures realistically and make her choice.

Indeed, there are times, especially prior to her trip to Lagos, when Kehinde's allegiance tilts too much toward her African roots, as happens in the way she relates to Mary Elikwu, a more educated woman than herself. She expresses bitterness towards Mary during the send-off party held for Albert in London. She rejects Mary's compliments and labels her "a fallen woman who had no sense of decorum" (38). Mary's unpardonable sin is that, though she has six children, she abandons her abusive husband to live independently. From Kehinde's traditional perspective, such a loose woman is not worthy of an invitation to her party. Mary's unwelcome presence is accidental; she comes as a member of an invited group. It isn't until Kehinde takes a trip to Lagos that she realizes she has misjudged Mary, and that Mary's courage to get her education and live independently and successfully is praiseworthy. To an immigrant, tradition is a valuable asset, although it comes with its own danger, as in the case of Kehinde's misjudgment of Mary Elikwu.

Albert's dream for a new life of ease and comfort in Nigeria meets a dangerous obstacle that tests the couple's faith and resolve. Kehinde discovers that she is pregnant. This means that their savings will be depleted, and it would be impossible for Albert to save "for their home-coming on his income alone, to say nothing of feeding another mouth" (22). Being Igbo and Catholics, they are not expected to resort to abortion, for it is highly forbidden in both cultures. Igbo customs place much emphasis on children and regard abortion as an abomination (72). But nothing would stop Albert in his bid to go home and reclaim his birthright, and so he persuades Kehinde to have an abortion. Kehinde consents to please Albert, and we might say for the sake of peace in the family, but in so doing she compromises her conscience and spirituality.

An emigrant's ambivalent position is part of the concern of this novel, and is no doubt of particular interest to the author who experienced it personally. Albert and Kehinde weave in and out of two worlds of the Igbo tradition and the British western values. To intensify the tensions within these two Nigerian emigrants, Emecheta emphasizes the dichotomy in the choices they make. For Albert, whose whole preoccupation is with reclaiming his patriarchal rights of male dominance, going back to Nigeria is not negotiable. Emecheta's feminism is most visible in her portrayal of male characters in the two novels. In the first, Adah's husband is shown to be lazy, unproductive, abusive, and a total failure. In the second, *Kehinde*, Albert is unconscionable and manipulative, and it is likely that without a woman to lean on (Kehinde or Rike or the latest wife from the north), he would drown emotionally and economically. So self-centered, his sole objective is to return to Nigeria, where he will fly in his patriarchal glory, surrounded by a host of wives. Like Albert, many an emigrant male are myopically resistant to Western values as a result of their rigid fixation to traditional life patterns which invest them with power and dominance over women. Migration leaves no traces of transformation in them. They may tolerate a degree of acculturation, but that is quickly discarded the moment they step back into their patriarchal domain. It is the case with Albert who, as soon as he returns to Nigeria, resumes his position as an overlord, with wives and servants at his service.

The neocolonial image represented by Albert is a matter of concern in this novel. It is significant that Albert's decision to return to his country of origin is based on the invitation of his sisters who want him to come home to participate in the country's booming economy. We realize, of course, that the event in the novel takes place a few years after Nigeria's independence from Britain in 1960. Fully grounded in Western education, Albert is qualified to join the middle class, the elite that takes over the management of the country from the colonizers. In *The Wretched of the Earth*, Fanon warns about the educated national middle class, "the national bourgeoisie [who] steps into the shoes of the former European settlement," and whose self-interests conflict with those of the people (122). These neocolonialists will use their privileged education and position to replicate the colonial administration of the nation for their own personal profit. Given his character and motives, Albert is Emecheta's neocolonial type whose activities will place the newly independent nation in jeopardy.

The periodic intervention of Taiwo in the novel is important and says something about Emecheta's combination of Igbo and Yoruba traditions in *Kehinde*. Emecheta herself is familiar with both cultures; she is Igbo but raised in Lagos (Yoruba). Taiwo and Kehinde are twins, but Taiwo, the first of the two, dies at birth. In Yoruba "ibeji" myth, a Taiwo will continue to exert her spiritual influence over a Kehinde. The use of Yoruba and Igbo concepts of twins is best explained by Brenda Berrian: "Formerly, [the] Igbo abhorred the birth of twins and eliminated them and sometimes the mother, whereas the Yoruba have always revered twins. With the intervention of Christian missionaries and changing value systems, twins are presently cherished by the Yoruba and tolerated by the Igbo" (170). It might be an exaggeration to hold that the Igbo only "tolerate" twins in their postcolonial, Christian culture; they also love and respect twins. But the Yoruba tradition, ever rich in myths, does preserve the memory of a dead twin with an ibeji statue "carved to serve as the abode of the dead twin" (Opoku 107). Emecheta has combined the Yoruba belief in Taiwo with the Igbo belief in "chi"—one's spiritual double, a kind of guardian angel. From time to time Taiwo returns to chastise, to warn, to guide, and to direct her sister, Kehinde. One of those instances occurs right before she has the abortion. Feeling lonely and confused, she hears the warning voice of Taiwo: "Our mother died having you. I too died so you could live. Are you now going to kill your child before he has a chance of life?" (17). As Kehinde feels lonely and anxious about Albert after he departs for Nigeria, Taiwo, "that intrusive inner voice," intervenes again to confirm her fears and urge her to go back to Lagos and prevent Albert from getting another woman, because Nigerian men consider it manly to be unfaithful (46). Thus Emecheta uses Taiwo to represent spiritual vision and guide for her protagonist, but at the same time uses her as the author's persona in certain critical and controversial matters. As Berrian, who sees the novel as "a quasi-mystical novel of human identity, a search for self," has rightly observed: "Neither defeated by indigenous Igbo gender definitions nor constrained by Western gender definitions, Kehinde conjures up her own self-definition with the aid of her spirit twin Taiwo and embraces only those values which are the most beneficial for her lifestyle" (171).

While waiting to sell their house in London, Kehinde experiences life in the ditch, similar to Adah's ordeal in the earlier novel, except that she has no children for whom to provide. With Kehinde's husband and children all gone, she feels terribly divided and incomplete; "she was a half-person"

(59). Her feelings of isolation and marginalization are heightened by the fact that other Nigerians shun her. Even her best friend, Moriammo, avoids her company because her husband, Tunde, forbids her to associate with "a woman who had sent all her family away so she could have a good time" (56). Unable to sell the house, and getting mixed signals from Albert, who is insisting she should never resign her lucrative job, should first sell the house and then wait till he sends for her, Kehinde sinks deeper and deeper into depression. After she resigns her job, her state of insecurity and unbelonging makes her begin to understand the plight of widows and estranged wives like Mary Elikwu. Although well adapted in England, Kehinde still clings to her Nigerian traditional patterns as a model of existence. But when the factors that sustained the model collapse, life becomes a hell for her; in other words, when she is deprived of husband, children, and her Nigerian community, she feels like an exile, and London is no longer a place for her. She has to make a trip to Nigeria to reintegrate her sundered self, in short, to find a home.

Kehinde's homecoming is the most problematic and mortifying experience in her life. Albert is at the airport to receive her, but he is so detached. He has a new and imposing look, beaming with confidence. In his white "agbada" and matching skullcap, he surely presents a new image suggestive of the new male power with which the country has crowned him. It does not surprise us because this has been foreshadowed by his nonchalance after the abortion, his infrequent letters from Nigeria, and his angry phone call insisting that Kehinde should return only at his own time.

Lagos for Kehinde proves to be another hell, even worse than what she experienced in London. Albert has taken another wife—a beautiful and sophisticated woman with a doctorate in literature, who also lectures at a university. She and Kehinde will share Albert's bed in a polygamous relationship. Polygamy will prove a hard pill for Kehinde to swallow, especially after living for several years in England and being so Westernized. Nor can she put up with a number of other customs that sound ridiculous to her ears; for example, that she cannot call her husband by his first name, rather, she must address him as Joshua's father. She must also learn to call him "our husband," not my husband, because he is Rike's husband, too. These customs are obviously meant to "favor the man but demote her status as a woman" (Berrian 175). She is reduced to a small bedroom and deprived of the use of the expensive furniture she had shipped home from London. With no job to occupy her time, and being entirely dependent on Albert for all her needs, she gradually becomes despondent and disenchanted and sinks further into depression. Kehinde's case becomes hopeless when her only supporter, her very sister, Ifeyinwa, who loves her dearly and is out to protect her at all cost, sees the whole picture differently. As far as she is concerned, Albert is a good man, behaving like every other Nigerian man. Rike is also good, a generous woman to Kehinde's children; she visits them at school every Saturday and provides for all their needs. Even Kehinde's children, Bimpe and Joshua, feel at ease with the system. Bimpe understands why Albert had to marry Rike, while Joshua has quickly adapted to the Nigerian way; he "soon became reconciled" to his father's taking a second wife; besides, he has learned that in Nigeria "you don't talk to your father anyhow" (74). The general feeling is that Kehinde should be submissive and accept things as they are (75).

One of the themes Emecheta explores in this novel is the impact of tradition on women. Her commitment to feminism is manifested in the manner in which she experiments on this theme. She uses Kehinde, a migrant who originated in this tradition but has been transcended and exposed to its counter (the Western), to expose and condemn the excesses and superfluities of Igbo tradition, specifically, the way it serves men and oppresses women. Emecheta obviously trusts that her audience, an enlightened audience, will transcend the level of judgment shown by the patriarchal society, in which female oppression is accepted as normal.

Questions have been raised regarding Emecheta's position on the controversial subject of polygamy. From reading *Kehinde,* one might be tempted to think that, based on its general acceptance by everyone, including Kehinde's sister Ifeyinwa, Rike, and her daughter Bimpe, she condones the practice. Bimpe's compromise is clearly expressed in her letter to Kehinde (120–22), with particular reference to her father's polygamous action: "I know it was painful for you, what dad did. Joshua and I were shocked at first, but we soon learnt that it is very common here. And Rike is not bad at all. She prays for all of us all the time. And we are family" (121). It might even be strongly argued that polygamy is advantageous, because in some sense it helps a woman achieve freedom from her husband to do the things that please her—a position Emecheta has maintained in an article "Feminism with a small 'f'" (175). In Kehinde's case, polygamy contributes to her final initiative to search for independence and a new beginning (175). Attractive as this proposition might be, based on textual content in which Albert is portrayed in a very negative light and in which Kehinde, Emecheta's fictional other, abandons Albert and moves on with her life, it seems more accurate to say that Emecheta perceives polygamy as a form of female subjugation.

Kehinde's Lagos experience reminds us of T. S. Eliot's poem, "Journey of the Magi," in which one of the wise men who had journeyed to Bethlehem to witness Christ reflects on the event years later. The event of Christ has had such a radical transformation on the Magi that they are "no longer at ease" with the old dispensation. Their journey to Christ gives rise to their own rebirth, which in itself is a death to the old life (Williamson 164). Kehinde, disappointed and marginalized in her homeland with the patriarchal system that denigrates her as a woman, takes refuge back to London. Her romantic dreams of Africa have proved false, and she is compelled to choose between two evils, Lagos and London. She feels nostalgic for London, where although she might live as an "unwelcome" alien (96), she would at least have an environment in which she could fully exercise her rights as a person. Kehinde's migratory movements, which finally terminate in London, properly define her as a nomadic subject whose subjectivity "blurs boundaries, making transitions between categories, states and levels of experience" (Andermahr, Lovell, and Wolkowitz 184). This transgressive subjectivity is best described in Virginia Woolf's famous statement: "As a woman I have no country, as a woman I want no country, as a woman my country is the whole world" (197). Kehinde's nomadic subjectivity in no way suggests homelessness, for despite initial setbacks, she finally discovers her true home in London.

Freedom to choose for oneself, especially after experiencing contrasting situations, lightens the burden of immigration. As tough as the new beginning will be in London, Kehinde is equipped with courage and strength to succeed. In her new rebellious mood, Mary Elikwu becomes her icon of revolt. In a letter to Moriammo written in Lagos, she confesses that Mary has remained on her conscience since Albert's send-off party, and considering all she has experienced in Lagos, it has become clear to her that Mary's path to liberation via education should be the model for all women (95). Emecheta's opinion is most vividly expressed in this letter as well as in Moriammo's reply, which states that Mary is making tremendous progress with her new book and her involvement with the "Milk for our babies" campaign. She is very much in the limelight (101). And then she adds what appears to come straight from Emecheta: "She [Mrs Elikwu] must know by now, what we women are like. When we are married, we feel we have advantage over a woman who is living by herself, even if the latter is a million times happier" (101). Here, as well as in her interviews, Emecheta pursues the theme of women oppressing other women, women contributing largely in a man's world to the suffering of fellow women. Kehinde's late recognition that Mary has chosen the better path is the beginning of wisdom, the beginning of her quest for independence and self-reliance, indeed, the beginning of her salvation and freedom.

Kehinde's rejection of her husband and her assumption of full responsibility for her future remind us of similar situations in literature, particularly Edna's rejection of wifehood and motherhood in pursuit of her personal freedom in Kate Chopin's *The Awakening,* and Nora's slamming of the door at her husband and walking away from him and her children to sort herself out in the world, free of the constraints of husband and family, in Henrik

Ibsen's *A Doll House*. In each of these works, the husband is perceived as part of, if not the principal cause of, the protagonist's subjugation. But Emecheta's character is remarkably different; she stays in contact with her children by sending them money and exchanging letters. Her traditional role as a mother is seriously maintained, although she does not allow her freedom to suffer as a result. This in a way demonstrates Emecheta's balanced attitude towards traditional matters. She embraces the positive aspects of tradition and rejects its negative aspects. In his discussion of "interculturalism" in the new literatures in English, Bernd Schulte writes:

> 'Intercultural writing' takes place in a historical situation which confronts the countries of the former colonies with the problems of finding 'national identities' somewhere between tradition and modernity—in a sort of sociocultural moratorium. Orientation and identity formation seem to be staged within processes of intercultural oscillation. Thus, on a structural level, authors of 'new' literatures in English often develop patterns of motivational dispositions and they conceptualize their protagonists by fictionalizing such processes within the framework of distance and participation. The writers' own attitudes towards Indian, African or other traditions turn out to be part of their biographies and a literary principle at the same time, as is demonstrated by their autobiographical as well as fictional works. (qtd. in Hawley 334–35)

In *Kehinde*, Emecheta is celebrating this "intercultural oscillation" alluded to by Schulte; what is even more important is that her protagonist is doing it by negotiating her cultural identity formation. Emecheta seems to "speak for all migrant women throughout the world who have taken root in the West but have maintained their 'twin' identity in their homeland. These women refuse to sever their connection with the nation of origin" (Hawley 336).

As soon as Kehinde steps her foot in London, she feels one with the natural surrounding. Notably, it is spring, symbolically, time for a fresh start. Everything welcomes her back; the immigration officials are most friendly, and "the smell of the London terrace house welcomed her like a lost child" (107–8). Once again, she merges with her twin, Taiwo, who had not spoken to her since she went to Nigeria. Strengthened by this reunion with Taiwo, she wrenches the "For Sale" sign in the front yard with this powerful declaration: "This house is not for sale. . . . This house is mine" (108). Her transformation into a new woman is obvious. Within three years she earns a degree in sociology, thus truly following the footsteps of Mary Elikwu, her new mentor. Since a befitting job is not easily available, she assumes menial jobs, for example, housekeeping at the hotel. The hotel job is not without its own trial: a rich but perverse Arab Sheik demands to see her naked to fulfill his longing to view a black woman in the nude. This form of prostitution is beyond what she had bargained for in her quest for independence and freedom. Kehinde walks away from the job and maintains her dignity, which is Emecheta's subtle and feminist suggestion to all women that true freedom must fly on the wings of morality and self-esteem.

Further evidence of her freedom and empowerment is shown when her son Joshua, prompted by Albert, arrives in London to claim his birthright—their house. This proves unsuccessful, and soon the message is driven home to Joshua that he is dealing with a rebellious mother who can no longer be intimidated by the corban of tradition; hence, she tells him in clear terms, "This is my house, though it may be yours one day" (137). An important change that Joshua discovers is that the new Kehinde, now properly in tune with her reintegrated Taiwo, makes her choice of what is good for herself. She chooses to befriend her Caribbean tenant, Michael Gibson, and when Joshua wants him out, she insists that in her house "whoever she wanted to stay, stayed" (137). Taiwo's voice has at this point become "a permanent part of her consciousness" (135) and also a source of illumination and wisdom assisting her in making tough choices, particularly reaffirming her sexuality by taking as a lover a Caribbean man five years younger (136). This permanent merger with Taiwo is indicative of her complete reintegration of the self. Rehabilitation of the self or the redefinition of one's identity is the beginning of real and meaningful existence. In *Kehinde*, such rehabilitation is achieved in London far away from the protagonist's country of origin. Emecheta stylistically uses space and movement to resolve the conflict introduced at the opening of the novel.

That Emecheta is a feminist is an incontestable fact, for she uses all her resources to deal with the process of changing the gender relations in society, and more especially in situations that invest power on men and marginalize women. What needs further clarification is her brand of feminism, for feminism has assumed various colors since its inception. Black women theorists are prone to resist the imperialistic imposition by the so-called Western or First World feminists who claim to blow the final whistle on the criteria of struggle. African feminism is recently taking a center stage in feminist criticism, even with all its differences and emphases. By whatever name it goes—womanism, a term popularized by Alice Walker and much written about by Mary Modupe Kolawole, or nego-feminism (literally, "the feminism of negotiation; no ego feminism"), a concept much favored and propagated by Obiomma Nnaemeka (377)—African feminism, "a hybrid of sorts" (Davies and Graves 12), has come to signify a humanistic, collective, and culturally wholesome expression of African female (and sometimes male) concerns.

As Kolawole aptly puts it, "African womanism cannot be separated from humanism. Rather, it seeks to enrich the female gender through consciousness-raising while giving a human touch to the struggle for the appreciation, emancipation, elevation and total self-fulfillment of the woman, in positive ways.... African women can take whatever is positive in the encroaching modern values and simultaneously retain the essence by preserving what is good in their culture and establishing it" (204). Emecheta's feminism, as demonstrated in the two novels under consideration, mirrors the attitudes shown in these statements. Her protagonists, seeking to define or rediscover themselves in migratory space, are prepared to cross boundaries and negotiate their ways with no taint of "egocentricity and individualism that undermine collective action" (Nnaemeka 364). Their ability to combine modern values with authentic and salubrious traditional values is a major part of their success. Through migration experience, Emecheta and her fictional characters fulfill Nnaemeka's vision of African feminism, especially in their willingness to negotiate and compromise and ultimately achieve balance.

Critics are nevertheless baffled by the complex or, rather, seemingly shifting complexion of Emecheta's feminism. On the one level, she seems to favor Western (individualistic) approach, for example, Kehinde's final rejection of her traditional marriage with Albert. But on another level, Emecheta seems to accommodate the traditional practice, like polygamy, which might be shown to be a patriarchal instrument of oppression. She seems to condone polygamy by making it acceptable to everyone except the rebellious protagonist, Kehinde. To resolve this issue, we need to be clear on one point: In her novels Emecheta is not out to attack Nigerian culture but to affirm it, a critical point Katherine Fishburn consistently makes in her book, *Reading Buchi Emecheta* (58, 60–61). Fishburn further explains that independent women "may well be the heroines of Emecheta's novels, but her fiction is no paean to rebellion. More than is obvious at first glance, her novels are a reaffirmation of her received African concepts of community" (56).

Another point to remember is that Emecheta has a great deal in common with Western feminists. On a large scale, she presents her novels on a feminist frame (Fishburn 58). If judged, for example, by the way she represents African husbands in her novels, she would look like a feminist Shylock in hot pursuit of male writers for the dreadful pint of blood. But in reality, Emecheta, though with a touch of Western feminism, is an African feminist. In an interview with Kirstern Holst Petersen, she makes the point clear: "I will not be called a feminist here, because it is European.... I just resent that. ... If you look at everything I do, it is what the feminists do, too ... my books have the same ideas.... It is just that it comes from outside, and I don't like people dictating to me. I do believe in the African kind of feminism" (19).

Thus, she identifies with African feminism or what some call womanism, for although she is deeply concerned with the oppression as well as the social and economic upliftment of women, she still has a profound respect for African values and tradition. We must bear in mind, of course, that between Western feminism and African culture, there is a point of contact vis-à-vis their common emphasis on community. As Fishburn rightly points out, "If we recognize . . . that traditional Igbo culture values community in much the same way we feminists do, we can perhaps begin to rethink our own relationship to society at large and not to be judgmental" (58–59).

Emecheta goes even further beyond her mutual interests with Western and African feminists to promote the cause of the individual woman, and in doing this she is ready to sacrifice Western and African feminist ideologies. In other words, she is prepared to expunge a traditional custom, which impinges on her protagonist's freedom and welfare, no matter how strongly the custom is entrenched in society. Such compromises are common in *Kehinde* and *In the Ditch*.

The Bride Price, however, presents a different picture. Here the individual is sacrificed in the interest of the community. Fishburn has observed correctly that in her fiction, Emecheta "continually reaffirms the value of community" and that she "does prescribe certain limitations for women that in real life she herself has soundly rejected" (59). Discussing this conflict in *Head above Water*, Emecheta explains why her protagonist is doomed to die for challenging tradition: "I had realized that what makes all of us human is belonging to a group. And if one belongs to a group, one should try to abide by its laws" (166).

The complexity of Emecheta's feminism is rooted in her tendency to shift grounds and emphasis, depending on what her ultimate goal is. Generally, her goal is to "encourage solidarity among women" (Fishburn 58), to show women how to struggle against and overcome all forms of oppression, including those arising from tradition and modernity. In pursuing this goal, Emecheta is apt to negotiate courses. To gain self-fulfillment, her heroines would weave their ways between Western and traditional values, trading off and combining as need arises. Emecheta is therefore a seasoned pragmatic feminist or a typical negofeminist.

Albert's weakness, made very explicit in *Kehinde*, serves one major purpose: it helps to clarify the principles inscribed on Emecheta's female protagonist, Kehinde. Albert, the unfulfilled immigrant, seizes the opportunity of his homecoming to attempt to reassert himself. Back in Nigeria he becomes the real macho man, the master/husband of three wives, and the one who calls the shots. There are attendant problems, however, which include the sudden abdication by his first wife, who had largely provided for him for about twenty years, and then the loss of his lucrative job with the ugly possibility of his having to depend on Rike's income. Albert may not eventually succeed in solving all his problems, yet we cannot imagine him going back to settle in London. He has found his home in Nigeria, a place where he belongs, where he feels fulfilled enough to exercise his manhood. In the eyes of Emecheta, Albert is a failure. Like Obi Okonkwo who fails to make the best use of his privileged exposure to Western and traditional ways in Chinua Achebe's *No Longer at Ease,* Albert fails because of his fixation to patriarchy and his inability to negotiate between the boundaries of space and culture. For Kehinde, however, the situation is different. Opposed to going back home from the start, she later changes her mind following her Taiwo's advice. But in Nigeria she quickly discovers that, having been relegated to the back seat of social and family affairs, a situation that threatens to destroy her completely, she no longer belongs there. She rebels and returns to London, where she reorganizes herself and moves on. Although at the end of the novel Kehinde has not yet secured a permanent job in her professional field, the prospects are good. On the whole, she is liberated, confident, and happy. For her, therefore, London is the real home.

Thus, Emecheta's fiction fulfills Schmidt-Grozinger's notion of "progressive" in immigrant literature. Among the three modes of orientation Schmidt-Grozinger discusses, two reflect the direction taken by the two major characters in *Kehinde:* 1) the retrospective mode, in which a person defines himself through his origins, as Albert does when he takes refuge in the patriarchal system of his homeland; and 2) the progressive mode, in which a person critically examines his or her past and present situations and decides on what is best for his or her progress (112). Kehinde fulfills this second mode because, to borrow from John Hawley, she is "doubly rooted" in the African and Western traditions, having formed "a psychic bridge across the metaphysical space separating them" (339). We maintain strongly that it is this double rootedness that finally enables Kehinde to reconstruct her splintered self in her immigrant country just as it does for the immigrant writer, Emecheta.

In the end, the two women, Adah and Kehinde, follow the same pattern. Both follow their husbands to migrate to England; both are disappointed by them; both go through a period of bitter struggle and discovery; both finally find solace in freedom and self-rehabilitation; and both find London to be their true home, indeed, a new space that allows them to blend old and new, tradition and modernity. In these two novels, Emecheta is attempting to resolve her personal life issues. Adah and Kehinde's plights closely reflect her own experience in her migration from Nigeria to England. With these two novels she seems to resolve a persistent question for herself as well as for millions of other women migrants, namely, that true home is any place or country where the self is liberated and fulfilled, an idea so succinctly expressed in Grace Nichol's line, "Wherever I hang me knickers—that's my home" (qtd. in Davies, "Black British Women Writing the Anti-Imperialist Critique," 112).

[CHAPTER 4]

Gloria Naylor's North/South Dichotomy and the Reversal of the Middle Passage

Juxtaposed Migrations within *Mama Day*

Kathryn M. Paterson

In "Rootedness: The Ancestor as Foundation," Toni Morrison observes that "there is something very special and very identifiable" about black literature, even if the style is "elusive" (200). Morrison laments the fact that few scholars or critics acknowledge this quality in the work of African American writers, and that such scholars prefer to praise or condemn the work "based on criteria from other paradigms" (200–201). Morrison urges scholars to consider a new paradigm when evaluating black literature, a paradigm that often includes a choral voice, which threatens critics who view the artist as a "supreme individual," who is "always in confrontation with his own society" (201). This de-centering of the narrative subject often confuses scholars, many of whom wish to see the black writer as an independent agent negotiating through dominant discourses in order to assert his or her own identity.

Black women's writing presents even more challenges to scholars operating under white theory; as Carol Boyce Davies argues, "black women/'s writing cannot be framed in terms of one specific place, but exist/s in myriad places and times, constantly eluding the terms of the discussion" (*Black Women, Writing and Identity* 36). The dissonance that results from such "multiple voicings" may well make Eurocentric theorists uncomfortable, but this "radical Black diasporic subjectivity" deserves to be read and examined, even if its agency is elusive (Davies 37). Even though such a dialogic vision contradicts the European notion of the protagonist as a heroic isolate who embarks upon a dramatic quest, its plurality should be studied, even if scholars do need to utilize a different paradigm to do so. In particular, we must become more adept at interpreting the nuances of the first person plural point of view, a perspective that often embodies the collective voice of the

African community, and forges a "conscious historical connection" to what Morrison calls the ancestral past (202). It is therefore the "job" or sacred duty of the African American writer to preserve those historical ties, since "when you kill the ancestor, you kill yourself" (202).

Gloria Naylor's 1988 novel *Mama Day* "forges" just such connections, "among other African-American writers, other female writers," and "other classical literary figures" (Felton and Loris 3), echoing Morrison's premise. Indeed, if there is a single common thread running through the diverse scholarship on *Mama Day*, it is in the linking of the historical and the spiritual through the processes of community and genealogy. For Naylor, the spiritual and the historical are not distinct cultural elements, but inextricably linked, as the spiritual becomes historical, and histories become infused with spirit. The catalyst for this process is genealogy: the spiritual and its historical context are transferred from one generation to the next, in the process providing a portal through which the spiritual can break into and act upon events in the present, in turn generating new histories.

In *Mama Day*, Naylor uses the intricate ancestry of the Day family to forge connections between the capitalist, white world of modernist New York and the insular, black community of Willow Springs. As readers of the novel, we are invited to enter into Cocoa Day's conversation with George Andrews, a dialogue that he participates in posthumously, and a narrative that forms the bulk of the novel's forward action, even though the events narrated occur strangely outside of time. As Lindsey Tucker observes, "Cocoa's words are spoken in a time which has not arrived and addressed to a person who has been many years dead" (173). Indeed, by setting the moment of "story-listening" (Donlon 34) in 1999 rather than in 1988 when the novel was initially published, Naylor "stitches past, present, and future together" in what Susan Meisenhelder sees as an "unfinished, dynamic story" of "black experience" that is "as culturally autonomous as Willow Springs itself" ("The 'Whole Picture' in Gloria Naylor's *Mama Day*" 418).

Such a dynamic structure allows Naylor to enfold the narratives of George and Cocoa together, allowing them to call and respond to one another romantically while at the same time juxtaposing the individual journeys of each. Through the call and response dialogue of Cocoa and George, Naylor can also focus on a particular "dichotomy" of philosophies—"the clash between" the "rationality" or "nonbelief" that has shaped the identity of George, and the intuition or "belief" that characterizes Cocoa (Harris, "Shaping a Narrator to an Audience, an Audience to a Tale," 95). By allowing these philosophies to collide, Naylor examines the factors that have contributed to each character's distinct identity and provides points of departure from which each will travel. As Cocoa and George call and respond to one another, they must reconstruct both their separate and collective pasts, as such reconstruction allows them to articulate their respective migrations, trajectories that first collide with their initial meeting in New York City. In Cocoa's journeys back and forth between North and South, Naylor exposes the myth of the free and cosmopolitan North, as represented by Manhattan Island and New York City, and in George's migration to the South from New York, she further challenges history by metaphorically reversing the journey of the Middle Passage through George's integration into the African culture of Willow Springs. By giving up his dependence on the rationality and beliefs of the dominant American culture, George aligns himself with the African roots of Willow Springs, therefore reclaiming his own heritage as he is both physically and spiritually grafted into the genealogy of the island. Thus, in juxtaposing the migrations of Cocoa Day and George Andrews in *Mama Day*, Naylor explores the connection between history, genealogy, and African American identity, and provides an alternative narrative framework that allows for the reinterpretation of some of the darkest moments within the collective American past.

It is no coincidence that the romance between Cocoa and George begins in New York, since Naylor's urban North represents not only monetary opportunity and the promise of advancement but also a place ripe with opportunities for romance as well. It is only in this urban North that Cocoa can find a plethora of potential partners, where she can meet "quite a few" men in diners and coffee shops by offering them mint-flavored toothpicks from the little box she always carries around with her. Only in the urban North can she have the kind of job where she can spend the day under the air conditioner and be a "crisp butterfly" (14) and not out in the fields picking cotton or at the drive-through window of a fast food restaurant.

This urban North, and in particular the city of New York, embodies both the ambition and failure of the modern city, as it is the center for high finance, high fashion, and high art. Its skyscrapers point upwards, and its citizens inhabit those buildings, with little connection to one another despite such close proximity. New York may be, as George tells Cocoa, "a network of small towns" (61), but it is a network often divided and devoid of genuine community, a network of warehouse apartments and complicated intersections, where people are isolated by schedules dictated by trains and office clocks rather than the seasons of an agricultural economy. Such isolation and regimentation "exacts" from humanity "a different sort of consciousness than does rural life," notes sociologist Georg Simmel, who examined the role of the modern city in shaping consciousness as early as 1902 in "The Metropolis and Mental Life" (130). According to Simmel, the metropolis creates "psychological conditions" that "use up" more consciousness than do the slower, more habitual "life and sensory imagery" of the rural community (131). For Southern blacks during the Great Migration, the impact upon the psyche was especially distressing, since, as Farah Jasmine Griffin notes, "the arrival of Southern blacks is marked by an immediate confrontation with a foreign place and time, with technology and urban capitalism, with the crowd and the stranger" (51). Such a confrontation "assaults" what Griffin calls the "migrant psyche" and changes the way that the African American conceives "time and space" (52). And though, as Simmel observes, "metropolitan man" may be "free" of the prejudices and preconceptions "which hem in the small-town man," this freedom is not necessarily comfortable, as "the bodily proximity and narrowness of space" in the city "makes the mental distance" between individuals all "the more visible" (133). Indeed, all too often caverns exist between the citizens of a city, and in New York those caverns can seem insurmountable.

This alienation and lack of community are precisely what Cocoa experiences in New York, as she discovers that many of the opportunities held out by the large city turn out to be far more elusive than she imagined. Cocoa must spend a desperate six months searching for work, begging for job leads from friends when she nears the exhaustion of her unemployment benefits and discovers that jobs through temping agencies will scarcely pay the rent, let alone all the other necessities of life (15). And romantic possibilities often fizzle as well; although Cocoa's toothpick strategy has already resulted in two dates in one month, one turned out to be a "creep" and the other a "half creep" (16), causing Cocoa to conclude that she is living in "awful times for a single woman in that city," (17), awful times that make women "desperate and sad" (17), and she wants no part of such desperation.

Such a façade of possibility highlights the crumbling American ideal of the self-made man, an ideal never more promoted than in the image of Lady Liberty thrusting her torch into the clouds above Ellis Island. "Give us your poor, your huddled masses," the engraving at Liberty's feet reads, but at the time of that engraving those "huddled masses" certainly did not include the chained rows of slaves, legs shiny with sweat and urine, crowded onto the decks of slave ships on a forced pilgrimage to the New World. Neither did they include the regiment of Africans fighting in the Civil War against their own freedom or the myriad of Negro slaves harvesting corn and cotton to boost the Southern economy. While it was fashionable during the height of the industrial revolution to believe that individuals could advance beyond their stations given the right education and set of skills, by the mid-twentieth century many people were beginning to question such a premise, arguing that even if the ideal did exist, it only applied to white men who were born into situations of privilege. Instead of leading to a close examination of racial relations and a genuine understanding of the accumulated horrors of slavery, this challenging of ideals prompted yet more false structures, designed to appease white guilt by attempting, on the surface, to promote equality. Cocoa is all too familiar with such empty gestures, as she acknowledges that firms who hire African Americans as front desk receptionists often hire no other black people for the more advanced positions, believing that by hiring just one person, "they'd put the ghost of Martin Luther King to rest" (20).

In the case of the Andrews and Stein office, however, it is a white woman who is at the reception desk, and George Andrews himself is black, hinting at real potential—in Cocoa's case, the potential both for a job and for the significant interpersonal connection she has lacked ever since she left Willow Springs. She is attracted to him immediately, and although she tries to repress this attraction, especially when she realizes he is the interviewer whom she is scheduled to meet, she cannot help but think about him both sexually and romantically. His hands linger during their post-interview handshake, and as she stumbles out into a reception area filled with other applicants, she is filled with the promise of both a salary and a love interest (31).

What the handshake is not filled with is the potential for Cocoa to connect with her heritage, and it is because of this lack that she readily defends her yearly trip back to Willow Springs. Instead of altering her plans when George tells her that she will have to start Monday if she is hired, she informs him that the trip is nonnegotiable. Cocoa must go back home, not only because her position as only remaining grandchild obligates her to, but also because she needs to observe the tradition she has created for herself. The references throughout the novel to the annual nature of Cocoa's journey transform the typical two-week vacation of the working professional into a ritual pilgrimage into the inner workings of the soul, a time for the kind of renewal and invigoration that can only result from the clarity of reconnecting with one's family of origin.

In forcing Cocoa to choose between honoring her tradition and unconditionally accepting the position with Andrews and Stein, Naylor juxtaposes the city of New York, and in particular Manhattan Island, with the island of Willow Springs. In the chimerical meritocracy of New York, opportunities are diverse and plentiful but elusive and often insubstantial. In Willow Springs, there is little opportunity for advancement, but there are tangible ties within the community and to its heritage. As Meisenhelder observes, Willow Springs is "culturally independent," standing outside of white traditions and even outside of America ("Whole Picture" 405) in its location among what Trudier Harris calls the "mythical, southern territories" of fictional spaces ("Shaping a Narrator to an Audience" 62), spaces that, like

Faulkner's Yoknapatawpha County in Mississippi, serve as ripe soil for generational sagas (63).

Willow Springs's independence both from the mainland and from the politics and culture of statehood forces upon it a certain kind of insularity, but, as George points out to Cocoa during and after their first date, pockets of circumscription exist even within a place as large as New York. According to George, Cocoa has come to New York "following a myth" (Naylor 61) that she has to be quick, aggressive, and competitive, because New Yorkers are always rushing. The reality of New York that George sees, however, is of "a network of small towns" within whole blocks, a couple of alleys, or a single apartment building, in which the people have lived for generations and are bound together by a single language, "code of behavior" (61), and set of laws. George also challenges Cocoa with the idea that she has isolated herself, by choosing to venture no further beyond her apartment building than an area the size of Willow Springs (65).

The difference, then, between these neighborhoods of New York City and the town of Willow Springs lies simply in connections; because Willow Springs is not geographically or politically connected to the area around it, its citizens must seek internal connections, reaching back through history to the events and characters of the past. In New York, Cocoa can learn that a "Kumquat" is really a Korean and that a "taco" is a Puerto Rican (62), and she can begin to appreciate those external and cultural differences, but in Willow Springs, she can internalize the legends of Sapphira Wade and the mysteries of the Other Place. Thus, what Naylor points to through Cocoa and George's mutual education of one another is that with big city diversity comes the crux of the problem inherent in the industrial condition. Cocoa will become an island unto herself if the goal of the place is merit and progress—tradition and heritage are less important and must often be compromised, leaving the individual isolated and alone. And this is the problem for Cocoa with New York: the freedom she wants is there, but she must relinquish a little bit of her identity in order to have it, a sacrifice she is not willing to make—for a job or for a man.

In order for the capitalist world of New York and the mystical community of Willow Springs to coexist in the narrative, Naylor must bring them together in the marriage of Cocoa and George, a marriage that she sensibly initiates in a neutral location, New Orleans. Although New Orleans is southern, it is a very different South from that of Willow Springs, and George himself remarks that it is not the "real South" (129). Naylor takes little pains to describe the city, caring instead to reveal the whirlwind nature of Cocoa and George's marriage by her lack of detail. Cocoa and George get married so suddenly that George only remembers the week as "an exhilarating blur"

(140), and Cocoa's only recollection of New Orleans is of "fifty thousand people running up and down Bourbon Street screaming, 'Go Eagles. Go, Raiders,' flapping green wings on their backs and waving tinfoil swords" (147). And even though neither George nor Cocoa has significant attachment to the culture or geography of the city, Naylor superficially aligns the marriage trip with George. After all, the trip is not only his suggestion but also the condition upon which he accepts Cocoa's proposal in the first place. If either member of the couple can claim any connection to New Orleans, it is George, but only in a peripheral way, as the crowds at football games only serve for him as a surrogate and temporal community. Thus, while New Orleans is a place where the wedding itself can take place, such a neutral space does not allow the kind of spiritual growth that both characters must undergo if their marriage is to blossom and bear fruit. For this kind of growth, ancestral connections are needed, and it is only when Cocoa finally brings George to Willow Springs that both characters can reconnect to their spiritual heritage.

When Cocoa first introduces George to the island community, she is nervous and uncomfortable, rather than excited and proud, knowing that she faces the sudden clash of the two different worlds she has inhabited. Her life with George suddenly collides with her past from the island, and this collision prompts her to doubt whether or not George can love and accept the essence of Willow Springs that dwells within her. To Cocoa, Willow Springs is not just a hometown but also the living essence of her soul. She knows that George loves part of her—the part he has become acquainted with during the six months they've known each other in New York, but she questions whether he can accept "the rest" of her, "the whole" that is "here" in Willow Springs (176). Interestingly, this slippage of terms—from "rest" to "whole"—reveals in microcosm the slippages in Cocoa's identity. Before she revisits the island with George, Cocoa has never questioned the role Willow Springs has played in determining her identity. Until that moment, she has been content to exist in two separate personas, never allowing for a discourse to take place between the two. George's presence in Willow Springs forces her to acknowledge the "transformation" (176) that she undergoes every time she returns to Willow Springs, and enables her to step outside of herself and examine the part of her that has become urbanized. She stands in "Cocoa's bedroom" (176) watching "Ophelia's husband carefully unpacking his clothes" (177). This sudden shift to third-person reference suggests that the first-person narrator of the passage—Cocoa's essential self—is neither wholly Cocoa nor wholly Ophelia, but an authentic being in her own right, one who has assumed the differing personas necessitated by the roles she has been given by each community.

In assuming these differing personas, Cocoa has also developed different patterns of behavior for each community, and George's presence in Willow Springs also prompts her to reexamine those patterns. Like any young woman bringing home a new love, Cocoa fears the exposure of her flaws and the failure of her relational strategies, and in particular her methods of manipulating others. In New York, for example, she has found that she can effectively manipulate George's emotions by throwing temper tantrums. But in Willow Springs, those tantrums, "whether coddled or dismissed" are "never taken seriously" (177). When Cocoa looks at her bedroom through George's eyes, she sees its rustic character, flaws and all. For the first time, "the slope in the wooden floor" unsettles her and all she can think about is the "dripping shower head that left a blue-green stain in the base of the tub" (177), a dripping showerhead that engineer George will likely want to fix.

While Cocoa wonders how her past and familial ties will affect her relationship with George, she also acknowledges that George's presence in her bed transforms her room from a girlhood sanctuary to a "world where only Ophelia and George belong" (177). After all, with George, Cocoa is Ophelia, but beyond Cocoa's immediate family, no one on the island knows "who in the hell Ophelia" is (176). This childhood bedroom is the place where the Cocoa of Willow Springs collides with the Ophelia of George's New York. It is only after experiencing the force of this collision that she can temporarily reconcile her two disparate identities and realize how fortunate she is to belong in both worlds: "Ophelia and Cocoa could both live in that house with you [George]" (177).

Cocoa's acknowledgment of how fortunate she is to belong to both George and to the island community reveals the multifaceted nature of her identity, a complex nature that may be mistaken for what Homi Bhabha calls hybridity, but in actuality is something very different. Bhabha's concept of hybridity relies upon the notion that the hybrid emerges from a negotiation between two or more different cultural identities. Out of this negotiation flowers a reevaluated cultural identity that incorporates this confrontation of difference: "The social articulation of difference, from the minority perspective, is a complex, on-going negotiation that seeks to authorize cultural hybridities that emerge in moments of historical transformation" (*Locations of Culture* 2). While it may be easy to see Cocoa Day as a character who exemplifies this negotiation, a close reading of this and other passages within the novel reveals that Cocoa's development lends itself more to the position of syncretism, as articulated by Becquer and Gatti in "Elements of Vogue," and further discussed in Carole Boyce Davies's *Black Women, Writing and Identity*. Syncretism, as Davies explains, describes an "antagonistic relationship," where the process of relating to an opposite awakens that which is "Other within the Self," so that both identities can simultaneously be "enabled and prevented from full constitution" (48). If we look closely at this explanation, we can read what happens within the pages of *Mama Day* between George and Cocoa as "antagonistic," as each character certainly stirs recognition of Other within the Self. However, even this position of syncretism is not an entirely fitting theory for Cocoa and George's relationship within the novel or for either character's pathway to integration and self-actualization.

What Naylor does in *Mama Day* with black identity is something even more complicated: Cocoa and George do awaken Otherness within each other, but instead of paralyzing that Otherness within the Self and inhibiting integration, Naylor enables full integration by spiritualizing their relationship and allowing the two characters to participate in a dialogue that transcends not only time and space, but death. By having readers eavesdrop on a dialogue that George can only participate in posthumously, Naylor suggests that there is an essential self—or soul—that transcends all boundaries of identity and therefore relegates racial limitations to the flesh. If Cocoa experiences a collision of worlds, it is not only because she has been operating, in New York City, according to white limitations and expectations, but also because her role in Willow Springs demands its own set of expectations. Only after death can all of these limitations be transcended, and that which is Ophelia fully integrated with that which is Cocoa. *Mama Day*'s pages close before we see this take place, but by "listening" to George's process of transcendence, we can at least somewhat glimpse Cocoa's as well. Such glimpses parallel the prediction that Mama Day herself makes, that Cocoa will come back to the island, in time realizing her true identity. But what we do not see is whether or not that realization will take place before Cocoa's death. What Naylor suggests, then, is that Cocoa, like George, may only be wholly integrated with her ancestral past beyond the boundary of life and death. Thus, George's presence in Cocoa's life and in Willow Springs itself prompts us to expand our notions of hybridity and double-consciousness, suggesting that there is a spiritual dimension that transcends such anthropological classifications.

George's presence in Willow Springs also prompts Cocoa to examine the complex nature of her membership in the community; while she does belong to the community in spirit, her ambitions, and the consequent time she has spent off the island, have distanced her from the everyday lives of the people. Perhaps it is because of this isolation that Cocoa's voice is not the first we hear; our introduction to her comes not through her own narration but through a mention by the communal voice of Willow Springs that narrates chapter 1. Interestingly, although Mama Day claims Cocoa as "like her very own" during this opening segment of the book (9), the communal voice refrains from doing so. As long as Cocoa remains geographically separate from the island, she cannot be fully a part of its narrative. Furthermore, even though we do hear her side of the story, it cannot be told fully from the perspective of the communal voice, since Cocoa is both an insider and an outsider to Willow Springs. Although many of the townspeople still align themselves with her and consider her a part of them, her time in the urban North has sent her into a state of permanent limbo between communities—a limbo that, while allowing her to be the arbiter of certain kinds of information, prevents her from being privy to others.

Though Cocoa sees herself as being whole only when she is on the island, she is not fully integrated into the island culture, a move that Mama Day hints will only happen in the fullness of time. Through George, Cocoa gleans information that she would not otherwise be privy to, and through George, she recognizes the limitations her gender has placed upon her knowledge of certain portions of community lore. Although Dr. Buzzard and the rest of the men in the barbershop have never actively kept secrets from the women in their lives, there are tales they deliver more readily to other men (189–90). Cocoa does not know these stories in part because she is a woman and therefore not likely to be told them directly, but also because, like Reema's boy in the opening chapter, she has not asked the right questions of the right people, choosing instead to get her information about these men "filtered through their daughters or wives" in "bits and pieces from Grandma and Mama Day" (190).

What Naylor points out through Cocoa's realization of her limits as a member of Willow Springs is the failure of any one voice to provide the entire narrative of the community. This is why Naylor must narrate her novel through both the dialogue between Cocoa and George and the consciousness of the island's collective voice. All three perspectives are needed. All three woven together make the whole, "multi-faceted truth," which according to Meisenhelder forms a "complex narrative quilt of distinct voices" ("Whole Picture" 418). The obvious Otherness of George thus does not find its counterpart in Cocoa, who is portrayed as neither fully Other to George, nor fully Same. Rather, it is found in the collective Self, represented by the "we" of the island's communal voice. Naylor uses the plural first person to establish the collective consciousness of the Willow Springs community, a consciousness that holds in tension multiple versions of its own history. Each member of the community knows, for instance, the name Sapphira Wade, and that she is the grand ancestral figure from whom many of them are descended. From this point, however, the legends diverge: in one, Sapphira smothers Bascombe Wade, her master, and lives to tell her story for a thousand days afterwards; in another, Sapphira marries Wade, bears him "seven sons in just a thousand days," puts "a dagger through his kidney," and escapes "the hangman's noose, laughing in a burst of flames" (3).

This lack of consensus is acknowledged by the collective voice, who understands that histories are likely to splinter and shift "down through the holes of time," but who quickly points us to the two "facts" that remain unaltered: Bascombe Wade is dead, and Sapphira had seven sons. The competing legends about Sapphira exemplify the plurality of perspectives within the communal voice, a plurality that theorist Mikhail Bakhtin would find doubly heteroglossic. Here the voices of many are compressed into a single narrative and translated to us via a mostly omniscient narrator who can see into the hearts and minds of all, but who resists providing an overarching narrative that will expose an objective truth. Naylor's omniscient narrator is neither human nor divine but rather an amalgamation of spirits that holds within itself a multiplicity of perspectives and impressions. Instead of privileging one narrative, this collective entity is content to give equal weight to all, allowing multiple histories the chance to exist simultaneously and enhance rather than detract from one another.

If Naylor distinguishes the communal voice by its reliance upon the heteroglossic, then she provides a nice contrast to that heteroglossia in the character of George, who attempts to collapse all the voices that inform his consciousness rather than allowing them to remain unique. George has grown up with the monoglossia of the Wallace P. Andrews Shelter for Boys, a place where rules are not only to be respected and followed but also internalized as one's own inner voice. Because most of the boys have come to the Andrews shelter from either abusive or unknown pasts, the prevailing ethos of the community is "only the present has potential" (23). Mrs. Jackson, the woman who runs the orphanage, exhorts the boys to "keep it in the now," and therefore divorces them from their painful pasts and the ensuing emotions those pasts create.

Because George knows nothing of his parentage except for the fact that his mother was a whore (130), he grows up accepting and even depending upon the monoglossia of the shelter. The shelter's rules are predictable, its structure implacable, and George begins to internalize the "facts" of life that Mrs. Jackson teaches (26). Because he has no authentic heritage, George allows his concept of rules and laws to supplant his concept of self, as he discovers a spiritual underpinning in the Western (often white) system of logic and science. Because scientific principles are universals, they are the only ideas he can trust, and he places his faith in them accordingly. Until he meets Cocoa, he eschews the intuitive and the supernatural in favor of what is purely rational and empirical: "I had what I could see; my head and my two hands, and I had each day to do something with them. . . . I may have knocked my head against the walls . . . but I never knocked on wood" (27).

George's choice of profession clearly reflects this dependence upon the literal present and the potential within it. As a mechanical engineer, he must manipulate materials according to their physical characteristics (which are scientifically invariant) and their environment of use. George so associates himself with the principles of engineering that he has commissioned a silver tie clip that he wears on his first date with Cocoa (60), a tie clip that is the essence of his identity. He is proud of the precision with which it is crafted, that is, of the precision expressed in the use of the laws of physics. It represents his identity as a mechanical engineer (60), which in turn represents his identity as a thing in the "now." It also represents the claim of absolute laws to universality, since they operate across ethnic and racial boundaries, and also across time; they are good for the past, present, and future. No genealogy is required to understand their importance. No spiritual linkage is required to make them relevant to the present. The question is, whether there is something missed by the laws. This is hinted at in George's indication that not many of the boys in the shelter went on to be artists. The world of art is a world of great power but also of great danger (26–27).

Cocoa's initial rejection of the tie clip is a rejection of George and the world of laws that he inhabits. Although the internalization of such laws has confined George's thought, the world in which he operates these laws is in theory broader than Cocoa's—or at least more diverse. He grew up in a population that was mixed African American and Puerto Rican; thus he is able to appreciate the contributions of different groups. Appreciating these contributions, however, is different from internalizing them into a heteroglossic inner voice, which is what Cocoa has done with the plurality of voices she brings with her from the island. Growing up in Willow Springs has kept Cocoa from an objective knowledge of heterogenic cultures, but in so doing has allowed her to explore fully the diversity of her own culture, something that George has yet been unable to do. Indeed, George even admits to Cocoa after the storm that "words spoken" in Willow Springs "operated on a different plane through a whole morass of history and circumstances that I was not privy to" (256). Although George is not fully aware of the existence of this "different plane" early on in his relationship with Cocoa, it is her language and the promise of authenticity she offers that he is drawn to upon their very first meeting.

Cocoa's authenticity opens George to the possibility of a genuine heritage for himself. Until he meets her, he has so divorced himself from the African community that he has even been involved with Shawn, a white woman, for five years. He does not see Shawn as Other, but he does recognize something within her that distances her from him. George never specifies what it is that "ultimately couldn't bring" him "to marry her," and even insists that it is not her race: "She had stopped being a redhead with freckles a long time ago and had become just Shawn" (53). Yet, Shawn has never inspired in him the visceral physical reaction that Cocoa does when he passes by her in the coffee shop; it is Cocoa, not Shawn, "who has the power to turn" George's "existence upside-down by simply running a hand up the back of her neck" (33). George's confrontation with such power makes him realize what is lacking in his relationship with Shawn, and makes him "question silently" whether or not he is just using her (53).

It is not until Cocoa has been married to George for over a year that she is able to bring him fully inside her heritage by taking him with her to Willow Springs. Once there, George finally realizes the connection between genealogy and history, as he watches Cocoa interact with the island and its people, particularly Abigail and Miranda. When George first meets the Day women, he is astonished by their ageless appearance. Like the fragrance of Willow Springs itself, which "smells like forever" (175), Miranda and Abigail radiate an aura of eternity. Strong, steady, and almost free of wrinkles, they possess a mythical quality that contrasts with George's own ephemeral nature and causes him to ponder whether they will ever die. George is also surprised to find Miranda smaller than he imagined, "barely five feet and could have been snapped in the middle with one good-sized hand," because she has "loomed" a "big, tall woman" in his imagination based upon the stories that Cocoa has told him (175–76).

From the beginning of their relationship, George has been envious of Cocoa's ties to her heritage, especially since these ties expose his own lack of ancestral connections. While Cocoa was born in her grandmother's house and grew up in a community where she could visit the birthplaces of several of her ancestors, George doesn't "even have a real last name" (129). To George, what Cocoa has is not just a family but a history as well, a history that George himself cannot begin to match. Thus, what Cocoa has that George lacks is a visceral connection to her past; she not only holds within her the folk traditions and legends of her people but also the internalized memories of personal contact with living ancestors. It is the lack of such connections that prompts "a lump" to form in George's throat at the "gentle pressure" of Abigail's hands upon his face, as she claims him as one of her own: "Up till that moment, no woman had ever called me her child. Did they see it in my eyes? The intense envy for all that you had and the gratitude for their being willing to let me belong?" (176)

George has never before experienced such a sense of belonging. After all, the only woman who was a constant presence in his early years was Mrs. Jackson, who ran the shelter where he grew up. Although Mrs. Jackson does care for the boys in the shelter, she effectively distances herself from the role of mother in their lives, even reminding them directly, "I am not your mother. I am paid to run this place. You have no mothers or fathers. This is not your home" (26). By including these statements as part of the list of "facts" she recites, Mrs. Jackson not only underscores her lack of maternal connection to the boys but also the anonymity of the shelter itself. The shelter exists without a past or a future, and with no folklore to bind its inhabitants together, save the suggestion that Mrs. Jackson once killed a dorm director who had raped some of the young boys. Such lore serves only to increase the presence of Mrs. Jackson as a foreboding figure, one who does care deeply for her charges but who only displays that concern beyond the confines of her relationship with them.

Mrs. Jackson is also a woman without a race—or at least that is how Naylor portrays her. Never does Naylor provide a physical description of Mrs. Jackson, so there is no clear indication of her race one way or another. Thus, Mrs. Jackson bears no kinship to George—emotionally, racially, or spiritually. He has grown up in a household that is not a home, a place that positions him, along with all the other boys who live there, as Other. They are Other to Mrs. Jackson, to the dorm directors, to each other, and finally, to both the state that pays Mrs. Jackson's salary and the world outside the shelter's doors. As Mrs. Jackson says, the boys are not "delinquents, rejects, or somebody's garbage" (26), but they are not necessarily valuable either, and certainly do not possess the physical kinship that would validate them. As critic Suzanne Juhasz contends, throughout the entirety of *Mama Day*'s Part I, George exists "beyond the bridge" that leads to Willow Springs, dwelling in a modernity that represents patriarchical hegemony and that remains forever "separate from the magic circle of mother love" (136).

The belonging that George gains on the island extends beyond the bounds of blood relationships. What George gains in Willow Springs is an ancestral heritage that transcends genealogy; when he aligns himself with Cocoa and her living ancestors, he becomes spiritually grafted into their lineage, a lineage that extends beyond the physical boundaries of the island to the continent of Africa itself, of which the island is an extension. This process of spiritual grafting metaphorically reverses the Middle Passage, providing an authentic, rich, and heteroglossic past for George that replaces the provisional, narrow, and monoglossic rule of rationality that has hitherto existed for him as a surrogate heritage.

This grafting is credible because Naylor has positioned Willow Springs from the beginning of the novel as, in Miltonian terms, a paradise regained, or, in this case, an Africa regained. The island's ambiguous location off the coast of lower South Carolina and north Georgia places it geographically in the middle of the real-life Gullah islands, Sea Islands off the Atlantic coast that linguists and historians recognize for their unique preservation of African American culture and history. As theorist Lene Brøndum argues, "once a 'reverse Ellis island' to the African slaves, the islands today have been reversed again into a more positive cultural 'bridge' to Africa" (153). In *Mama Day*, Naylor, according to Brøndum, uses "the rich Sea Island heritage" to identify Willow Springs as an extension of Africa. The tiny island community operates as a microcosm of the continent at large, complete with tribal remedies and customs, reverence for ancestors, and a designation of a particular location, the Other Place, as possessing a concentration of spiritual power due to its ancestral ties.

This continuity of African tradition into the Americas is only made possible by Naylor's initial depiction of the island as independent, a fact she makes evident in the novel's prologue. Because, as critic Hélène Christol contends, a "journey back to origins" must "start with the reappropriation of the land" that has once been lost to the black community, *Mama Day* begins by establishing Willow Springs as a "free" and "black territory," emphasized in the text by "the importance of . . . the 'deed' that confirms" black ownership (160). From the Willow Springs map that is, according to researcher Cheryl Wall, "itself a sign of black self-sufficiency" (1452), to Mama Day's larder, which "is always full" (1457), the black community of Willow Springs is heroically independent—liberated in every sense of the word (1457–58). But, as Christol insists, "owning the territory is not enough; reappropriation of land has to go with the reappropriation of time and thus of history" (161), a history that Mama Day will continually reinvent and tie to genealogy. Thus, the book's structure involves a "creative dialogue between public and private life, history and biography, the past and the present," with genealogy itself at the center of these intersections (161). Christol contends that such genealogy can only be reconstructed by the recovering of the names of the Day family, names that "the Days own . . . as they own their land" (162). Once this genealogy is reconstructed, Christol concludes, the "lost unity of man and nature, of men and women," and perhaps even of black and white, can finally be restored, and "the peace which has been lost" regained (162–63).

George, of course, cannot recover the names of his forebears the way that Miranda and the rest of the Days are able to, since he has no name to connect him to the past. His last name, Andrews, is merely the last name of the man who founded the shelter where he grew up; like the slaves ripped from their heritage and given the names of their white masters, his surname is disjointed from his reality as a man of African descent. George's redemption into his lost African heritage depends upon a storm that sweeps across the same ocean that the African slaves once traveled. It is this storm that finally severs

George's ties to the patriarchy of America, literally washing out the bridge that connects the island to the mainland. Meisenhelder sees the storm, like the Genesis flood, as a process of purification ("False Gods and Black Goddesses in Naylor's *Mama Day* and Hurston's *Their Eyes Were Watching God*" 1445), sweeping with it the "false gods" that have hitherto existed within the novel "as well as false models of masculinity" (1446). According to Meisenhelder, Naylor sees George's "rigid masculinity" as having "no place in the purified new worlds born out of the storms" (1446).

The storm, however, is not merely a means of purification. Naylor goes to great lengths to emphasize the storm's African heritage and its parallels to the Middle Passage. It "starts on the shores of Africa, a simple breeze among the palms and cassava, before it's carried off, tied up with thousands like it, on a strong wave headed due west. . . . Restless and disturbed, no land in front of it, no land in back, it draws up the ocean vapor and rains fall like tears" (249). It is almost as if the storm gathers up in itself the ancient tears and the pain of the Middle Passage that created them. After all, the storm traverses the exact path that many of the slave ships took to America from Africa. But the storm does not only gather up spirits lost along the Middle Passage—it begins with the murmuring of the spirits in Africa as well; as they groan through the leaves of the palms cassavas, we can almost hear the cries of grief of the African ancestors whose descendants have been lost to them. After all, the reason that the Middle Passage is so traumatic to begin with is that it does not just encompass the horrors of the transatlantic journey, but the reality of the historical events and separation of families that take place on both the African and American coasts that are its borders. As Maria Diedrich, Henry Louis Gates Jr., and Carl Pedersen argue in *Black Imagination and the Middle Passage*, the Middle Passage "emerges not as a clean break between past and present, but as a spatial continuum between Africa and the Americas," a spatial continuum that "extends" topographically "from the interior of Africa across the Atlantic and into the interior of the Americas" (8). In *Mama Day*, Naylor, like many other Black writers, has "reconceptualized" the Middle Passage to include what Diedrich, Gates, and Pedersen term a "syncretic notion of a space in-between that links geographical and cultural regions" and transcends "ethnic, racial and national boundaries"(9). Thus, Naylor's storm itself experiences and contains the trauma of the Middle Passage, resulting in such a fury that it obliterates the superficial ties that Willow Springs has to America, ties born of convenience and circumstance rather than shared affinity.

Psychologically, it is this fury that George experiences as "God," or in this case, "Goddess," as Naylor explains that such fury "could only be the workings of Woman" (251). Such an understanding of "God" adds a new layer of meaning to George's experience of the storm. On the face of it, George is undergoing a spiritual crisis of the sort well understood in the mainstream American religious tradition: is there "some presence that might be governing what was beyond my own abilities?" (251). Trained in rationalism and self-reliance, George has tried to "engineer" life as he engineers water systems, choosing his beliefs like construction materials to maximize the occasions when "things were under control" and leave him in the position of "a comfortable amnesiac," desiring only to be "left alone to seek happiness where I could find it" (251). For George, concrete religions like Buddhism, Christianity, and Islam shared a similar goal: control of their adherents through politics and fear (252). Only now, faced with the awesome "pure power" of the storm and his own impotence to do anything other than witness its destructive capabilities, George can recognize the limitations of his rationality.

The storm's force exceeds all of George's established parameters, with an untamable wildness and a center at which there is no possibility of negotiation. Faced metaphorically with the force of the voices and tears of millions upon millions of his own forebears betrayed and dehumanized, George can now realize an authentic heritage of his own, a heritage which cannot be destroyed due to "amnesia" or negotiated away through the adoption of a surrogate culture. The storm allows George to experience the Middle Passage for himself, for only in so doing can he regain what has been denied him from birth, and importantly, the revelation of his heritage comes not through his own searching but from Africa itself. The power of the horror of the Middle Passage takes matters into its own hands and forces itself upon George unasked and initially unwanted, an irresistible and inescapable grace no less potent than John Calvin's. Only now that the past has irrupted into the present is there a chance of peace. Only now, since George has felt "the growing and pervasive realization of my own insignificance" (252) can he stand in proper relation to his ancestors, living and dead, and gain spiritually the position of community member that he holds physically by his marriage to Cocoa.

George's spiritual transformation is not initially evidenced in his behavior, however. Despite his experience, George longs for nothing more than "to return to work," to escape back to a world of phones and hospitals, a longing made desperate by Cocoa's illness. Circumstances dictate otherwise. A possible voyage in a washed-up boat is foiled when the citizens of Willow Springs tear the boat apart to use the wood in rebuilding the bridge. George works tirelessly on the bridge, all night at one point, only to see the work of several days destroyed by a lightning strike. There is clearly a force that will not suffer George to leave the island until he can properly understand the nature of his transformation; George has experienced the Middle Passage and the return to "Africa regained," but he has not yet accepted his heritage as his own.

It is not inevitable that George must die on the island to fulfill what is required. Mama Day knows that if he so chooses, his self-belief may be guided by her "so she can connect it up with all the believing that had gone before" (285). George chooses otherwise but nevertheless enters the community of spirits that dwell on the island, just as his ashes dwell in the waters around it, a sure confirmation that his transformation was complete, if unrecognized. As Fred Metting observes, "although George remains skeptical . . . he does participate long enough, and with enough will, to protect" Cocoa (165). In order for George to be capable of this saving power, Metting argues, "Mama Day must convert" him by linking him "to the legacy of the Day men" (165). Because of this grafting into the genealogy of the Day family, in future years, Cocoa will talk with his spirit, as only Mama Day can do now. In future years, George will contribute to the narrative that is *Mama Day,* a voice from the dead combining with the voices of the living. In future years, perhaps, there will be a variety of legends built upon the basic facts of Cocoa's recovery and George's death, a recognition that, as Cocoa says, "there are just too many sides to the whole story" (Naylor 311). In the "now" of George's death that is mere present, the "now" of the rational, of the Wallace P. Andrews Shelter for Boys, there is room only for tears, for the mourning of the one who has left, for individual loss. But in the "now" of the island that wraps up in one past, present, and future, there is a rope of a million variegated strands stretching across time and the Atlantic, each lending strength to and drawing strength from the whole, and here they mourn only lost possibilities.

Thus, even though Cocoa still does not live on the island by the chronological end of the novel, Abigail and Miranda Day do not mourn her absence, because they know that Cocoa, no matter where she is, embodies possibilities that are not lost, since her spirit is bound up with the other spirits of the island, which are in turn bound with Africa. Even if Cocoa does not fully understand this bond at the time of the story's telling, she will one day, and, as Miranda reassures George's spirit, Cocoa will return both to him and to the island community itself: "One day she'll hear you, like you're hearing me. And there'll be another time—time that I won't be here for—when she'll learn about the beginning of the Days. But she's gotta go away to come back to that kind of knowledge. And I came to tell you not to worry: whatever roads take her from here, they'll always lead her back to you" (308). For Cocoa, then, George's death is a catalyst that prompts her to grow, but this growth requires that she leave Willow Springs. She cannot "bury" herself "in Willow Springs forever" (308), nor can she divorce herself from it entirely.

Although she still does not realize that the spirit of Willow Springs lives within her, she understands that she needs to be rooted somewhere—and that New York is not a place that allows for such stability.

Not only does New York remind Cocoa too much of the George for whom she grieves; the city cannot function as "familiar ground" the way that Charleston does. Charleston's proximity to Willow Springs allows Cocoa to live apart from the island but close enough to maintain some connection to it, even if she still does not fully participate in such a connection. Charleston also allows Cocoa the opportunity to meet another man and to fall in love again, even though she admits that he can only be "second best" to George. As Cocoa continues to live and grow emotionally, she not only learns to abide the loss of George, but she is able to begin her own family, thus continuing her strand of genealogy.

Just as it is George who attempts to rebuild the bridge between the island and the mainland, George becomes the means by which Cocoa can confront the sublation of her own disparate identities. By aligning George with the white European world of engineering and mechanical logic, Naylor places him as outsider or Other to Willow Springs, forcing Cocoa, in turn, to negotiate between her own Otherness and her sense of belonging. As George reunites with his African past, Cocoa becomes aware of the tenuousness and superficiality of her own ancestral knowledge, and it is only with this awareness that she can begin the process of being genuinely integrated into the core of the community. Such a process of integration must culminate in a final move away from Willow Springs before Cocoa can return; once away, she can finally see the rift between her own understanding of her community and the spiritual realities of her heritage.

Once Cocoa can see this rift, she will be able to understand, like Miranda, that her ties are inescapable, no matter how tenuous her knowledge of them is. After all, Cocoa's "pure black" skin "brings back the great, grand Mother" spirit of Sapphira Wade, even if Cocoa herself does not know the story of the Day family by the end of the novel. Her "18 & 23" blackness is her heritage and her destiny, absorbing "all the light in the universe" and "even" swallowing "the sun" (48), but her journey must continue beyond the end of the novel before she can fully realize her destiny and fulfill all of its possibilities. Once she realizes that she is truly the kind of gold "only an ancient mother of pure black" (48) can spit out, once she can see where her own lineage fits within the cord of her ancestry, then she will be able to return to Willow Springs for good, because it is only then that her own spiritual journey will be complete.

Cocoa's and George's migrations, then, like their narratives, are interdependent and complementary. While George begins his journey completely alienated from his spiritual past, Cocoa begins hers insisting upon observing traditions she has been physically part of but does not fully understand. Cocoa's initial migration out of Willow Springs to New York enables her to experience the inauthenticity of the modern city and allows George the possibility of reclaiming his spiritual heritage as he becomes grafted onto the genealogy of the island. In turn, George's integration with the ancestral community initiates Cocoa's remigration out of Willow Springs in preparation for final reintegration into her spiritual community and thus a fully integrated identity. By suggesting that both characters' spiritual development depends upon a return to the South, Naylor also aligns herself with several other writers, such as Toni Morrison, Alice Walker, Ernest Gaines, and Maya Angelou, who create what Farah Jasmine Griffin calls "artistic" narratives of remigration (146). Such writers, Griffin argues, "are influenced, but not bound by the dominant migration narrative," and often resist focusing "on the continued racism of the South" (182). Rather than depicting a South that "continues to suffer from a racist legacy," these "literary" migration narratives portray a South that is both "a place of possibility" (146) and a "homeplace" that offers "a haven of safety" (181).

Ultimately, both Cocoa and George have had to exist within conflicting modernities—the conflict between their African American ancestry and the dominant American culture that neither recognizes nor values it. Although this conflict produces schisms of the self, and the consciousnesses of both characters reflect such fragmentation, in Naylor's world, there is a way for both of them to reintegrate their fragmented selves into an authentic whole. In Naylor's world, the dominant culture, then, plays the role of Other, which leads the alienated African American to a crisis of understanding where a lack of integration becomes clear and where reintegration is now possible. Such reintegration functions as a reversal of the Middle Passage, since the individual does not merely return to the ancestral community but also opens up new knowledge and forges new connections.

[CHAPTER 5]

Reconfiguring Self

A Matter of Place in Selected Novels by Paule Marshall

Marie Foster Gnage

"From Poets in the Kitchen," an essay published by Paule Marshall in 1983, speaks to the importance of reinventing oneself, even though for Marshall's mother and her friends, it was a recurring two hours in the basement of a brownstone in Brooklyn. Marshall observed the "poets"—women of her mother's generation who had migrated to the United States from the West Indies—as they reconfigured themselves, transcending the daily grind. At least for the few moments that they gathered together in the kitchen over tea, they became problem solvers, sociologists, psychologists, counselors, politicians, and even poets in the use of language (Marshall, "From Poets in the Kitchen," 26–27). Marshall has transferred the lessons she learned from the "poets" to the women in *The Chosen Place, The Timeless People* (1969), *Praisesong for the Widow* (1983), *Daughters* (1991), and *The Fisher King* (2000), for whom place, be it physical or psychological, is a catalyst for reconfiguration. Marshall's creations reconfigure themselves with help from others and in places that feed or fuel their spirit—not unlike the women in "From Poets in the Kitchen." The characters, however, have different vocations in life and cross waters in an almost formulaic pattern in route to becoming. The migration to a different place actualizes the reassembling of the "puzzle pieces" of their lives—self-discovery, cultural discovery, and historical reference.

In four titles listed above, women characters sort out their lives that have somehow become as murky as the seas and oceans they cross and as dense as the fog that drapes their memory. Marshall uses many "devices" to suggest that they are in serious psychological trouble and are without a "kitchen" similar to one that provided a safe haven for Marshall's mother and her friends wherein to sort out their life conditions. Knowledge of their cultural, psychological, and sociological selves is either unknown or buried in their psyche. This lack of knowledge of self makes them need mentors, or medicine.

The outcomes of women's journeys to reconfiguration are equal to their ability to understand the need for appropriate physical and psychological places, and their willingness to be supplicant. Sometimes their bodies physically reflect the effects of migration on their reconfiguration. Olmstead notes that in *The Chosen Place, The Timeless People* and *Praisesong for the Widow*, "Marshall spends a great deal of time describing Merle's and Avey's bodies as the sites for radical transformation, not only of the self but of the community as well" (2). Ursa-Bea Mackenzie's and Hattie Carmicheal's physical bodies reflect their transforming experience: an abortion for Ursa and hair loss for Hattie. They experience physical and psychological upheaval in their literal and figurative passages, and place either defines or destroys them.

Reconfiguration for all of the women characters addressed herein seems to begin with restlessness, with a simmering discontent that will not be appeased by the circumstances of present life. If the restlessness converts into a quest, then—either through self-inquiry or discourses with spiritual guides, mentors, or friends—the result can be revelation and transformation. Reconfiguration seems to require the slow, steady infusion of vision into a reality. It is, in essence, moving from seeing anew to being anew.

Marshall wrote *The Chosen Place, The Timeless People* after many trips to Barbados and much research on the islands in the Caribbean and the challenges faced by the people. Edward Braithwaite comments that Marshall's ancestry influences her work: "in it we find a West Indies facing the Metropolitan West on one hand, and clinging to a memorial past on the other. Within this matrix, she formulates her enquiry into identity and change" (225). Ancestry more than likely influences Marshall's ability to blend fiction and history to make readers see not just the character or setting being described but all that they represent. Geta Leseur writes in "'Read Your History, Man': Bridging Racism, Paternalism, and Privilege in Paule Marshall's *The Chosen Place, The Timeless People*," "[m]ore than layers of place and time and persons, it is an interlocking crystalline structure that teaches history, mediates on the consequences of slavery and colonialism, and presents a vision for potential reconciliation and change on the personal, social and even international levels. . . . True to her storytelling heritage, she creates characters that speak and act realistically in their fictional world, reacting to historical and international forces as they confront local and personal, social, economic and political issues" (90–91). The historical forces that Marshall has her characters react to are those properties of post-colonialism that have affected the Caribbean Islands that are her settings. In *Colonialism*,

Postcolonialism, Ania Loomba defines postcolonialism as "the conquest and control of others' land and goods" (2). Postcolonialism on Bourne Island is apparent in new governmental structures as well as in the estate owners who take advantage of a people bowed low. Gina Wisker writes: "A country can be post-colonial, i.e. independent, and yet neo-colonial, i.e. still economically dependent on the relations and links with those who operate colonial rule over it. It is sometimes debatable whether once-colonized countries can be seen as properly post-colonial because their ideas and economies are still tied to the colonizer" (15). The setting of Marshall's novel, the fictional Bourne Island, is still dependent upon both the country responsible for its colonization as well as the United States, which contributed to colonialism on the island. Joy M. Lynch notes that people and place in Marshall's novel were "shaped by the colonizing of their land, culture, and history. The population of this island has inherited the economic, psychological and political by-products of being twice colonized, first by British colonial system and, more recently, by American economic interests. The traffic between nations—economic and racial—that constitutes imperialism results in a colonial condition reflected in individual identity" (174). Marshall seems to indicate that colonialism is interwoven into the identity of those like Merle whose birth and rebirth take place in countries where vestiges are still evident.

Central to an analysis of Merle Kinbona in *The Chosen Place, The Timeless People* is Marshall's explanation of what she accomplishes in the novel: "After struggling for some time, I was finally able in my most recent novel to bring together what I consider to be the two themes most central to my work; the importance of truly confronting the past, both in personal and historical terms, and the necessity of reversing the present order" (Miller 49). Marshall's female characters in all of the novels discussed herein experience identity crises because of their choice to install memory blocks to overcome their personal and historical pasts. However, they leave home and travel the heroine's journey, if they have the physical and spiritual strength, and a guide/mentor.

Robert Bone, in his review of Marshall's *The Chosen Place, The Timeless People*, refers to the novel as a "parable." He notes that the setting, "Bourne Island, as the name implies, forms a symbolic boundary between the cultures of Europe and Asia, between the forces of progress and tradition, between town man and country man, rich and poor, white and black" (4). Bourne Island is a land of contrasts; the character, Merle Kinbona, is a clearer reflection of this than other characters, male or female, in the novel. The island is described by characters as "painfully familiar" with "two equal unequal parts"—"neatly ordered fields and the town poised at its southern edge" in the west and a "kind of valley" that resembles "a ruined amphitheater whose other half had crumbled away and fallen into the sea" to the east, a "ravaged sea bottom" (*The Chosen Place, The Timeless People* 13–14, 21).

Merle Kinbona says of her beloved island, "This whole damn place needs to wash away" (5). Perhaps it is because she recognizes that the "damn place" and the haves and have-nots are the ravages of colonialism. But her return and her actions indicate that she loves her homeland. A stay in England, a place where her intellect was challenged and her spirit was broken, influences Merle's opinion of place. Merle needs healing, and although Bourne Island is an unlikely place, it is the place she chooses.

Dr. Saul Amron describes Merle Kinbona shortly after meeting her as "a woman who had not learned how to live with her bitterness and pain, how to control and disguise her rage; and who, moreover, insisted on holding every stranger accountable" (90). He later tells Allen Fuso that Merle "is a whole damn research project in herself" (118). Merle Kinbona, like Bourne Island, is a study in contrasts. She drives a beat-up Bentley car once owned by the colonial governor, wears earrings given to her by her English female lover and benefactress, peasant bracelets and African print fabric dresses. Her complexity is noted in the following: "She had donned this somewhat bizarre outfit, each item of which stood opposed to, at war even, with the other, to express rather a diversity and disunity within herself, and her attempt, unconscious probably, to reconcile these opposing parts, to make them whole. Moreover, she appeared to be trying to recover something in herself that had been lost; the sense and certainty of her self as a woman perhaps" (5). Merle is made of the "stuff" she has lived and that of her life's journey—from Bourne Island to England and back. Literally and figuratively, Merle Kinbona embarks on a journey that takes her to and from Bourne Island and Bournehill to England, Africa, and America: at novel's end she is making plans to travel to Africa. Like the island of her birth, Merle has been affected by the new colonialism just by being the daughter of a teenage laborer and a landowner.

Bournehills is much like an illegitimate child that everyone attempts to take on as a social cause. Merle's psychological warfare with herself begins with the knowledge of her illegitimacy and what it means to be her white father's child or a landowner's property—or a social case to be passed among relatives. Also, like the island, the imperialism of both England and America affects her. The white women she encounters represent England, America, and the Bourne Island colonialists: the unnamed English woman representing England, Harriet Amron representing the United States, and the murderer of Merle's mother—allegedly, the wife of her father—representing the effects of colonialism. Marshall indicated in an interview with Joyce Pettis that she wanted the novel to reflect "what is happening to all of us in the

Diaspora in our encounter with these metropolitan powers, the power of Europe and the power of America" (Pettis, "A *MELUS* Interview," 124). An appropriate conclusion is that Merle is a reflection of that diaspora with her "disjointed and fractured life" and her "serious psychological trouble" (Pettis 124). Her journey is interwoven with the history of Bourne Island: she has claimed the bitterness and pain of her beloved Bournehills as her own. However, until she is able to deal with the personal aspects of that history, she can only be ineffective in addressing the effects of a new colonialism on her land. Marshall's women who are able to tell their stories are able to transform and reconfigure themselves with some guidance. Until she meets her priest in Saul Amron, Merle is unable to escape her bitterness and frustration.

Merle migrates to England to become educated and enlightened. She finds happiness in exploring beyond the boundaries of the university, sampling politics and history, confronting issues and rebelling against the authorities that fostered them. England, then, serves as the setting of her coming of age. It is in England that she falls in with a wild group. If not for her Bourne Island connection, Merle could probably be seen as just another young adult having fun and defying adult authority. However, her exploitation is an opportunity for Marshall to punctuate the power of the wealthy over the "little fella." Merle seems so intrigued by the wealthy woman who gives her money that she is spellbound by her. She thinks more about what she is able to get than about the fact that she is prostituting herself. She literally substitutes her father's "hush money" with the paid exploitation of the English woman: "Good little brainwashed West Indian that I was, I thought it quite something to have a rich Englishwoman taking such an interest in me, an almshouse child, who couldn't remember her mother and whose so-called father had for years passed her on the road without so much as a word" (*The Chosen Place, The Timeless People* 328). The white woman, nameless and faceless, similar to the cane plantation owners in their effect on the present factory owners and the Bournehills people, renders Merle dependent. Fifteen years later, Merle returns to Bourne Island and Bournehills a psychological mess, looking for a healing. Eight years after her return, as she relates her story to her newfound and unlikely confidant, Saul Amron, she displays signs of guilt at being taken in, for being made into entertainment.

In England, she meets Africa, which for a time is her salvation. Marshall indicates in an interview with Maryse Condè, which was translated by John Williams, that experiencing the spirit of Africa is not enough; one must go there. Marshall states, "a spiritual return to Africa is absolutely necessary for the reintegration of that which was lost in our collective historical past and the many national pasts which comprise it" (Condè and Marshall 52–53). Merle experiences the spirit of Africa in her relationship with and marriage to a man from Africa and perhaps begins to find a means of understanding her history. Her husband is her first connection with Africa. Ketu is not her savior but he is someone who is wholly good, the epitome of integrity. Unlike her English lover and her father, he does not exploit either her or his land. Rather he believes it his duty to find "ways of improving the lot of the Little Fella" (*The Chosen Place, The Timeless People* 331). In England, Merle has the opportunity to interact with someone from Africa who stands in sharp contrast to the Bournehills bourgeoisie, Lyle Hutton and others, who believe that their homeland is beyond help, or who are in essence neocolonialists taking advantage of a new government. Her passage also includes experiencing love and childbirth and gaining the strength from the two to defy returning to the white woman even as the white woman's revenge causes the end of her marriage. Merle acknowledges this in a conversation with Saul about the two years with her husband: "In a way you know they made up for all of the others before—and since. There's no describing them. Let's just say I became a different person with him. Softer, for one.... After years of not being sure what I was, whether fish or fowl or what, I knew with him I was a woman and no one would ever be able to make me believe otherwise. I still love him for that" (332). Even Ketu's inability to forgive her is part of her passage, but when he leaves her, taking their child with him, insanity becomes her step towards reconfiguration. Insanity causes her to return to the wild life before heading home to Bournehills for healing. However, by then, England has provided a foundation for her personal growth.

Nothing about Merle is orderly. Leseur writes that Merle needs to "find herself to establish order and find wholeness among the fragments of her shattered personal life" ("'Read Your History, Man'" 92). Her experiences in England, especially her connection with Africa, require that she take steps to recognizing that her life is in shambles and finding herself. The latter connection gives her the strength to shake off England as personified by the white woman. Orderliness and wholeness can only be achieved by facing the anger and the guilt that Saul Amron finds Merle harboring eight years after her return to Bournehills.

Merle's anger at the white woman and her father, and perhaps her disdain of her illegitimacy, keep her from wholeness. She had expected a kind of healing from reverse migration—upon return to Bourne Island: "I hoped that I might have been able to sort it out once I was back—and not only every thing that happened those years away, but when I was a child. I wanted to go all the way back and understand" (*The Chosen Place, The Timeless People* 229). Adam Meyer believes that Merle is "restricted by a moment in the past, one that she must transcend before she can live in the present" (22). Unfortunately, the most impacting moment in the past is her illegitimate birth. Coming to terms with her past means coming to terms with a father whose death she seems to applaud. She tells Saul, "that man was no father of mine. He got his in the end though.... [W]ith all the land and houses he owned he died without a soul he could call family at his side" (*The Chosen Place, The Timeless People* 357). His room, which she moves into without making changes, is the chamber to which she retreats to fall apart and to rejuvenate.

The catatonic states that she escapes into and her confession to and affair with Saul Amron encourage her journey to wholeness. The catatonic state—"limp, like someone dead"—is as much a defense mechanism, like her talking, as it is an opportunity to reenergize for the next fight (336). When she cannot address the situation to her satisfaction, she bows out of life in her father's old room amid artifacts of the past, sinking into "one of the long, numbing depressions," and remains indisposed for several days (215). Merle finds in Saul Amron the father-confessor—her JuJu man—and is able to free her conscience of past transgressions, to move beyond dispossession by parent and husband and anger at those who have exploited her. In a way, he functions as her spiritual guide on her quest for understanding and strength to live, even when they make love and he removes her earring, her symbol of subjugation by the woman lover. Merle's confrontation with Harriet Amron regarding her affair with Saul emphasizes that she is well on her way to order and wholeness. Merle reacts to another white woman who is attempting to subjugate her, to control her life. The confession, the catatonic state, and the love affair strengthen her resistance to such efforts. Merle tells Harriet, "I can't be bought or bribed . . . and I don't accept handouts. Not anymore at least. I used to. You might have doubts about that, but I did. And for the longest time. And because of it I lost two people who meant life itself to me. I've gotten wise in my old age. . . . Poor as the devil, but proud" (441). Marshall notes, "Harriet permits me to find a means by which Merle will finally be able to overcome that relationship with the English woman. So technically it was important that she reflect in an American way the same pattern of dominance and exploitation that the English woman represents in the novel" (Pettis, "A *MELUS* Interview," 125). Merle sells her possessions and leaves for Africa to see her husband and child. But she will return to Bournehills because it is home, and home is where one should take a stand. The route of her journey to Africa indicates her continuous growth: "And she was not taking the usual route to Africa, first flying north to London via New York and then down. Instead, she was going south to Trinidad, then on to Recife in Brazil, and from Recife, that city where the great arm of the hemisphere reaches out toward the massive shoulder of Africa as though yearning to be joined to it as it had surely been in the beginning, she would fly across to Dakar and, from there, begin the long cross-continent journey to Kampala" (*The Chosen Place, The Timeless People* 471). Merle emerges a woman who recognizes her strength but also recognizes others' contributions to her reconfiguration. Before she travels and after she determines that she will "live," she discards the bracelets and earrings. Marshall writes that when Merle leaves Bourne Island for Africa, she is "embarking on another leg of the journey back to the historical self" ("Shaping the World of My Art" 106). Barbara Christian believes that Merle is "journeying towards 'self-renewal'" (133).

In her interview with Pettis, Marshall explains Merle Kinbona: "One of the really fitting descriptions for her, I think, came from the person who did the review of it for the *New York Times*. He called her part saint, part Obeah woman, and part revolutionary. That really sums it up. What she is symbolically is the black man/woman of the Diaspora" (125). Garvey in "Passages to Identity: Re-Membering the Diaspora in Marshall, Phillips, and Cliff" writes that Marshall implies that Merle, born at the crossroads between Africa and both Britain and the United States, will succeed in the transatlantic passage and fit the disparate pieces of herself together to form a coherent identity" (260). The past must be recognized and dealt with or there can be no future, a lesson that all of Marshall's heroines must learn from their migratory journeys.

While Merle's migration takes her from Bourne Island to England and back, Avey Johnson—even though her journeys take her to a number of places—essentially migrates from Harlem to North White Plains, New York, with anticipation that she will soon migrate to Tatem. In *Praisesong for the Widow* (1983), when Avey, an elderly widow who is on her third cruise with friends, leaves the cruise, David Pinckney writes, "Avey is, one assumes, on the verge of a nervous breakdown. She has withdrawn tendencies of someone in a paranoid state. She is repelled by people and things, anxious to keep her mental balance" (26). As is the case with Merle Kinbona, this "state" is but a stage in her transformation, the journey home. In *Black Women, Writing and Identity: Migration of the Subject*, Carole Boyce Davies writes that Avey's "development is centered on journeying. All of the journeys, from the walks with her Great-aunt Cuney to the tourist ship journeys and her journey to Carriacou and her subsequent journey back to the US are central to her being able to place her various identities in context. Avey, beyond the impetuousness of youth, has to be more fully engaged in the rituals of identification. These identifications are of gender, nationality, heritage, race, age, sexuality, and class" (119). With each journey comes a different place psychologically as well as physically. Ebele O. Eko posits that "the plot delineates the archetypal journey into awareness from "Runagate" (running away from) to "Sleepers Wake" (awakening to shocking reality); to "Leve Tete" (washing away false mentality); to "Beg Pardon" (the reconciliation with one's own heritage)" (143). One could also note that the journeys take her across waters leading to diasporic and spiritual experiences that are necessary in order for her to reconfigure into wholeness.

An earlier journey to Tatem, South Carolina, and the Landing, where and when she learns the apocryphal story, establishes the context for the journeys that follow. It is because she has no concept of the importance of the setting that all of the other journeys have to take place. Great-aunt Cuney shows her the way to identity and home: the realization that such is the case comes many years and journeys later. Great-aunt Cuney, whom Gay Wilentz refers to as "a spiritual Africanized mother," serves as guide for Avey's journey around Tatem and to and from Ibo Landing in her younger years—before her first migration from Harlem to White Plains. She is also Avey's historian/storyteller and connects her to her past in her mature years. She tells Avey about the Ibos, their grandness, and their ability to see and foresee summer after summer, refusing to allow Avey to complete the story even after hearing it numerous times. "But how come they didn't drown, Great-aunt Cuney?" is Avey's naïve response to her aunt's final coda, spoken with an amazed reverential laugh: "Those Ibos! Just upped and walked on away not two minutes after getting here!" (*Praisesong for the Widow* 39). Even the look that her aunt gives her, a look she remembers even at present, does not cause her to understand or to reach conclusions about the importance of the story or its setting. Its relevance to her is that it was her great-aunt's tale—until she makes the journeys that end with her self-knowledge, and thus her reconfiguration.

Avey's transformation is years in process—almost a lifetime. The final stages take place in the journeys made after the death of her husband, Jerome. Avey seems totally unaware that reconfiguration is imminent. She simply recognizes that something is driving her to abort one journey in order to undertake another—the journey home. The story of Avey's reconfiguration is content and context for psychoanalysis: the pressures of inner consciousness build in a woman who has had a lifetime of being "Avey" without recognizing that "Avatara" has unrealized and unresolved issues. Avatara "Avey" Johnson recalls her "demons" in the people she knew and loved, and they appear to her to chastise and even punish her in her dreams and nightmares, almost forcing her to remember the importance of place and to transform.

Avey Johnson's migrations begin with her marriage: she begins married life with Jay Johnson in Harlem, moves to Brooklyn, and ends in North White Plains with Jerome Johnson. Harlem was a time of friends. Brooklyn was first a place of carefree existence that became the site of suffering both economically and psychologically. In the weeks before making the move from Brooklyn to North White Plains, Avey "found herself thinking not so much of the new life awaiting them but of the early years back on Halsey Street, of the small rituals and private pleasures that had lasted through the birth of Sis [their first child]" (122). Lacking rituals, life for Jay and Avey changes to blind acceptance of life. Something seemingly as simple as Jay shaving off his mustache symbolizes that Avey has lost Jay, the partner with whom she experienced passion, fun, as well as economic struggles. Jay Johnson in North White Plains becomes Jerome Johnson, who does not dance to the music of favorite black artists while fantasizing about being in dance halls. Instead, Jerome makes statements such as, "If it was left to me I'd close down every dancehall in Harlem and burn every drum! That's the only way these Negroes out here'll begin making any progress!" (132). The distance to Tatem, South Carolina, becomes greater when summer vacations are no longer spent there in the old house inherited from her Great-aunt Cuney. The trips and thus her connection with the Landing and the story of the Ibos end one fateful Tuesday evening when she challenges her husband about his faithfulness. Life then becomes focused on economic security and the drive never to return to Halsey Street, where they were among the struggling poor. Therefore, at the time of her cruise when Jerome Johnson appears to her in her sleep and chastises her for being frivolous and wasteful, it awakens memories, fragments of her life with both Jay and Jerome Johnson. Their lives, and Avey's journey, are affected by the purely Western influence that encourages them to seek security in personal wealth in their migration from Harlem to North White Plains.

Great-aunt Cuney, whose cultural and history lessons are central to Avey's reconfiguration, is first to make a haunting appearance in Avey's dreams. Perhaps the appearance and events that follow remind Avey that she is named for her great-aunt's grandmother, Avatara, a woman whom people swore was crazy. Martinique and the sound of the patois that Avey hears spoken there subliminally remind her of the language of the Landing and possibly prompt the dream. The dream follows a long day ashore in Martinique when she hears the "peculiar cadence and lilt of the patois," which "fleetingly called to mind the very way people spoke in Tatem long ago" (67). In the dream she fights with her great-aunt, who tries to force her to return to walk on the Landing. Ironically, in the dream Great-aunt Cuney's request competes with Avey's plan to attend the celebration of her husband's achievement of Master Mason. She is dressed for the dais at the Statler, not trudging the landscape of Tatem and the Landing. The setting of the fight is both Tatem, where she learned her heritage, and North White Plains, where it was forgotten and replaced by middle-class mores and the persona, Jerome Johnson's wife. Perhaps the role of Great-aunt Cuney is to awaken her and to force her to remember a past that is affecting her present, that is causing her not to know the person she sees in the mirror—the woman with the Marian Anderson "poise and reserve," stylishly dressed, a matron, a woman "who clearly kept her thoughts and feelings to herself" (48–49). Great-aunt Cuney disrupts her so-so life, and while it looks like Avey is on a downward spiral, she is in essence on the road to home, which must include a few stops for healing in places with history that is conducive.

One of those stops is Grenada, the place where Avey encounters two men: the man who was her companion in her life of confusion, Jerome Johnson, and the man who points the way out of her confusion, Lebert Joseph. Jerome Johnson appears in Avey's nightmare as she attempts sleep in a hotel on the island. He accosts her with his fear of being back on Halsey Street, where they were struggling poor. Lebert Joseph saves her life by providing water and guidance in her literal thirst for life. His question to her is "And what you is?" . . . "What's your nation?" (166–67). This he asks a woman who hours earlier does not recognize the reflection that she sees in the mirror—does not recognize herself. Abena P. A. Busia writes, "the answer to this is established for Avey Avatara Johnson at birth, but journey to 'sacred' places are needed for the character to come to an understanding of the answers" (196).

Lebert Joseph transforms his rum shop into both a couch and a confessional where Avey confides in him: "Could this be Avey Johnson talking so freely? It was the place: the special light that filled it and the silence, as well as the bowed figure across the table who didn't appear to be listening" but seemed to know of her Gethsemane (*Praisesong for the Widow* 170). In his eyes she can see that he is "someone who possessed ways of seeing that went beyond mere sight and ways of knowing that outstripped ordinary intelligence (*Li gain connaissance*) and thus had no need for words" (172). Renu Juneja and James Kingsland argue that "He [Lebert Joseph] is very evocatively connected to Papa Legba of Vodun, the Eve god of thresholds and the Yoruba god of crossroads, a messenger of gods to earth, one who links the early and spiritual realms together" (64). Lebert Joseph assumes the role of priest in listening somewhat detachedly and then as psychologist as he attempts to help her address the questions he asks about her identity. Saul Amron's engagement of sexual activity with Merle aids in her transformation. Perhaps Lebert's taking Avey on a trip serves a similar purpose. Lebert Joseph convinces her to make the trip to Carriacou. Busia writes, "The interrupted journey and the unexpected journey take on great significance as metaphors of the progress of her life, a life whose meaning she no longer understands" (196). Grenada then becomes a setting that is a stepping-off point for self-discovery, a turning point where her psychologist/guide prescribes travel with him to the Carriacou Excursion and dancing the dances of her ancestors as the appropriate cure for her. On the boat to Carriacou, she is overwhelmed by dreams and memories and experiences a great fullness that is followed by nausea—a continuation of physical show of her transformation: old women on the boat help her through this, thinking that perhaps it is the crossing of the channel that has caused her illness. These women remind her of the presiding mothers of the Mount Olivet Baptist. Just as the old women of the church were there to help mourners "come through," these women "set about divesting her of the troubling thoughts, quietly and deftly stripping her of them as if they were so many layers of winter clothing she had mistakenly put on for the excursion" (*Praisesong for the Widow* 197). They help her to continue her battle with her own demons on the "threshing floor" as both body and mind are purged. Gay Wilentz writes that "the process of healing comes through the old women who are in touch with their African/Caribbean identity, and after the healing of the middle-aged, upper middle-class Avey Johnson in *Praisesong*, she returns to New York to tell this tale to all the upwardly mobile black youths who think success means denying their culture" (400).

In Carriacou, Avey Johnson completes her reconfiguration as she experiences first the bathing at the hands of Lebert Joseph's daughter, Rosalie Parvay, and then dances to beg pardon of the elders and to honor the nations, in accordance with the Carriacou people's custom. She dances the ring shout that she remembers from her experiences in Tatem, never recreating the move that caused the church to reprimand her great-aunt. During her dance, the community embraces her, and she experiences and witnesses the importance of connection with one's history and perhaps realizes that she has been running from her own history. The setting and the dance that is both a remembrance of culture and spirituality complete her reconfiguration into a woman who becomes Avey, short for Avatara, as her Great-aunt Cuney taught her, a woman resolved to return to Tatem and to continue to tell the story of the Ibos. Jane Olmstead writes that Marshall emphasizes the importance of place in two interrelated ways: "first Carriacou locates the forces of memory, history, and the spirit, channeling them in order to reclaim the widow, Avey Johnson, from despair and alienation from her ancestors; second Avey's body becomes the site for her own transformation" (254).

Avey's acceptance that things were not in order on the ship is a bridge that leads her to higher levels of self. Her dreams and visions mirror a past fraught with mistakes, negative responses to events. Once she recognizes it as such, she becomes free to become, to transform and reconfigure her way of thinking and her direction. Marshall juxtaposes memory of the past with the present, and Avey is seen very much caught in a middle passage of her own. She cannot do as the Ibos in her Great-aunt Cuney's story and simply see reality and walk back across the water homeward. Wilentz believes that Avey "finds her past and takes the spiritual middle passage back to Africa via the Caribbean, and it is here that the circle of the diaspora is completed" (400). What Avey seems to need for her transformation is an encounter with people who understand and appreciate their history, culture, ancestry, and homeland.

The issues of migration and healing are underscored in Marshall's *Daughters*. In an interview with Darryl Cumber Dance, Marshall states that "like most of my novels, *Daughters* is about people, politics, culture, history, race, racism, morality, marriage, children, friends, love, sex, the triumph and sometimes defeat of human spirit, as well as a few other things I threw in for good measure" ("Interview" 2). She indicates that the novel is "in part, the story of Ursa's struggle to come to terms not only with her family, but with the two worlds, the America where she lives and the island where she spent her childhood" (2). Ursa Beatrice Mackenzie is the daughter of a West Indian politician, Primus "the PM" Mackenzie and a Hartford, Connecticut–born mother, Estelle Harrison Mackenzie. Ursa's journey offers a migratory pattern very different from that of other women in Marshall's fiction. She is conceived in the postcolonial Caribbean island, Triunion, born in the United States, raised to teenage years in Triunion, and attends high school, completes college, and settles in the United States. Also, unlike Marshall's other women protagonists, Ursa's migration does not end in her homeland but in her mother's country of birth—as willed by her mother. Estelle Mackenzie prepares her daughter for life in the United States, symbolically and ceremonially, with an air of defiance and a goal of creating a radical young woman. Along her journey Ursa must come to terms with the conflicting feeling of disdain and respect for her father, the abandonment of her country, and the abortion of her child to achieve peace and order in her life.

Setting or place—the island of Triunion and the United States—has much to do with Ursa's reconfiguration. The island where Ursa is born is yet in her thirty-fourth year a bastion of postcolonialism or neocolonialism that rivals that described in Marshall's earlier novel, *The Chosen Place, The Timeless People*. Triunion, like Bourne Island, is a land of contrasts, magnified by the effects of postcolonialism from Garrison Row to Armory Hill to the Morlands, each supporting a different lifestyle—a different way of surviving. The PM's government job and his politics give his family the benefit of a home in Garrison Row, the ritzy part of the island as well as his home place in the Morlands—where Estelle invited in some of the poor children as playmates for Ursa, and the PM chases them away. Ursa's island has its slum area, which Estelle notes is very similar to the slums in the United States, Armory Hill. In "Legacies of Community and History in Paule Marshall's *Daughters*," Joyce Pettis writes, "familial relationships, character locus, and memory constitute the primary components through which the author explores a persistently debilitating postcolonial mentality in communities on the island of Triunion" (2). Estelle Harrison, in the early days of her marriage to the PM, romanticizes the impact that she and her new husband will have on the island, thinking that they can successfully battle the existing government and its postcolonial behavior of exploiting the poor, and the poor's resignation to things as they are. It is on this island in the sun that Estelle's body seemingly reacts with miscarriages, or "slides" as the islanders call them, until she goes to America for the term of her pregnancy. Ursa romanticizes the land and conditions until upon her return for a visit she confesses: "I can't hide from it anymore. . . . You never saw this when I was small, Viney. That's what this government has come up with by way of progress. That woman [a prostitute], the U.S. Navy [with guns readied to fight rebellion during elections] and tourists [some of whom would occupy her father's Mile Tree Colony Hotel at Government Lands that his keep-miss managed]" (*Daughters* 107).

Ursa's reconfiguration is also affected and possibly even framed by settings in the United States. New York figures as prominently as Triunion; Hartford, Connecticut, as indicated by Viney's inability to remember that Ursa went to high school there, has little relevance except as her mother's birthplace. Ursa migrates to New York, also a land of contrasts based on socioeconomics. New York is where she meets, loves, and breaks up with Lowell Carruthers; moves to a very small apartment after quitting her job with National Consumer Research Corporation, a Fortune 500 company; has her thesis proposal on slave rebels, Will Cudjoe and Congo Jane, denied; has an abortion in a beautiful clinic dissimilar to the one that Astral Forde must use in Triunion; comforts her friend, Viney, when her nine-year-old son is handcuffed by a policeman who is trying to scare him; and accepts grant funding to study a community and its politics, Midland City, New Jersey, which has in common with Triunion's Armory Hill the fact that a highway was built for the benefit of the wealthy to the detriment of the poor. She crosses the waters to the United States, her mother's homeland, the setting of her journey to clarity.

Ursa's odyssey begins with her mother not only because she was born to Estelle, but because Estelle raised her. At birth, Estelle determined that she was raising a child to be more radical than she, one who would return to the United States prepared to wage war against racism. She writes to her mother excitedly about "the Movement" in the United States: "the Movement, I love it! I'm going to send Ursa-Bea to take my place at the barricades as soon as she's old enough. Nobody here knows it, but I've already got her in training. . . . I'm going to hold out for Weaver High so that she can learn how to walk the walk and talk the talk. To get her ready for the barricades. As you saw in the picture of her I sent you last year she's already got her afro" (224). Until Estelle needs Ursa to defeat her husband, thus dealing a blow to the postcolonial regime, she does not see a role for Ursa in Triunion or its politics. She tells Ursa about her Uncle Grady who was crippled by a beating he received in Alabama during the marches and voter registration drives. She dresses Ursa in American clothing, directs servants to let her wait on herself as soon as she is able to do so, shapes her hair into an afro, not only teaches her the story of Will Cudjoe and Congo Jane but takes her to the monument to touch the statues placed out of sight in the Morlands, and sends her to the United States for schooling. Moira Ferguson notes in "Of Bears & Bearings: Paule Marshall's Diverse *Daughters*" that "to preempt her daughter being permanently lost, Estelle teaches Ursa as a child to spot the constellation of the North Star and of Orion" (3). Perhaps this emphasizes the desire of Ursa's somewhat eccentric mother to prepare her to be a strong woman capable of rejuvenating at the end of a battle lost to fight another battle and net a possible win. While Ursa is the sum of all of the women in her life—the grandmothers for whom she was named, Celestine Marie-Claire Bellegarde who helped to raise her, and even her father's keep-miss—she is indeed her mother's daughter, guilty of stasis only with men that she respects and loves despite their weaknesses. In addition to her roles as mother, teacher, historian, and mentor, Estelle Harrison is also cheerleader, cheering her daughter along on her transformative journey.

Marshall's heroine seems to have several defining moments that form the map—or log—of her journey. She was born—the only time that her mother does not have a miscarriage. This makes her the "great Mistress Ursa," as Astral Forde calls her, and places her as the star in her parent's constellation (312). She challenges her professor regarding her thesis topic to no avail but deals with him in her dreams; resigns her job with the National Consumer Research Corporation, much to the chagrin of her father, and in the same spirit she decides to stop her visits to Triunion after being disillusioned with what was happening on the island; has a second abortion and breaks off her relationship with her boyfriend; receives grant funding for her study proposal; helps to end her father's political career; and makes peace with her father's keep-miss. All are decision points that show her ability to make tough and necessary judgments. However, they all pale in comparison to ending her father's career, an action that is perhaps foreshadowed when she sees the parallel between the Midland City, New Jersey, politician and her father as pawns of a power structure. She sees both as having betrayed the women who helped them to success and the people who trusted them to save them: Sandy Lawson in Midland City with Mae Ryland and the PM in Triunion with Estelle. Nadia Elia notes, "in the intimacy of a woman's bedroom, away from man's hearing, mother and daughter engage in a long-overdue conversation about their dissatisfaction with the PM's politics" (106). One could add that they are also dissatisfied with his morals. Ursa's boyfriend in his last harangue at the time of their breakup possibly causes her disdain for her father to erupt as he—weak person that he is—proclaims: "Why not write and say look here, PapaDaddy, you've been in government too long, its about time you gave up your seat and let somebody else try to do something for the poor constituents" (*Daughters* 26). Her body heals from her second abortion when she returns to her home island for the election, carries out her guerilla tactic of sharing a planned development with her father's opponent, and makes peace with the woman who needs to be assured that she will have gained something from her more than thirty-year relationship with the PM. The abortion becomes complete even as she grabs hold of her life by helping another let go of his. The pain that did not follow immediately upon the heels of her abortion comes as she deals with her feelings for her father and her homeland, and as she seemingly looks forward to resolving issues with her former boyfriend, Lowell Carruthers, the father of her aborted child. Paule Marshall explains that Ursa's abortion is symbolic: "It's meant to suggest her attempt to cut away the subtle seduction and domination that has long characterized her relationship with her father. . . . It's only at the end of the novel, when she brings about the PM's political defeat that she's finally free of this incubus" (Dance, "An Interview with Paule Marshall," 6).

"You're like that place you're from, you know that. Still taking orders from Big Daddy England, America, and whoever. Still got that mindset. Would be scared shitless to stand on their own feet if they could. That's you allover" (*Daughters* 268). Lowell Carruthers's words no doubt capture the essence of Ursa before she reconfigured. However, she is the daughter that Estelle prepared for "the Movement"—prepared to be radical, and with that preparation Ursa Beatrice Mackenzie's transformation is inevitable.

Hattie Carmichael in Marshall's last novel, *The Fisher King*, is not the heroine. She is primarily a vehicle for Marshall to relay the story about family reunion and legacy. However, like the other women characters, she embarks upon an odyssey. Paule Marshall was inspired to write *The Fisher King* by the photograph of her cousin Sonny, whom she never met due to a familial feud. That cousin was a jazz saxophone player—"phenomenally brave to do in my part of the world," where children wanting to be artists were not tolerated (Stander 2). Her cousin was drafted into the Army in World War II and died soon thereafter. Marshall said, "his willingness and determination to be an artist stayed in my mind. I knew that I had to write a book about it, just in the way of exorcising it. So I decided to invent a life for him, in part to make up for the life he had been denied" (Stander 2). Marshall creates Everett "Sonny-Rett" Payne, a reason for and a major influence on the odyssey of Hattie Carmichael. He is her Saul Amron—although not as wise—her Lebert Joseph—even though not as mentoring—and her Lowell Carruthers—although not as self-consumed.

The title of the novel comes from an Arthurian legend about a wounded king who is imprisoned in his castle waiting for a knight to come heal and protect him. Hattie Carmichael is the knight in shining armor who, at the very least, watches over Sonny-Rett and his family. This role changes Hattie Carmichael from city child to family member and causes her migration from the United States to Paris and her transformation—a metamorphosis partly reflected physically in her baldness and in her need for medicaments.

Hattie Carmichael's journey is complicated by her social status at birth and a lack of family history. Avey and Ursa have family members—women—as cultural/historical models. Hattie, like Merle, is a daughter without a mother. The women from her other novel indicate that Marshall considers mothers and mothering to be very important in the lives of women. However, Merle is a part of her island's history: Hattie has no anchor in either personal or communal history. Merle's mother is murdered, and she is shuttled among family members until her father decides to own her. Hattie has a pretty mother who has been committed to a mental institution and whom she may visit at the mercy of her menagerie of foster parents. She is a ward of the city—one of the city children—due to her mother's institutionalization. She is the foster child of many: Mis' Dawson "who had been prevailed upon by her church, St Peter Claver, Catholic, Colored, to open her roomy third-floor apartment and her heart to one of the City's children"; the short-tempered Mis' Rayburn, "so quick with her hand or the strap"; "that old West Indian Mis' Motley, who used the money for the children to pay her mortgage"; Mis' Hamilton who used her like a drayhorse at age seven, sending her to pick up 25-pound blocks of ice to be transported in an old baby carriage; the really nice Mis' Porter who "was the only one who ever took her out to Creedmoor State Hospital to visit her mother with the pretty name, Dawn," but had an "old husband who liked for her to touch him down there" (*Fisher King* 68–69). She is not a part of the clashes of culture in Brooklyn between African Americans and West Indians, represented mainly by Florence Varina McCullum-Jones and Ulene Payne, the mothers of her two best friends. She peeks into the window of Florence Varina McCollum-Jones's home with its claw and ball-footed table, brass chandelier, and crystal, china, and silver place settings and fantasizes about being a family member even when she does not like some of the members of the family. She envies Edgar and Everett Payne, even though they have a "mean old mother acting like she owns the City's sidewalks" (70). As a foster child, she knows what she cannot aspire to; she imagines acceptance, and she develops a resilience that supports her survival. The lens with which Hattie sees her native Brooklyn is obscured by her social status as one of the city children.

She, like Merle Kinbona and Ursa-Bea Mackenzie, leaves her native land, but the reason distinguishes them. Merle is sent to Europe to attend school as her father's debt to her, and Ursa is sent to the United States for schooling as her mother wishes. Hattie chooses to be an expatriate because of the deliverance from her early history that it promises. She migrates from Brooklyn, New York, to Paris, France—a city where jazz people can live—at the invitation of her friends, Sonny-Rett and Cherisse Payne. She leaves Brooklyn, the place where she is a visitor to many families, but a member of none. She began leaving the Brooklyn that was her world in junior high school when "stuck-up, show-off, siddity Cherisse who never came out to play" became her best friend (70). As a child peeking into the Joneses' home, she is sure that had Cherisse been brave enough she would have abandoned mother and father, the pretty room, and the best house on the block to join her on the sidewalk. Cherisse's abandonment of home comes later. In junior high, she and Cherisse Jones become inseparable best friends, popping doohickeys, painting nails and mouths, and practicing kissing and touching "in ways that went beyond little kids playing doctor-and-nurse" (72). Hattie is a poster child for studies that indicate that foster children tend to have internal conflict and low sense of self-confidence. She derives her confidence from her relationship with Cherisse, "losing her ordinary-looking self and becoming with each deep kiss and caress the much-loved, dressed-up, prized daughter at the dining room table" just as she had fantasized years earlier (72). Florence Varina McCollum-Jones's show of displeasure did not deter the affections of the two: "Is that the only friend you could find? Some foster care child? Couldn't you pick someone better than that?" (72). The friendship is a gift that Hattie rewards the giver for time and time again. And when Sonny-Rett Payne chooses Cherisse as his mate, she sees "the three of them like the connected sides of the triangles she used to draw in geometry in high school, with her as the base, joining them to herself. It might be the way—the only way—to have them both" (143).

Harriet's migration to Paris boosts her sense of importance, of belonging. Paris tolerates race and unconventional relationships and provides opportunity for artists. Vowing never to cross the Atlantic again, she follows

Sonny-Rett and his jazz—tabooed by his family—to Paris. Martin T. Williams writes, "jazz is the music of the people who have been told by their circumstances that they are unworthy" (256). John Gennari notes that jazz was seen by some as "the devil's music" and as "the seedbed of narcotics, abuse and anonymous sex" (451, 467). In Paris, Harriet becomes a valued member of a family. In the grand immeuble near the Sorbonne, the Luxembourg, and the movie theaters at Odeon in Paree Cinq, she serves as "fathermothersisterbrother," lover, and live-in manager for both Sonny-Rett and Cherisse (*Fisher King* 158). The three of them are inseparable. She is no longer one of the city children, an outsider. Paris supports her movement from foster child depending on others for her self-esteem, to a codependent woman, living a dysfunctional life with her partners. She is dependent on the Paynes, overly involved with them, and is confused about her identity and the boundaries within her relationship with them. Her codependency has all of the usual attributes: "(a) martyrdom—sacrifice of one's own needs to meet the perceived needs of others; (b) fusion—loss of one's own identity in intimate relationships; (c) intrusion—control of others' behaviors through caretaking, guilt, and manipulation; (d) perfection—unrealistically high expectations of oneself and others often resulting in overachievement or inadequacy; and (e) addiction—use of compulsive behaviors for emotional self-management" (Hogg and Frank 2). Hattie sacrifices, loses herself in her friends, takes care of them, is the base of the triangle of friends, and takes drugs. She indulges Cherisse, who is beautiful but constantly needs to be reassured and admired. Hattie needs to be consulted by both Sonny and Cherisse: she needs to feel that she is the only one trusted, the only one whose opinion matters. Sonny needs someone to consult and to trust. Sonny asks, "'What's you think, Hattie?' . . . As always she gave her opinion—the only one he trusted, she knew, the only one that mattered" (*Fisher King* 186). Hattie travels Europe with Sonny, while Cherisse stays at home and works on her French. Cherisse whispers in Hattie's ear, *partager*, the French verb meaning "to share," and Hattie takes it as a directive and shares Sonny with her: "When he was ready, she slowly drew him into her wonderfully complicated, inexplicable self, proving to him, as she did each time they were together, that even an ordinary, unremarkable body such as hers possessed a kind of music, its own rhythms, harmonies, tonalities, crescendos—more than one, and that at times, her special music had the power to leave him in tears afterward on her breast. Pleasure that great" (195). It is Hattie who decides when Sonny and Cherisse should have a baby, who raises the child named JoJo, and who decorates the living quarters to replicate Cherisse's home on Macon Street in Brooklyn. When Sonny is killed, she becomes the decision maker, taking care of Cherisse until her death four years later. Paris is home for Hattie, even when she has to move to the seedier side of the city to a "poor, abject, treeless rue Sauffroy with its crumbling walk-ups that looked as if they predated Ancien Regime; rue Sauffroy, with its erupted, crippling paving stones, choked gutters, and ragtag laundry hung out front to dry" (61). Her journey is so interwoven with the Paynes that she never lives a life independent of theirs. It is in Paris that Hattie truly becomes the base of the friends' triangle, loving first Sonny-Rett and then Cherisse as she lies dying and raising their daughter and grandson. Migration gives her family and life. That is her Paris, the setting of her reconfiguration to a "somebody" even if it is a codependent.

The object of her codependence changes with the deaths of her friends and the estrangement from their daughter. Medicaments are her means of mentally escaping her losses. Sonny-Rett and Cherisse's grandson is their daughter's way of punishing Hattie for the love scene she sees between Hattie and her dying mother. Little Sonny becomes her reason for living. She responds to a request from the Paynes and Joneses, who had recently learned of his existence, to bring him for a visit and for a celebration of his grandfather, without recognizing that she had come full circle—back to Brooklyn where she was a city child. Africa figures into Hattie's migration in the form of young Sonny, who by birthright spans three cultures: African American, West Indian, and African. His African American great-grandmother, Florence Varina McCullum-Jones remarks: "You got some of all of us in you, dontcha? What you gonna do with all that Colored from all over creation you got in you?" (36). Africa gives to her, in Paris, a reason to emerge from her emotional despair. The return to Brooklyn puts her in the position of remembering the past and being impacted by a future that does not coincide with her plans. She asks, "Could somebody please tell me what I'm doing back here? How I could've let myself be talked into coming near this place again?"(73). Her journey brings her to a place where what is left of who she lived for is going to be taken from her. Her past is revealed long before she commands Sonny to keep the secrets about where they live, her job in a downscale nightclub, his babysitter, and her *medicaments*. Now she will receive punishment for the lives she and her codependents lived: the loss of her earned status as motherfathersisterbrother.

Like Marshall's other women characters discussed herein, Hattie could be accused of being mad. One questions whether Hattie is an enlightened guardian or an addict in denial. She has psychological challenges, which she addresses in different ways. As a child, she found it comforting to be a voyeur pretending to be a member of the families she observed through the windows of homes along Macon Street. Her response to the death of her friends is to withdraw into her Paris apartment—until Sonny saves her from herself. As she tells Sonny about a place where she once lived, she drifts off: "She wasn't really talking to him. It often happened. He knew, by now, to simply wait until she returned from wherever she had drifted off to and noticed him again" (*Fisher King* 67). Recognizing her state of being, Sonny "did what he always did when she was upset or feeling low and didn't have her medicaments with her. To soothe her and to restore her to herself and to him, he quietly slipped his hand into hers" (73). Hattie's response to loss and all other emotions is to allow drugs to aid in her escape from the world and the problems heaped upon her.

Hattie does experience transformation. In migration, she achieves a goal: she becomes an insider. The psychological effects are still felt by her in the end as she has to take medicaments to deal with memories of the life and death of her friends, and the child—a gift from her friends—that she must fight to raise as her own.

The novels *The Chosen Place, The Timeless People; Praisesong for the Widow; Daughters;* and *The Fisher King* are rich with psychological and sociological case studies of women on their journeys to selfhood—journeys that cause or shape their migration. Merle Kinbona, Avey Johnson, Ursa-Bea Mackenzie, and Hattie Carmichael migrate to places that help them to become whole. During their migration, each "touches" Africa: Marshall believes that contact with Africa is crucial to self-identity and self-understanding. Marshall presents characters who demonstrate the necessity for a "journey back" through history and migration to a place where an individual is able to come to terms with one's past, present, and future. Reconfiguring is something that happens *to* Hattie Carmichael, but it happens *for* Avey Johnson, Ursa-Bea Mackenzie, and Merle Kinbona. Their bodies reflect the stages of their reconfiguration: their bodies cry out for the relief that comes when they have "come through" as surely as one who experiences a spiritual awakening.

[CHAPTER 6]

"What a History You Have"
Ancestral Memory, Cultural History, Migration Patterns, and the Quest for Autonomy in the Fiction of Jamaica Kincaid

Julia De Foor Jay

The women in Jamaica Kincaid's works illustrate the burden of colonized women in Caribbean cultures, the women in Dominican and Antiguan colonial and postcolonial societies specifically, and their heroic struggles to transcend the past to create new, autonomous selves and to locate new spaces in which to flourish. In the process, the women experience profound emotions of anger and despair in response to colonialism and its legacy of exploitation, poverty, disease, and corruption. Annie in *Annie John*, Lucy in *Lucy*, Xuela in *The Autobiography of My Mother*, and Elaine in *Mr. Potter* are weighed down by a history of powerlessness and the legacies of English colonization. Their quests for empowerment inform these major works.

Importantly, these fictional works are somewhat autobiographical in nature, paralleling many of the episodes, memories, and feelings of the author herself. Kincaid admits that her writing is autobiographical, "down to the punctuation" (Kreilkamp 54). In *My Brother* and *A Small Place*, nonfictional accounts of her island experiences, Kincaid continues her explorations of colonizing influences. Curdella Forbes concludes, "Kincaid has sought to work through the problematics of a personal literary and historical (West Indian) identity. These texts represent a series of journeys that paradoxically end where they begin: with the conviction that a radical form of self-empowerment is necessary and capable of achievement only through the rejection of antecedents—that is to say, through a credo of a new self in imperative disjunction from the histories from which it was produced" (172–73).

In their quests the women must finally reject the family, in particular the mother, the embodiment of English rule. The mother who has absorbed English teachings imparts to the daughter English beliefs, standards, and practices and thereby undermines the daughter's path toward self-realization, self-definition, and independence. The questing women in Kincaid's fiction reject the biological mother and migrate to other places, other paths, and other mothers.

These surrogate mothers (what Diane Simmons calls "othermothers" and Angelita Reyes calls "mother-women") provide the emotional and psychological bedrock on which the women find the strength and will to move away from the oppressive and restrictive nature of the biological mother (encoded as "mother country"). Often, grandmothers fulfill the role of surrogate mother, serving as catalysts for growth and change. They also act as transmitters of cultural history and ancestral stories. Importantly, they know and practice ancient rituals and ceremonies from Africa and the Caribbean. An integral part of the maturation processes, these rituals and ceremonies bring healing and renewal.

Kincaid also gravitated toward a nurturing grandmother and surrogate mothers and moved away from a domineering, oppressive biological mother in her identity quest. These women validated her sense of worth and acted as catalysts for change. Like Kincaid, her main characters despair of the powerlessness effected by place, by colonialism, and by family. Their quests for freedom take them to other places, awakened self-consciousness, and to other mothers. Ultimately, their migrations are movements away from powerlessness toward autonomy and opportunity.

Whether from Dominica or Antigua, the women in Kincaid's fiction desire freedom from place in their quests for self-determination. The mother and grandmother in *Annie John* and *Lucy* and Xuela in *The Autobiography of My Mother* are from Dominica. Although ostensibly an island paradise, Dominica signifies ugliness and oppression to the women. For example, the mother in *Annie John* left Dominica to escape her father's domination. She packed all her belongings in a trunk and "left not only her parents' house in Dominica but Dominica itself for Antigua" (105). Xuela calls Dominica a "false paradise" (*The Autobiography of My Mother* 32), the injustices hidden under a façade of beauty. Considering Roseau, the capital of Dominica, Xuela suggests that "there were then many places like Roseau, outposts of despair; for conqueror and conquered alike these places were the capitals of nothing but despair" (61). Here lived "people for whom history had been a big, dark room" (61–62). Fleeing an oppressive situation with an explorer, Xuela walks across sections of Dominica, noting, "I walked across my inheritance, an island of villages and rivers and mountains and people who began and ended with murder and theft and not very much love" (89). Negative images of Dominica crisscross the novel: Xuela describes it as a "small world"—a world "of sharp, dangerous curves in the road . . . of people who had never been regarded as people at all; we looked into the night, its blackness did not come as a surprise, a moon full of dead white light traveled across the surface of a glittering black sky" (177). Even the Dominican sea Xuela calls a "tomb" (185), recalling the Middle Passage and the resultant turmoil and ultimate defeat.

Antigua is also regarded negatively, "a geographical and psychic reality that constantly serves as a backdrop" for the women's pain (Ferguson, "Jamaica Kincaid," 7). Generally regarded as a paradisaical setting also, Antigua is, nonetheless, a place of negativity to the women, a place where negative creatures and situations abound. Images of snakes and serpents traverse the novels *Annie John* and *Lucy*. Although at the beginning of *Annie John*, Annie declares, "It was such a paradise that I lived" (25), she soon becomes aware of troubling features of the place.

Annie increasingly becomes rebellious and defiant in this island "Garden of Eden." Like Satan in Milton's *Paradise Lost*, Annie resists restrictions, engaging in a series of outrageous acts. When Annie sees her reflection in a store window, her skin black, "as if someone had thrown a lot of soot out of a window," and her "plaits stuck out in every direction" (*Annie John* 94), she remembers a painting, *The Young Lucifer*, and equates herself to his likeness. The painting "showed Satan just recently cast out of heaven for all his bad deeds, and he was standing on a black rock all alone and naked. Everything around him was charred and black, as if a great fire had just roared through. His skin was coarse, and so were his features. His hair was made up of live snakes, and they were in a position to strike" (94). Although Satan wears a smile, to Annie, he is "lonely and miserable" (95)—the smile hiding his true nature. This episode encapsulates Annie's low self-esteem and deep-seated despair, shaped by a history of marginalization/otherization. Annie has absorbed colonial teachings, reiterated by the adults in the community, of the superiority of whiteness. Frantz Fanon relates this feeling of inferiority in *Black Skin, White Masks*: "Sin is Negro as virtue is white" (139).

In *Lucy*, Lucy's name joins her with Lucifer and his rebellion, also. Her mother tells her, "I named you after Satan himself. Lucy, short for Lucifer. What a botheration from the moment you were conceived" (152). Understanding fully the implications of the name, for Lucy had studied the Book of Genesis and *Paradise Lost*, she notes, "The stories of the fallen were well known to me, but I had not known that my own situation could even distantly be related to them" (152–53). Lucy realizes that exile in Hell would be better than subservience under the mother/colonialism: "For Lucy, Hell is her isolated independence, and Heaven is her West Indian past ruled by her mother. Lucy flees Heaven to become her sole authority in Hell" (Chick 97). Ironically, this reference transforms Lucy from a feeling of failure to triumph: "I did not grow to like the name Lucy—I would have much preferred to be called Lucifer outright—but whenever I saw my name I always reached out to give it a strong embrace" (*Lucy* 153).

Among the troubling features of the place is the sun. The Antiguan sun, in particular, signifies oppression through much of Kincaid's works. At the end of *Annie John,* Annie states as she leaves the island, "[H]ow much I never wanted to see the sun shine day in, day out again" (127). Although born in St. John's, Antigua, Annie regards the island as oppressive, a daily reminder of cultural repression, restrictions, and marginalization. She sees the island through a different lens than most of her peers, who seem to accept the biased teachings of the colonial masters. After arriving in New York, Lucy (an extension of the Annie character) embraces clouds, snow, and seasons, observing that all the prosperous, happy people seem to live in the parts of the earth with seasons: "I was born and grew up in a place that did not seem to be influenced by the tilt of the earth at all; it had only one season—sunny, drought-ridden. And what was the effect on me of growing up in such a place? I did not have a sunny disposition, and, as for actual happiness, I had been experiencing a long drought" (*Lucy* 86). Referring to the sun in her own island experience, Kincaid asserts, "But the sun is almost hellish, really. Sometimes it would turn from something wonderful, the light of the sun, into a kind of hell" (Cudjoe, "Jamaica Kincaid and the Modernist Project," 231).

The sun is also a negative presence in Kincaid's nonfictional accounts. In *My Brother,* the sun is menacing: "That sun, that sun. On the last day of our visit its rays seemed as pointed and as unfriendly as an enemy's well-aimed spear" (75). In Kincaid's *A Small Place,* references to the sun begin the work. Tourists, she sarcastically relates, will look forward to "this place (Antigua) where the sun always shines," but tourists do not see that the islander suffers "constantly from drought, and so has to watch carefully every drop of fresh water used (while at the same time surrounded by a sea and an ocean—the Caribbean Sea on one side, the Atlantic Ocean on the other), [but this] must never cross your [the tourist's] mind" (4). She goes on to canvas the island, noting the poverty, the neglect, the corruption—the spiritual drought. At the end, she calls Antigua a negative place, a "prison" (79). Antonia MacDonald-Smythe notes, "While she has not given up her Antiguan citizenship or her right to criticize freely her island home, Kincaid is equally adamant that it is a place where she could never live, that there, her creativity would be stifled, her individuality submerged beneath the weight of her mother's personality" (18). Voluntary exile has empowered Kincaid, argues MacDonald-Smythe (18). In an interview with Selwyn R. Cudjoe, Kincaid relates, "I knew ... that I would never go back to Antigua, that I would never be able to live comfortably in Antigua again. I somehow felt free of the West Indies. . . . I thought that I could never go home because it would kill me, drag me down. It was a total act of liberation" ("Jamaica Kincaid and the Modernist Project" 223).

In addition to place, Kincaid's protagonists seek freedom from colonialism, its oppression and domination. Even as a child, Annie rebels against English rule and English domination of the island—domination of culture, language, and politics. The socialization of the young minds with English imperialist power and glorification permeates the novel. Books read, poems recited, songs sung, holidays observed—all mark British power and preeminence. Annie's intuitively questioning these practices of the English teachers—and of the teachers themselves—are signposts of her developing subjectivity. For example, in *Annie John,* Annie views most of the teachers negatively, describing Mr. Slacks, the physics teacher, as "dingy-toothed" (73); Miss Edward, a "bellowing dragon" (78); the piano teacher, a "shriveled-up old spinster" (28); and Miss Moore, the headmistress, "a prune left out of its jar for a long time" (36).

In conjunction with Annie's negative views of the teachers are her views of some of her classmates and their icons, especially those from England; one in particular is Ruth, the white minister's daughter. She is particularly dense, according to Annie, for she does not know even the basic history of the island territories. Annie considers Ruth a representative of English exploitation: "Perhaps she wanted to be in England, where no one would remind her constantly of the terrible things her ancestors had done. . . . Her ancestors had been the masters, while ours had been the slaves. She had such a lot to be ashamed of, and by being with us every day she was always being reminded" (*Annie John* 76).

Besides the teachers and classmates, Annie resents any vestiges of the monarchy. When she enters a new school, she happily destroys her old notebooks, "which had on their covers a picture of a wrinkled-up woman wearing a crown on her head and a neckful and armfuls of diamonds and pearls" (40). She also resents special occasions that honor the ruling family, such as the particularly odious holiday honoring a princess who came to the islands to get over a love affair.

Furthermore, Annie denigrates the textbooks, in particular, *The History of the West Indies,* in which explorers such as Christopher Columbus are glorified. She defaces a picture of Columbus in the history book, a reaction to colonial domination and abuse. Ironically, the picture features Columbus in chains, reinforcing Annie's perceptive view of the explorer as an imperfect, perfidious, occupier. She sees through the heroic idea of the explorer perpetuated by the teachers to the historical truth of the conquest, brilliantly deducing that the conquest has left a trail of betrayals, violations, and indignities in the West Indies.

Annie also finally rejects some elements of Obeah practices and rituals in the island culture. Obeah, a "system of beliefs grounded in spirituality and an acknowledgment of the supernatural and involving aspects of witchcraft, sorcery, magic, spells, and healing" (Frye 198), is practiced by many of the inhabitants of the West Indies. Alan Richardson calls Obeah, or Obi, a "religion" (171). Archie Bell contends that "no one seems to be able to explain exactly what is meant by the word Obeah, or what is the belief, as it appears to have variations in the different islands, all descended, however, from African fetishism" (qtd. in Frye 197). Reyes maintains, "But as an extension of West African animism and cosmological beliefs in the New World, obeah not only influenced the personal lives of the people but their political agendas as well" (82). Anxiety, fear, loss, and revenge often surround the references to Obeah in *Annie John*. One in particular regards the "bad spirits" the father's former lovers cast on Annie and her mother. For example, Annie's mother concludes that one of the former lovers is trying to harm her because of a series of mysterious mishaps: a sore on Annie's instep had been slow to heal, Annie was bitten by a dog, and a cherished bowl had suddenly slipped from her hands and had broken. To counter the spell, Annie's mother consults an Obeah woman who recommends a special ritual that includes a bath in a special concoction created from roots and flowers boiled in oils and a "strange-smelling" candle burning in a darkened room (14–15). In the novel *Lucy*, Lucy also considers the spells placed on her and her mother because of the father's past lovers: one woman had tried to kill Lucy when she was still in the womb; earlier the same woman had tried to kill her mother; another woman had tried to kill Lucy and her mother several times. To thwart these attempts, the mother consults an Obeah woman regularly (80). Lucy also refers to the ritual baths, which were taken "to protect me from evil spirits sent to me by some of the women who had loved my father and whom he had not loved in return" (124).

The Obeah women also know the causes and cures for illnesses; they know about death and dying. Annie's/Lucy's mother lost a beloved brother, John, who died of "something the doctor knew nothing about, of something the obeah woman knew everything about" (*Annie John* 69). Later, when Annie is ill, Ma Chess, Annie's grandmother, pronounced in French patois that Annie would survive because she was "Not like Johnnie. Not like Johnnie at all" (124).

In the section "The Long Rain," Obeah women, including Annie's grandmother, perform various rituals and ceremonial rites to cure Annie of her depression. These include special candles, incense, crossmarks on the soles of the feet, sachets to wear inside night clothes, and ointments to rub on the skin. They also ceremoniously "bless" her jewelry and underclothes to protect her "from evil spirits and every kind of misfortune" (134). After Annie recovers and prepares to leave the island, she vows to leave behind most Obeah beliefs: "I placed a mark against obeah women, jewelry, and white underclothes" (135). To Annie, these aspects of Obeah represent outmoded beliefs—baggage that Annie refuses to carry. Angelita Reyes considers the leaving behind of ancestral traditions, rituals, and beliefs: "If they must reject the laws of the ancestors' religion, then so be it. Nevertheless they remain spiritual as they seek new ways to define spirituality and religion. They want to make new pathways for wellness" (155).

Like Annie, Lucy also seeks freedom from colonial oppression and dominance, realizing that "the origin of my presence on the island—was the result of a foul deed" (*Lucy* 135). Although the novel begins with Lucy's arrival in America and her subsequent negotiations in a new hybrid space(s), her memories and perceptions of colonial rule and its aftermath are ever-present and mimic, in most respects, Annie's. Having received a colonial education, she also rebels against English rule and culture. In particular, she resents the privileging of everything English. One hated poem, probably Wordworth's "I Wandered Lonely as a Cloud," features rows of daffodils, a nonexistent flower in the tropics. As a pupil at Queen Victoria Girls School, Lucy memorizes and recites the poem at a public function. Afterwards, she vows "to erase from my mind, line by line, every word of the poem" (*Lucy* 18). Later, upon seeing these in the United States, Lucy is incensed at her employer's (Mariah's) love of these flowers, especially her imposition of these flowers on Lucy's psyche and senses as if the flowers should be, must be, appreciated by the viewer. But to Lucy, the flowers signify the colonizer's indoctrination, even brainwashing, of the inhabitants of the island colony. They reveal the insensitivity of the colonizer to island experience and culture. Diane Simmons suggests, "[S]he [Lucy] is not fooled by the pleasing masks donned by colonial power to trick and manipulate its subjects. The beautiful and innocent form of the daffodil, for example, no longer masks the fact that by glorifying the daffodil in poetry and by ignoring Caribbean flora, colonial education has used the daffodil as a tool to 'erase' everything that is native to the colonial child" (33). Simmons notes further that "Lucy, coming into her own powers of vision, can see that a daffodil may not be a daffodil but a weapon" (33).

Perceptive and precocious like Annie, Lucy, as a young school girl, resents all vestiges of English indoctrination, English iconic representations, and Columbus's legacy. At fourteen she refuses to sing "Rule, Britannia! Britannia rule the waves; Britons never, never shall be slaves," declaring, "that I was not a Briton and that until not too long ago I would have been a slave" (*Lucy* 135). At this, the choir director wonders if she would ever be "civilized." Lucy also resents the English ruling family: the queen on a stamp is pronounced a "stony-face, sour-mouth woman" (136). She especially resents Columbus's impact upon Antigua: "It [Antigua] was discovered by Christopher Columbus in 1493; Columbus never set foot there but only named it in passing, after a church in Spain. He could not have known that he would have so many things to name" (135). Ironically, she adds, "A task like that would have killed a thoughtful person, but he went on to live a very long life" (135). Certainly, Columbus was not a hero to the island natives, the Carib Indians, who were almost decimated by the disease and brutality. A Carib Indian from Dominica, both Annie's and Lucy's grandmother is one of the few remaining indigenous people.

Similarly to Annie and Lucy, Xuela, in *An Autobiography of My Mother*, also seeks freedom from colonialism's legacies. She laments, "My mother was a Carib woman, and when they looked at me this is what they saw: The Carib people had been defeated and then exterminated, thrown away like the weeds in a garden" (16). Xuela is actually an allegorical figure of the near genocide of all Carib people, her mother having died at her birth. Caroline Rody contends, "Xuela's motherless identity is associated throughout with a brutal, persistent, irreversible history of 'defeat'" (128). Lizabeth Paravisini-Gebert agrees that the mother is "representative of a race doomed to disappearance from history from the moment of the colonial encounter" (151). Fanon posits, "If the other seeks to make me uneasy with his wish to have value (his fiction), I [the Colonizer] simply banish him without a trial. He ceases to exist" (*Black Skin, White Masks* 212). Because of her giftedness, a teacher proclaims Xuela "evil," "possessed," placing the blame on her Carib ancestry (*The Autobiography of My Mother* 16–17) and negating her very existence. Xuela, marginalized in multiples as a Carib, an African, and a woman, states that "the ones who look like me, had long ago been reduced to shadows; the forever foreign, the margins, had long ago lost any connection to wholeness" (*The Autobiography of My Mother* 132–33). Xuela muses, "For me history was not only the past: it was the past and it was also the present (138).

Xuela's father, allegorically realized as European colonialism, is "the color of corruption" (181). But he is also of mixed blood: "[H]is father was a Scots-man, his mother of the African people, and this distinction between 'man' and 'people' was an important distinction, for one of them came off the boat as part of a horde, already demonized, mind blank to everything but human suffering, each face the same as the one next to it; the other came off the boat of his own volition, seeking to fulfill a destiny, a vision of himself he carried in his mind's eye" (*The Autobiography of My Mother* 181). Troubled by this duality of his heritage, he considers the sea: "the blue sea, the gray ocean will take him along with all that represents his earthly happiness (the ship full of people) and all that represents his unhappiness (the ship full of people)" (137). Her father, named after Alfred the Great, chooses to follow the route of the oppressor, becoming a policeman, a "jailer" (90), and speaking the "language of the conqueror" (110). To Fanon, "this self-division is a direct result of colonialist subjugation" (17).

Xuela's sense of defeat, linked with historical realities, underscores all three novels—defeats linked inextricably with the diaspora, the Middle Passage, slavery, and colonialism—the unending repercussions reverberating through the centuries. In fact, Annie's depression and anger stem from these realities. Likewise, Lucy, upon arriving in America, considers the maid's room, in which she is confined, a box: "a box in which cargo traveling a long way should be shipped" (*Lucy* 7). Orlando Patterson, in *Slavery and Social Death: A Comparative Study*, explores the atrocities of the slave trade, the tight packing, "the length of the time at sea, the quality of food and water during the passage, and epidemics and health conditions at the point of embarkation in Africa," that led to the high mortality rate of the people (163). Lucy, although having chosen to travel to the "New World," temporarily feels a profound depression from the journey and a sense of loss of her ancestral home. Memories of—and identification with—the diaspora, in which African slaves had been confined to tight, suffocating spaces and had been transported like cargo, link Lucy to old stories and old wounds.

In addition to freedom from colonial oppression, the women seek freedom from family, in particular, the mother, whose control is aligned paradoxically with colonialism. Kincaid states, "It became clear to me that the mother I was writing about was really Mother Country" (Ferguson, "A Lot of Memory," 177). Although the mother in *Annie John* had migrated from Dominica to escape family oppression herself, specifically her father's tyranny, she exerts a similar oppressive stance toward her daughter, Annie, continuing the cycle of abuse. The father had absorbed colonial teachings and postures and, in the process, had made the daughter's life unendurable. The only route out of such oppression is rebellion and/or escape. However, no escape seems possible. On Antigua, she is still subject to the legacies of colonialism and patriarchal notions of male/female relations. She is still subdued and subjugated by the immediate men in her life and by the society at large. In defense, she lashes out at her daughter, Annie, establishing a pattern, a repetition of inherited responses.

In retaliation, Annie begins to rebel. Ironically, Annie's "acts of severing from her mother can be exposed as the predetermined imitation of a rebellion which her mother, also named Annie John, has already enacted—an imitation, in a sense, of a language her mother has already spoken" (Byrne 279). In particular, Annie rebels against the mother's admonitions to be an exemplary girl in the English mode. Keith Byerman contends that the training of the daughters is cultural: "The training of the daughter in true Antiguan womanhood carries on the established pattern.... Female identity within Antiguan culture can only be defined in terms of the mother, and, since the mother passes down the culture, she is the source of national identity as well" (97). The social construction of Annie by the mother includes lessons in domestic chores and deportment: "This is how you set a table for tea; this is how you set a table for dinner; this is how you set a table for dinner with an important guest; . . . this is how to behave in the presence of men who don't know you very well, and this way they won't recognize immediately the slut I have warned you against becoming" (*At the Bottom of the River* 4). Her mother insists that she practice Christianity and attend a European-style educational system. She is also sent to various teachers to learn good manners and take piano lessons—all in preparation for a middle-class marriage and a middle-class lifestyle. In "Adolescent Rebellion and Gender Relations in *At the Bottom of the River* and *Annie John*," Helen Pyne Timothy observes,

> [T]he Caribbean mother who is bent on seeing her daughter rise from the lower classes to the middle ranks must not only teach her useful housekeeping tasks, cleanliness, good manners, and practical knowledge of her environment but also European norms and the need to desist in the practice of African ones. The girl perceives these paradoxes inherent in the mother's relationship to her own Caribbean culture, and they become part of the negative features that help reinforce the split between the egos of the mother and daughter and the daughter's subsequent rebellion. Thus in the mother's perception, Christianity, Sunday school, good manners (the ability to curtsy), and piano lessons are all essential to her daughter's acceptability and respectability. (240)

Annie's rejections of this lifestyle reflect her growing independence and fierce spirit. Intuitively, she senses the colonial weight borne by the mother; the mother has become a transmitter of colonial ideology. The mother, like her father before her, has absorbed the teachings of the colonial masters and is perpetuating and preserving English traditions, ways, and norms—and, ultimately, English power and its implied subjugation over defenseless people.

Annie's affiliations with the Red Girl, who is the antithesis of her mother's ideal, mark a major phase in her identity construction. Annie relates,

> I soon learned this about her: She took a bath only once a week, and that was only so that she could be admitted to her grandmother's presence. She didn't like to bathe, and her mother didn't force her. She changed her dress once a week for the same reason. She preferred to wear a dress until it just couldn't be worn anymore. Her mother didn't mind that, either. She didn't like to comb her hair, though on the first day of school she could put herself out for that. She didn't like to go to Sunday school, and her mother didn't force her. (*Annie John* 57–58)

The Red Girl, dirty, free-spirited, and amoral provides a perfect catalyst for Annie's growth and development—a secret friend to defy the mother and to begin the process of differentiation. In addition, the Red Girl may be a metaphor for the pre-Colombian native, a free spirit, unfettered by European influences. In her quest for self-definition, Annie temporarily embraces the Red Girl as an antidote for the mother's invidious and injurious invasiveness. Annie's conflicted nature is evidenced by the Red Girl episode. These conflicts will be in evidence again when she must come to terms with her beloved grandmother's pre-Columbian religious beliefs.

Other rebellions against the mother's/society's strictures follow; the marbles incident is the most notorious. Annie's playing marbles, a game her mother strictly forbids, marks a serious breach of "feminine" etiquette, for marbles playing means behaving like a boy, squatting or kneeling in dirt, instead of sitting or standing in a "lady-like" position. Marbles playing means games of chance, betting, winning, and losing, "lower-class" activities, not meant for proper island girls trained in the English tradition. Annie's marbles playing also aligns her with the Red Girl who climbs trees like a boy and runs free. Annie notes, "I took winning for a sign of the perfection of my new union with the Red Girl. I devoted my spare time to playing and winning marbles" (*Annie John* 60). Her proficiency at marbles indicates her growing independence and "boyish" leanings, for Annie's behavior is nontraditional or noncolonial. It is outside the English traditional practices of "civilized" English ladies.

Thievery and lying are offshoots of the marbles incident, and they continue the trajectory toward freedom from the island culture. Lying to the mother about the marbles and stealing money to buy favors for the Red Girl constitute a physical and moral betrayal of the mother's indoctrination. In other words, Annie takes a stand, albeit not a conscious one at the time, against the entire colonial experience. It is an allegorical rebellion of slave consciousness.

Annie's leading a group of girls in forbidden acts among the old tombstones of white Europeans buried before slavery had been abolished in 1833 continues her quest for an identity apart from the mother, especially the mother's directive, to behave "like a lady." She leads the girls in dancing, singing bawdy songs, and shouting obscenities among the headstones. These acts indicate Annie's defiance of the colonial past—a complete rejection of old ways, old histories, and old legacies of colonialism: "What perfection we found in each other, sitting on these tombstones of long dead people who had been the masters of our ancestors!" (*Annie John* 50). These acts connect the girls to a long history of resistance and rebellion in the Caribbean. In fact, in 1736 the graveyard in Antigua was the meeting place of the rebelling slaves, who recited an oath of war and drank liquor mixed with grave dirt and blood: "The manner of administering the Oath, was by drinking a Health in Liquor, either Rum, or some other kind, with Grave-Dirt, and sometimes Cock's Blood infused. . . . The Words were various, but the general Tenor, was to stand by, and be true to each other, and to kill the Whites, Man, Woman, and Child and to assist in the Execution of this" (*A Genuine Narrative of the Intended Conspiracy of the Negroes at Antigua* 13). Many of the ritual ceremonies were performed at the graves of slaves in order to seek the blessings of the ancestral spirits (Gaspar 231). The girls' subversive acts also parallel uprisings by slave women in the early 1800s, for in about 1831 slave women rose up to protest the abolishment of the Sunday markets in St. John's, Antigua, a prelude to the general emancipation in 1834 (219). Likewise, Annie's acts prefigure her own emancipation from colonialization and its aftermath.

Annie's lying, playing marbles, stealing books, flinching money, and hiding contraband under the house differentiate Annie from the mother, who in Annie's eyes is subservient, domestic, and trapped—trapped by the psychical and social binds of colonial ideology. The mother is the subaltern, created by the dominant group in a systematic, centuries-long, educational and socialization process. Later, Annie considers an escape. If she stays on the island, she seems destined for life as a servant or a wife—destined for a life of subservience like the mother's unless she can break free. Caroline Rody posits, "Kincaid's heroines must escape this mother [Mother-Country] by leaving the mother-island" (127). The voyage is one of hope: Annie hopes to break the cycles of abuse and oppression, manifested in the novel in the form of the mother and the mother's father, specifically. Annie's journey is problematic, though; she will be confronting some of the same injustices in England she has experienced in Antigua; negotiating this new hybrid space will not necessarily bring the freedom for which she longs.

Similarly, *Lucy* parallels *Annie John* in its negative rendering of the mother and its close alignment of the mother with "Mother-Country" and West Indian colonial culture. According to Byerman, the "mother/culture must be challenged because it denies voice and true creativity" (101). Lucy declares, "My past was my mother" (*Lucy* 90). As a young girl on the island, she had grown to hate her mother and had wished her dead (93). One of the most egregious betrayals in the novel is the one in which Lucy's mother disregards her intellectual potential, favoring instead her younger brothers for university education. Her father (actually her stepfather) she could forgive since the sons are his biologically, but her mother she cannot forgive since her mother knew her well—knew her love of learning and her dreams of advancement. At the birth of each of the sons, the mother and father make plans for the boys to study in England to become doctors or lawyers or "someone who would occupy an important and influential position" (130). The nursing profession is the highest goal the family has for Lucy who laments, "Why did someone not think that I would make a good doctor or a good magistrate or a good someone who runs things?" (92). After this betrayal, Lucy calls her mother "Mrs. Judas" and begins "to plan a separation from her that even then I suspected would never be complete" (130–31).

Her escape to New York as an *au pair* for a wealthy couple, Mariah and Lewis, marks a turning point in her growing sense of autonomy and power: a sea passage of hope and renewal. Refusing to read her mother's letters represents a significant break with the culture and the past; burning the letters parallels the mother's burning of Lucy's/Annie's books—a purging of anger and despair. After the announcement of the death of the father and the poverty of the mother, delivered by a particularly hated emissary of the mother culture, Maude Quick, Lucy declares, "I am not like my mother. She and I are not alike. She should not have married my father. She should not have had children. She should not have thrown away her intelligence. She should not have paid so little attention to mine" (*Lucy* 123). She surmises that her father, who is thirty-five years older than the mother, married her mother because she was youthful and strong: she could serve him well. Her mother mainly served the family, cleaning, cooking, washing, ironing, and cultivating a small garden, her intellect and creativity undermined and stifled. Lucy's recognition of her mother's position in Caribbean society becomes a catalyst for her move away from these constricting spaces and definitions. Lucy experienced the phenomenon Carolyn F. Gerald calls "zero image." The protagonist's main images are that of whites, in this case, white Europeans, specifically English, "the result of white racial projection of its own best image upon the universe" (132). The black child experiences identity confusion, having no positive or powerful references with which to construct her or his world (Gerald 132).

Lucy, though, negotiates the new hybrid spaces of New York with strength and will. Determined to find the freedom she seeks, she, nonetheless, is often overcome with despair or anger, these emotions brought on by her recognition of injustices in her new environment. Colonialism's long arm extends to the household in which she works. Episodes with Mariah bring reminiscences of hypocrisy, oppression, and defeat in Antigua. For example, when Mariah says after catching a fish, "This is supper. Let's go feed the minions" (*Lucy* 37), Lucy's disdainful attitude (although she admits Mariah might have said "millions") denotes her deep-seated pain: "A word like that would haunt someone like me; the place where I came from was a dominion of someplace" (37). Throughout the novel the painful thread of memories weaves a sorrowful tapestry. Paradoxically, sorrow and anger become catalysts for redemptive passages of growth and achievement. Leaving Mariah's employment for better job opportunities, making critical decisions about friendships and lovers, and beginning to write her life stories constitute acts of grace and affirmation.

Like the mother, the father also employs all the vestiges of colonialism. In *Mr. Potter*, Kincaid explores the patriarchy within the colonial systems of the Caribbean Islands, particularly Antigua. Although labeled fiction, Kincaid's novel is essentially autobiographical, for Kincaid's birth name is Elaine Potter Richardson; her mother's is Annie Richardson. The woman in the novel bears the same name and historical references. Mr. Potter, however, is more than a rendering of Kincaid's biological father; he is an allegorical representation of the complex political, social, and economic junctures of island culture. Forbes contends, "That Mr. Potter is only one instance in a sociopolitical world governed by destructive patriarchies is signified in the tandem sketches of patriarchal/colonial/imperial figures whose lives impinge on Mr. Potter's" (173). For example, Mr. Potter is named after the English admiral George Brydges Rodney. Importantly, he is of mixed birth, African and European; his father's (Nathaniel's) "ancestors [are] from some of the many places that make up Africa and from somewhere in Spain and from somewhere in England and from somewhere in Scotland" (*Mr. Potter* 39). His birth signifies the first rupture, the first disjunction from Africa, results of the Middle Passage, colonialism, and slavery. And he bears a legacy of racial/ethnic complexities, cruelties, and sorrows. Mr. Potter "was born with a line drawn through him" (97); a line was drawn in the column where a father's name should have been written. That is, he is illegitimate; no father acknowledged him. Likewise, his own father had a line drawn through him as well as his daughter, Elaine. In fact, Mr. Potter has many island daughters, each unacknowledged, each with the ubiquitous line. This inheritance leads to a void of progress and fulfillment, a poverty of spirit and will. Again, an image of zero, or negativity (Gerald 131). There is no inheritance as such, only stagnation and death, major tropes interlacing the story. Mr. Potter encapsulates the vacuity and stalemate of most of the men's lives on the island, especially those of African descent; he has no spiritual center, no love, no humanity. The men are trapped in a cycle of neglect and abuse, handed down by the fathers and visited on the daughters. In an interview with Moira Ferguson, Kincaid posits that the cycles of physical and mental abuse are "a legacy of slavery" ("A Lot of Memory" 186).

One thread woven through the novel *Mr. Potter* is the subject of education. As a child Elaine asks her father for money for books and a writing tablet, one of the only times she confronts him; but he waves her away. Significantly, none of the men can read or write. Elaine breaks the cycle by learning both, a triumphant break with the past and its defeats. Forbes notes, "Mr. Potter's illiteracy focuses the revenge code inscribed in ritual repetitions throughout the narrative: 'Mr. Potter could not read and he could not write, but I can read and I can write'. . . . The ability to write Mr. Potter in her own image is the hurt child's revenge for having been abandoned" (174). Finally, Elaine migrates from the island. The novel gives no hint of her destination or her negotiations within the new space. However, the novel makes clear that she has triumphed through education. In fact, writing Mr. Potter's life authenticates her history and finally grants legitimacy to her own existence. Writing gives her a connection to her ancestors, a rootedness in family and culture. Writing also attempts to heal the rupture, the forced migration of the Middle Passage, the wrenching breakup of familial groups, and the painful loss of country.

Also, the brothers in *Annie John* and *Lucy* are family members who act as catalysts, spurring the women away from the island environment. *My Brother* (1997), Kincaid's account of her younger brother, Devon, dying of AIDS in Antigua, encapsulates all the wrongs bequeathed to her siblings and, by extension, to Kincaid herself if she had remained on the island: "[H]is life unfolded and there was everything to see and there was nothing to see; in his life there had been no flowering, his life was the opposite of that, a flowering, his life was like the bud that sets but, instead of opening into a flower, turns brown and falls off at your feet" (162–63). Kincaid suggests that separation from the mother and the colonizing influences she represents might have saved him: "[I]f only he could have seen his way to simply moving away from her [mother] to another planet, though perhaps even that might not have been far enough away" (117). Kincaid realizes that if she had stayed on the island, she would have experienced a similar fate: "[I]t frightened me to think that I might have continued to live in a certain way, though, I am convinced, not for very long. I would have died at about his age, thirty-three years, or I would have gone insane" (90). According to Louise Bernard, "Devon symbolizes, therefore, a parallel self, a self that Kincaid literally and figuratively left behind when she arrived in New York. 'Jamaica Kincaid' is born in a state of exile from both Antigua as an ideological space imbued with 'vulnerability and powerlessness' (*My Brother* 32) and from the family that represents not a homely place of refuge, but a stifling conformity to gendered expectations" (132).

Lastly, and perhaps most importantly, the women in *Annie John*, *Lucy*, and *The Autobiography of My Mother*, like Kincaid herself, seek freedom from powerlessness. In an interview with Kay Bonettti, Kincaid states emphatically, "I am writing about power and powerlessness" (139). In another interview with Ferguson, Kincaid reiterates: "I began to see that I was writing about the relationship between the powerful and the powerless. That's become an obsessive theme, and I think it will be a theme for as long as I write" ("A Lot of Memory" 177). Confronting her mother, the European invasions and occupations, and the history of slavery leaves Kincaid with life-long subjects for personal and cultural exploration.

Early on, Annie in *Annie John* begins to feel a sense of powerlessness. Her awareness of her mother's/England's power begins at puberty and increases until, at the end of the novel, she must escape or die. Laura Niesen de Abruna contends that "the alienation from the mother becomes a metaphor for the young woman's alienation from an island culture that has been completely dominated by the imperialist power of England" ("Jamaica Kincaid's Writing and the Maternal-Colonial Matrix" 173). Her mother's awesome nature looms large. Looming large also is a growing awareness of class and race issues, her mixed race heritage producing a complex cornucopia of master/slave, rich/poor, upper class/lower class polarities. In particular, Annie realizes her inferior position in the society at home and at large. Her mother/English imperialism has master status. This depends on Annie's maintaining/accepting the position of Other/slave: "[T]he European settler is able to compel the Other's recognition of him and, in the process, allow his own identity to become deeply dependent on his position as a master. This enforced recognition from the Other, in fact, amounts to the European's narcissistic self-recognition since the native, who is considered too degraded and inhuman to be credited with any specific subjectivity, is cast as no more than a recipient of the negative elements of the self that the European projects onto him" (JanMohamed 20). She also observes that her family/culture is poor; the English occupiers, rich. These polarities of upper class/lower class are directly related to the master/slave duality: to be a master is to be rich—and powerful. The only recourse Annie can devise is outright rebellion. Her rebellions register on the domestic and social fronts, specifically. Although, at the time, her rebellions seem to portend disaster in social terms, in the end her acts are positive, propelling out of, and saving her from, a lifetime of servitude, domesticity, and poverty.

Upon arriving in the United States, Lucy in *Lucy* also feels a sense of powerlessness, especially regarding class and gender issues. However, her migration to America is, at first, a problematic venture. Her reference to feeling like cargo in the small space she is allotted points to her identification with the Middle Passage experience of her ancestors and her depression and loneliness. Her lower status as a nursemaid in a wealthy family makes her aware of her vulnerable position. Studying a French painter, probably Gauguin, Lucy ruminates, "He is shown to be a man rebelling against an established order he had found corrupt; and even though he was doomed to defeat—he died an early death—he had the perfume of the hero about him. I was not a man; I was a young woman from the fringes of the world, and when I left my home I had wrapped around my shoulders the mantle of a servant" (95). She, however, does not intend to go back to Antigua: "I never wanted to live in that place again, but if for some reason I was forced to live there again, I would never accept the harsh judgments made against me by people whose only power to do so was that they had known me from the moment I was born" (51). Lucy's migration to America gives her a new perspective on the island culture she has fled; she feels empowered to take a stand against injustices in the Caribbean family and community if forced to return. However, Lucy's pronouncement, although courageous, would doom her, especially before English rule was abolished. No new space/place for the colonized could be realized in such an environment. Lucy's rebellion would parallel Annie's—and other slave rebellions'—courageous stance, but migration seems the only viable solution for the individual to counter the powers of an imperial state.

Xuela in *The Autobiography of My Mother* also confronts a situation in which her power is diminished. The novel "forcefully engages with the inequities of a world divided into 'the big and the small, the powerful and the weak'" (Kreilkamp 55). As part Carib from Dominica, Xuela's first source of self-reference is a negative one, associated with evil, abuse, and dispossession. However, Xuela declares, "I was not of the resigned" (93). Kincaid notes the resiliency of the Caribs: "The Caribs survived because they fought. They were fierce" (Ferguson, "A Lot of Memory," 174). In contrast, the natives of Antigua, the Arawaks, were dead within fifty years of Columbus's invasion. Kincaid's point seems to be that Xuela has the same fierce spirit of the native Carib people.

The women's awareness of powerlessness and the resulting despair and anger is partially addressed by grandmothers and substitute mothers who validate the young women's sense of self-worth and act as catalysts in their identity quests. Reyes in *Mothering across Cultures: Postcolonial Representations* states, "Many of us who come from New World African cultures know that if the natural mother is not able to provide, another woman will" (97). For example, the young girl in one of Kincaid's early works of fiction, "Antigua Crossings," journeys to her grandmother's home on Dominica, a movement away from a demanding, oppressive mother to a nurturing, natural figure, a "model of strength and serenity" (28). The girl observes that the grandmother, a Carib Indian, has not forgotten her heritage. She states, "I have seen the way she hunts agouti [a rabbit-like rodent] and I know that she has not forgotten the history of her ancestors and it makes me glad" (48). This character (the girl) seems a prototype of the later characters of Annie and Lucy, who also have strong, nurturing grandmothers. A Caribbean proverb states, "If your mother doesn't nurse you, your grandmother will" (qtd. in Reyes 97).

As a young child, Annie John has a strong sense of self, but it is undermined not only by the island environment and history but also by her mother's rejections and demands. Her outrageousness, her lying, her stealing are all ways to deal with a trapped, untenable situation. In the chapter "The Long Rain," Annie, weighed down by depression, stays in bed for three and a half months—three and a half months of continual rain, a metaphoric rendering of her despair. Only when her grandmother, an Obeah woman from Dominica, comes does Annie recuperate. The grandmother performs various healing rituals, but mainly she gives Annie love and comfort. Annie relates, "Sometimes at night, when I would feel that I was all locked up in the warm falling soot and could not find my way out, Ma Chess would come into my bed with me and stay until I was myself—whatever that had come to be by then—again" (*Annie John* 125). Simmons argues that the grandmother symbolically regestates Annie, that she uses her "transformative, and curative powers" to "restore [Annie] whose own connection [to the natural world] has been broken" (39). MacDonald-Smythe notes, "Annie's ensuing illness is a symbolic retreat to a womb where she is reborn into her own personhood, separate from the mother and as powerful" (58). Donna Perry agrees:

> This image of Annie as a fetus protected by its mother is an apt description of the "paradise" of the early part of the novel, when Annie and her mother lived in harmony. With the onset of adolescence came inevitable mother-daughter tensions, and Annie struggled to free herself from life in her mother's shadow. It is as though the maternal sheltering is surfacing again—symbolically—through the nurturance of the grandmother. This

nurturance does not smother the adolescent girl but serves as a source of strength, for she has already become a separate being. Her mysterious illness at the end of the novel corresponds to the death of child self—dependent self that must grow into freedom. (251)

Toni Morrison considers the importance of ancestors such as grandmothers in black literature: "There is always an elder there. And these ancestors are not just parents, they are sort of timeless people whose relationships to the characters are benevolent, instructive, and protective, and they provide a certain kind of wisdom" (201). She adds that "the presence or absence of that figure determined the success or the happiness of the character" (201). After the nurturing episode with the grandmother, Annie has the strength to leave the island and the family and migrate to England, albeit another hybrid space—one fraught with its own challenges and tensions.

Lucy finds strength in a substitute mother figure, Mariah, her employer in New York. Edyta Oczkowicz states, "Mariah serves as a surrogate mother for Lucy in this transitional moment of her liberation and self-invention" (148). At first, Lucy views her as the privileged "Other" "because she is inscribed by the dominant colonizer's world and accepts the conqueror's status" (Oczkowicz 147). But she soon grows to love Mariah, for Mariah's love for Lucy is unconditional, like Annie's grandmother's love. For example, Mariah does not approve of Lucy's friend Peggy, but she validates Lucy's choice: "I guess you like Peggy a lot, and, you know, you really should have a friend" (*Lucy* 63). Lucy notes that Mariah is superior to her mother because her mother "would never come to see that perhaps my needs were more important than her wishes" (64). Mariah's superiority to the mother is also evident when Lucy leaves her job with Mariah and moves in with Peggy, because Mariah gives Lucy her lifeline, a journal, in which to write her memories and dreams, her history: "As she gave me the book, she spoke of women, journals, and, of course, history" (163). Early in the novel, Mariah remarks to Lucy, "What a history you have" (19). This history—and the writing of it—will empower Lucy; writing will become a vehicle for self-realization and self-empowerment as she negotiates new spaces in America. Reyes states, "Memory is secular and spiritual. Memory is empowerment" (130). Finally, ruminations about leaving Peggy—and hints at the end about finding her own space—are trajectories toward a more independent status.

Like Lucy, Kincaid also experienced a rebirth in America. In an interview with Bonetti, Kincaid asserts that she was lucky to go to America and not to Britain; in America she was "allowed this act of self-invention, which is very American" (134). Kincaid also notes that writing was the primary act of self-invention, writing about the mother/daughter relationship in particular and, by extension, the colonizer/colonized experience: "It was the thing I knew. Quite possibly if I had had another kind of life I would not have been moved to write. That was the immediate thing, the immediate oppression, I knew. I wanted to free myself of that" (133). Bernard notes that "the freedom she ultimately achieves is one grounded in the recuperative process of a writing life. Her success is bound up in the formation and performance of a decidedly literary persona" (132).

Kincaid's own history parallels the history of her protagonists, a history of matriarchal domination and cruelty, a history of a mother inscribed with colonial signs and tropes. Like the mother in the novels, her mother had burned her book collection because while reading, she had neglected her younger brother: "my mother gathered up all my books I owned and put them on a pile on her stone heap, sprinkling them with kerosene and then setting them alight" (*My Brother* 197). Kincaid believes she has spent her life attempting to resurrect them from the ashes: "but it would not be so strange if I spent the rest of my life trying to bring those books back to life by writing them again and again until they were perfect, unscathed by fire of any kind" (197–98). Her mother also did not encourage her to seek higher education. Kincaid relates, "When I first started [writing] among the things I wanted to do was to say [to my mother], 'Aren't you sorry that no greater effort was made over my education? Or over my Life?'" (Bonetti 141).

Kincaid shares other parallels with her major characters, including a nurturing maternal grandmother, a Carib from Dominica, who provided psychological strength and a validation of self based on cultural and ancestral pride. One parallel is the association of the grandmother with the religious practice of Obeah. In an interview with Cudjoe, Kincaid reveals her own experiences with Obeah. Her mother and grandmother were believers although each adhered to some aspects of Christianity. Kincaid asserts that her Carib grandmother, though, was essentially pagan: "her deep belief was not Christian" (225). When her uncle (John of the novels) was dying, Kincaid notes that her grandmother's beliefs could have cured him, for he was "possessed," but the grandfather's Western medicine seemed to have been imposed. Kincaid maintains that he died from "obeah things" (226), implying that psychological problems could have been solved or lessened with Obeah practices—practices that involved a close relationship, even a hands-on relationship, with the suffering person.

Echoes of Kincaid's Caribbean and migratory experiences reverberate in the three novels, *Annie John, Lucy,* and *The Autobiography of My Mother.* Like Kincaid herself, the women protagonists of these major works must overcome a colonial legacy of oppression and dominance to begin the journey to a new land and a new self—a freer, more autonomous state of being. Annie migrates to England, which on the surface would seem a capitulation to English imperialism, but as K. B. Conal Byrne argues, "[T]he move to England is less of a giving in as it may be a further investigation and challenge on Annie's part of the imperial control over her culture.... Infiltrating the source of her domination, then, Annie will dismantle its authority" (298). Ferguson reminds us that Annie moved to London "roughly a year after the first major race riots, precipitated by discrimination against Caribbean immigrants, erupted in London in 1958" (*Colonialism and Gender Relations from Mary Wollstonecraft to Jamaica Kincaid* 117). Bryne suggests that she may have gone to England to align with these protests: "This may have been the final stage of her personal decolonization and the formation of her own identity" (298).

Lucy migrates to America, where opportunities for economic, social, and personal growth are possible. Like Kincaid, she negotiates the swells of several job experiences and relationships, developing a stronger sense of self along the way. Her relationship with Mariah, her employer, her relationship with Hugh, Mariah's brother, her relationship with Peggy, her unorthodox friend, her relationship with Paul, her lover—all bring, however, conflicting notions of self and place. Lucy's ultimate goal is autonomy; her quest is freedom. Even though she is often submerged in sorrow, Lucy's will to freedom is indomitable—a fixed star. At the end of the novel, she is sharing an apartment with Peggy, but she is contemplating a move to a new space—a space of her own.

Xuela, whose mother, a Carib Indian, dies at the beginning of the novel, migrates to the Carib Indian reserve on Dominica, a journey to her native Carib ancestors and her "other-mothers." She finally claims her identity with her mother's people. This act she calls a "victory," a revenge: "I am of the vanquished, I am of the defeated. The past is a fixed point, the future is open-ended; for me the future must remain capable of casting a light on the past such that in my defeat lies the seed of my great victory, in my defeat lies the beginning of my great revenge. My impulse is to the good, my good is to serve myself" (*The Autobiography of My Mother* 215–16). Because she has married an Englishman, because he worships her, because she does not love him, and because she has decided not to have children, she has a kind of figurative victory or revenge over English colonialism. At the end, she cares for him and then buries him, prefiguring the end of English rule in 1967. Xuela's identity formation is the most problematic, most conflicted, of the three. A hybrid of races (her mother Carib; her father African and European), she represents the interfacing of all cultures. In the end she triumphs in multiples when English rule ends. However, she chooses to align with her mother's people, the few indigenous peoples of the island; her final migration is to the bosom of her mother's people. One can only conjecture about this "transplantation"; Xuela may thrive; she may become a spokesman for the native peoples in their quest for autonomy and enfranchisement.

All of Kincaid's works represent her own journey toward self-empowerment, her own confrontation with her own historical legacies. *Annie John, Lucy,* and *The Autobiography of My Mother,* in particular, are clearly fictional autobiography. *Mr. Potter* is a fictional account of her biological father's attitudes and experiences. Nonfictional accounts such as *A Small Place* and *My Brother* are, of course, up-front accounts of her birthplace and family. In these works Kincaid explores what it means to be constrained by historical forces, made immediate by family dynamics. Migrations away from these forces are heroic acts of will and achievement. Sometimes subversive, sometimes confrontational, her writings explore the territory she has traveled, revealing the injustices found there and leaving a travel record of a gifted woman's trials and triumphs. Ivan Kreilkamp observes, "Kincaid has never forgotten what it felt like to be small, young and without power, and she uses that feeling of powerlessness as the material for her novels. Even as she's become a respected author, mother, and professor, she continues to write behind the authorities' backs—where she feels most at home" (55). Passionately, she writes about the anger and despair of the colonized woman and the conflicts inherent in migration. Importantly, in most of her stories, the woman prospers. Through her own effort and will, she moves toward greater freedom, opportunities, and empowerment.

[CHAPTER 7]

"Tee," "Cyn-Cyn," "Cynthia," "Dou-dou"
Remembering and Forgetting the "True-True Name" in Merle Hodge's *Crick Crack, Monkey*

Joyce Zonana

Trinidadian writer Merle Hodge's *Crick Crack, Monkey* has been called "the first major novel published by a black Caribbean woman" (Maes-Jelinek and Ledent 177), and "the first major novel by a post-colonial West Indian writer to problematize and emphasize questions of difference and the quest for a voice" (Gikandi 14). Appearing in 1970, "far in advance of any recognizable Caribbean feminist tradition" (Cobham, "Revisioning Our Kumblas," 46), it has been credited with "ushering in a new era in the writing of women in the English-speaking Caribbean" (Cudjoe, "Introduction," 43). Indeed, one of the first collections of Caribbean women's writing—*Her True-True Name* edited by Pamela Mordecai and Betty Wilson—took its title from a key passage in Hodge's novel. Yet, although the novel has been studied and celebrated by critics of Caribbean literature, it remains relatively unknown outside specialist circles. I hope that this essay will introduce the book to a wider audience and demonstrate its relevance for explorations of migration and identity in the specifically Caribbean context of the African diaspora.

Writing from an unspecified vantage point as an adult, *Crick Crack, Monkey*'s endearing first-person narrator dryly recounts her experiences as a child in colonial Trinidad, from the day of her mother's death until the eve of her departure for the "Mother Country," England. Deceptively simple, the short novel offers an understated but pointed critique of a world that teaches the narrator to be ashamed of the "ordinaryness" and "niggeryness" (105) of her Afro-Caribbean identity, insisting that she value instead the "Reality" and "Rightness" to be found only in books or "Abroad" (67). Torn between her working-class dark-skinned Tantie who lovingly calls her "Tee," and her middle-class, lighter-skinned Auntie who primly calls her "Cynthia," the narrator can find no authentic self—no proper name—of her own. Yet while the novel's plot offers no alternative but migration to the young girl's conflict, the text's narrative strategies suggest that the narrator's voluntary passage from Trinidad to England teaches her to value the elements of identity preserved by her ancestors during their involuntary Middle Passage from Africa to the Caribbean.

As Simone Alexander has argued, the European "Mother Country," the African "Motherland," and the Caribbean "mother'(s) land"—an "extension" of the African Motherland—provide a useful framework for understanding the fictional autobiographies of Afro-Caribbean women writers, including Paule Marshall, Maryse Condé, and Jamaica Kincaid (4). Hodge's work is no exception, though in *Crick Crack, Monkey,* the Caribbean "mother('s)land" cannot unproblematically be associated with the African Motherland. It is, rather, a complex and conflicted *new* land, with legitimate ties to *both* Africa and Europe (and Asia, in the case of Trinidad)—a place in which an indigenous, hybrid, "sovereign" identity is in the process of being formed (Hodge, "Challenges of the Struggle for Sovereignty," 203).

In the words of Martinican novelist and critic Edouard Glissant, Caribbean identity cannot be contained by the "fixed Being" of what he calls the "Sameness" of European ontology and epistemology. Instead, it partakes of a "Diversity" that "establishes Becoming" (98). Because "reversion" to the Africa before the Middle Passage is impossible for the Afro-Caribbean subject, and because "imitation" of the European colonial culture inflicts "insidious violence," it is only "diversion" that can lead the Caribbean self "somewhere" (Glissant 16–22). Yet, as Glissant insists, "Diversion is not a useful ploy unless it is nourished by reversion: not a return to the longing for origins, to some immutable state of Being, but a return to the point of entanglement, from which we were forcefully turned away" (26).

Thus, the Caribbean writer will not deny trauma by relying on what Dominick LaCapra calls "conventional" or "redemptive" narratives structured by the biblical model of "Paradise, Fall, History . . . and then redemption" (156); instead, practicing the "art of Diversion" (Glissant 85), she will write "experimental, nonredemptive" texts that work to come to terms with trauma (LaCapra 179). *Crick Crack, Monkey* is such a text, showing that the atrocities of the Middle Passage, slavery, and colonialism remain facts that cannot be denied or undone. The Caribbean subject must move forward, not back, creating a complex modern identity that neither clings to nor refuses the African past. As Silvio Torres-Saillant writes in *Caribbean Poetics: Toward an Aesthetic of West Indian Literature,* "the colonial condition has turned the Antillean man or woman into an existential migrant, a person who wanders between worlds, between spaces, between traditions" (32).

The narrator of *Crick Crack, Monkey* is herself a migrant, shuttling between different spaces and oscillating among a variety of competing identities. These competing identities are signaled by the variety of names by which she is called. Her "Tantie" calls her by the informal name "Tee"; her "Aunt" uses the formal "Cynthia." At school she is "Cynthia Davis," and when she over-invests in that institutional identity, her foster brother mockingly calls her "Ma Davis." In moments of heightened emotion, Tantie calls her "Dou-dou," using the Creole term of affection; other relatives playfully call her "Cyn-Cyn." And at the very end of the novel, a neighbor calls her "Cyntie," suggesting a possible resolution of her conflict. Naming—and who gets to assign those names—is foregrounded within this novel, which puts language itself at its center, exploring the interrelation of language and identity.

The plot is built around a series of migrations: first, that of the narrator and her brother from their parents' home to that of their paternal aunt, "Tantie"; second, that of their father to the Mother Country, England; third, the children's "capture" by their maternal aunt, Beatrice; fourth, their periodic journeys to their grandmother Ma's home in Pointe d'Espoir; fifth, the journey of Tantie's ward Mikey to the United States; sixth, Tee's voluntary migration to Aunt Beatrice's house; and finally, Tee's anticipated journey to England. Each of these migrations—with the exceptions of the visits to Pointe d'Espoir (Point Hope)—constitutes a rupture, a break in being, and each is accompanied by linguistic and psychological shifts.

As a very young child at home with her Tantie Rosa, "Tee" experiences a sense of belonging and unproblematic, unselfconscious selfhood. With Auntie Beatrice, with whom she lives while attending secondary school, "Cynthia" is at first dislocated and alienated, yet in time she comes to be ashamed of her earlier self. Tee/Cynthia experiences other worlds that give rise to other identities—the idyllic, sensuous landscape associated with her grandmother "Ma," and the idyllic entirely mental landscape she encounters in books. If the African Motherland associated with Ma, and the Mother Country limned in books, are extreme ideals, the contrasting realms of Tantie Rosa and Auntie Beatrice represent the conflicted but all too real aspects of the "mother('s)land" that does violence to those ideals, even as it evolves towards something new.

The novel begins with young Tee and her brother Toddan posted at Tantie's window, awaiting their mother's return from the hospital. "'We gettin a baby!'" the children shriek to all passersby (1). But both mother and her infant die, and Tee and Toddan become the center of a tug of war. The narrator recalls "a voice like high-heels and stockings" saying, "*We will take the children*" (2–3). These are the words and voice of Aunt Beatrice, condemning

Tantie ("Look at you, you aren't *fit!*"), with whom their father wants the children to stay. Tantie manages to prevail over "that bitch," and Tee's father goes off to "sea."

Much later in the novel we learn the source of the conflict between the two aunts. Beatrice tells Tee that her sister, Tee's mother, was a fair-skinned "beautiful little girl" who might have been taken to England by the people "up on the Grange"; instead she was adopted by "low-class" Godparents who lived in "the bush" (90). And then she chose to marry a dark-skinned man—Rosa's brother—a "misdemeanor" as far as Beatrice is concerned. Still, she wants to raise Tee and her brother, to give them a "quality" life and to win from them the love her own children deny her. For Beatrice's three daughters, having learned their lessons all too well, have turned their backs on their own mother as they work to be accepted by "nice" society.

In the aunts' competition for possession of Tee/Cynthia, Hodge dramatizes competing models of identity and modernity for Caribbean individuals as well as for Caribbean nations. Tantie Rosa is an emotionally expressive, sexually open woman who is happy to be who she is. She serves as a loving foster mother for the narrator and her brother, as well as for an older boy, Mikey. And she speaks in a colorful Creole—her very name in the novel, "Tantie," evoking the original French base of Trinidadian Creole. She is, in fact, one of the "self-possessed" Caribbean women Hodge admires, "women who did not seem to pattern their lives after the rules laid down by nice Trinidadian society, by the church or the storybooks" ("Challenges" 208). Aunt Beatrice, on the other hand, is a restrained and repressed married woman who carefully enunciates her formally correct Standard English sentences in her effort to be accepted. As Tee/Cynthia moves between their two worlds, she finds herself torn not only between their different value systems but also between their two forms of language.

While living with Tantie, young Tee listens to the singing of a drunken neighbor, "Gimme piece o' yu dumpling Mae dou-dou" (1); she hears her aunt lambasting Mikey, "An' before you look to help-out yu mother an' she forty-nine chirren no yu prefer siddong on yu arse wid them long wu'tless young men down at that bridge" (5); at the bridge with the "cream of Santa Clara's unambitious" (6), she follows a discussion of Westerns: "An' then the other guys reach, an' then, ol'-man, then yu jus' see Red-Indian falling-dong all over the place—ba-da-da-da-da—pretty, boy, pretty!" (9). In this environment Tee has days of glory, days when "it was the long, long walk with the sun all around and stinging and blurriness rising from the road and the smell of asphalt, and the road soft under you toes and the grass at the sides no cooler and just when it was getting too much we'd turn off the road and plunge between the bushes and down down the precipitous path to the water" (6). As she describes such moments, the adult narrator's language falls into the rhythms of Creole, the same rhythms she reproduces when recording Tantie's speech in free indirect discourse: "what she ain't tell that bitch is what she forget" (13).

In Aunt Beatrice's realm, on the other hand, Tee is introduced to the formalities (and hypocrisy) of Standard English. She overhears her aunt chastising a servant who calls a dress a "frack": "If you can't speak properly when you speak to these children then don't bother to say anything at all!" (38). Purchasing supplies at a country market, Beatrice makes "a systematic effort not to understand a word of what the shop-people said to her, and when she spoke to them it was loudly, slowly and emphatically, with much pointing and sign-language" (99); her daughters' voices "arch" through the house as they talk on the telephone: "so well I said well dorling why don't we just go and pick the others up orfterwards" (89). And although the book is not written in the exaggeratedly proper tones of Auntie's family, it is, for the most part, written in Standard English rather than Creole. Best to say, perhaps, that it is a hybrid of Creole and Standard English.

Discussing the title of her novel, Hodge explains that "the word *monkey* is meant to have all the associations of aping and imitation" (Balutansky 657). Aunt Beatrice's world is the "monkey" world, the "make-believe" colonial world in which children of the African diaspora strive to take on the attributes of the colonial master. As V. S. Naipaul puts it, "In the pursuit of the Christian-Hellenic tradition, which some might see as a paraphrase for whiteness, the past has to be denied, the self despised. Black will be made white" (63). Beatrice is a victim of the "alienation" Frantz Fanon attributes to the Caribbean person deformed by the "constant effort to run away from his [*sic*] individuality" (*Black Skin, White Masks* 60), in quest of a constantly elusive identification with the master that often takes the form of imitating the master's speech.

The distinction between Creole and Standard English is fundamental to the experience of Caribbean peoples. Jamaican writer Mervyn Morris notes that although Creole is the "language of feeling," the "most intimate language," Caribbean literature still privileges Standard English (9). Guadaloupan Maryse Condé argues that Creole languages are the "first example of the Caribbean syncretic culture," and reminds us that "language is power: who names, controls" (*Créolité* without Creole Language? 102). And Helen Pyne Timothy, in an important article, "Language as Subversion in Postcolonial Literature," catalogues numerous ways in which Creoles can function positively for Caribbean writers. Among other things, they assist the "creation and recreation of an identity" distinct from that of the colonizer; they assist "the reclamation and the recording of a history which is separate from that of the Master"; "they create a nexus" between oral and written traditions; and they "provide subliminal linkages to the slave past and the African ethos" (10). Hodge herself foregrounds the importance of using Creole languages to express the distinctive Caribbean worldview. "We speak Creole, we need Creole," she writes, "we cannot function without Creole, for our deepest thought processes are bound up in the structure of Creole, but we hold Creole in utter contempt" ("Challenges" 204). In *Crick Crack, Monkey*, she uses the interaction between spoken Creole and Standard English to demonstrate her narrator's self-division, as well as to suggest her ultimate integration.

Allied to the distinction between Creole and Standard English is that between spoken and written culture, oral folktale and written literary text. Thus, if the title of Hodge's novel points to what Glissant calls the "insidious violence" of imitation, it also has its roots in the very oral culture the European colonial masters (and their Caribbean imitators) sought to destroy (16–22). The title echoes the words sung at the conclusion of a "'nancy-story," one of the ubiquitous Caribbean folktales that take their collective name from Anansé, the spider-god of West African folklore who "survived the middle passage" (Jonas 51). These folktales, "outlawed by and in" colonial schools, celebrate the "artist-creator" trickster figure whose "subversive activity" is deeply "interrogative of the Anglo-inherited written culture" (Tiffin 56–57).

In *Crick Crack, Monkey*, Tee is told 'nancy stories by her grandmother, Ma—always at night, always outdoors, always under a moon. "If the night was too dark or if it was raining there was no story-telling—it was inconceivable to her that one should sit inside a house and tell 'nancy-stories" (15). In Hodge's second novel, *For the Life of Laetitia*, a schoolteacher shocks his students by expressing interest in their "moonlit world of people who were half beast, half spirit or half god," explaining that the *Tales of the Greek Heroes* "were just somebody else's 'Nansi stories" (52–53), and writing the names of "these beings whom we knew" on the board. "What would they be doing up here in our high-school literature class?" the narrator of *For the Life of Laetitia* wonders (53).

In *Crick Crack, Monkey*, the narrator recalls:

And when at the end of the story she said "Crick crack?" our voices clambered over one another in the gleeful haste to chorus back in what ended on an untidy shrieking crescendo:

Monkey break 'e back
On a rotten pommerac! (15)

In evoking this rhyme in her title, Hodge signals her interest in exploring "orature for the symbols and organizing principles" of her *written* text (Cobham, Revisioning Our Kumblas," 47). She also invokes the "trickster spirit" of Ananse as muse, a practice Joyce Jonas suggests is common among Caribbean writers (53). Edouard Glissant offers another possible gloss on the novel's title. "In a great number of folktales heard during childhood," he reports, "the storyteller tells about receiving at the end of the story a kick in his bottom that hurled him into his audience" (84). The oral storyteller becomes one with his or her audience, abandoning a position of mastery, all self-importance lost. Such a stance is particularly appropriate for a novel whose narrator reveals herself to be anything but a master of her own identity.

Tee is first brought to Ma's land after her temporary capture by Auntie Beatrice. This capture reenacts in miniature the forcible seizure of Africans by slave traders in the sixteenth and seventeenth centuries. It occurs when "The Bitch"—Tantie's name for Beatrice—arrives in a car offering sweets and smiles to the children. "Well how would you like to go for a nice drive in your Uncle Norman's car?" she offers, and while Tee is skeptical, Toddan enthusiastically accepts (12). Upon their return, Tantie is furious: "we had jus' nearly get we arse kidnap!"(14); the next day she packs the children off to Pointe d'Espoir, to stay with Ma, their paternal grandmother.

This migration brings Tee to an "enchanted country" (16), a timeless realm where the "air smelt brown and green, like when the earth was being made" (20). She imagines that the characters of the 'nancy tales—"Brar Anancy and Brar Leopard"—"roamed the earth" in just such a place (16). In this almost mythic world, the children become Ma's "acolites" (20), and Ma herself is endowed with the solidity of an earth goddess. "She rose at a nameless hour," Tee says, "and in my half-sleep I saw a mountain shaking off mist in one mighty shudder and the mist falling away in little drops of could" (18). Imperceptibly, the narration shifts from a description of one specific visit to Ma's land to an evocation of all the visits, year after year. "All the holidays at Pointe d'Espoir were one August month"; ordinary time becomes "fix[ed] into eternity" (19–20).

Although the narrator had been happy while living with Tantie, she is ecstatic while staying with Ma. At Tantie's, she was always wary of Tantie's rages; but Ma "equal to all the vagaries of childhood" never "rampage[s]" (17). And while life with Tantie is marked by the rhythm of all-night parties that are "loud" and "hilarious," life at Pointe d'Espoir follows the quiet rhythms of nature: Tee helps Ma as she harvests fruit "with a cutlass" and prepares preserves and jellies for the Sunday morning market (16). Ma's life is continuous with a rural African past. She is at one with her environment, capable of "rapture" as she communes with the natural world (20).

The narrator is first named for us during her visit to Pointe d'Espoir. At Tantie's, she was simply one of the children, absorbed in the collective "we" that dominates the narration of the earliest sections of the novel. At Ma's, among an even larger group of children, she is singled out as "Ma's own-own bold-face Tee" (21). The child and her grandmother engage in a playfully loving ritual:

> "Sometimes when the others were not about she would accost me suddenly:
> An who is Ma sugar-cake?"
> "Tee!"
> "An who is Ma dumplin'?"
> "Tee!"
> ... "Who tell yu that?"
> "Ma tell mih!" (21)

Thus it is with Ma that Tee acquires a firm identity, a self that is mirrored back to her in love.

Self-division and self-contempt—initiation into colonialism and racism—begin for Tee when she enters school. Although she had "looked forward to the day" when she could read (22), literacy brings with it the imprint of colonial power. Her textbook opens with "A for Apple, the exotic fruit that made its brief and stingy appearance at Christmastime" and continues with the "fortunes and circumstances of two English children known as Jim and Jill, or it might have been Tim and Mary" (27–28). Tee puzzles over nursery rhymes: "what, in all creation, was a 'haystack'?" (28), while her teacher, who has "been up in England in his young-days," instructs her to recite "Children of Empire Ye are Brothers All," "God Save the King," and "Land of Hope and Glory."

Tee's experience at school is typical of Caribbean children taught to value the "universal/imperial at the expense of things local" (Tiffin 44). As Jamaican poet Kamau Brathwaite writes, "We haven't got the syllables, the syllabic intelligence, to describe the hurricane; whereas we can describe the imported alien experience of snowfall" (qtd. in Talib 85). V. S. Naipaul recalls that "it seemed impossible" to turn the life he knew in Trinidad "into a book" (qtd. in Talib 96), and another Trinidadian writer, Sam Selvon, describes how he recited "English verse under a mango tree in the schoolyard" while dreaming of "green fields and rolling downs, of purling streams and daffodils and tulips" (qtd. in Talib 85–86). Hodge herself notes that "Caribbean people are capable of a kind of 'mental desertion' of their own environment, which is not matched, I think, by any other people on earth." ("Challenges" 206).

For Tee, the worst moment occurs when a teacher chastises a student who fails to recognize that the letters "g-r-a-p-e-s" accompanying a picture do not stand for "chennette," a local fruit. "You'll never get anywhere," Mr. Hinds thunders, "you'll never be anything but . . . *piccaninnies!* . . . *little black nincompoops!*" (32). Thus it is that a black man, imitating his colonial masters, initiates Tee into racism. Her education in self-contempt is furthered when at Sunday school she is offered "pictures of children with yellow hair standing around Jesus in a field of sickly flowers" (33). She quickly develops a "pretty good idea of what kind of a place Glory must be"—the place to which her mother has gone, the place which is the same as "The Mother Country and Up-There and Over-There" (33). With her classmates, she sings:

> Till I cross the wide, wide water, Lord
> My black sin washèd from me,
> Till I come to Glory Glory, Lord
> And cleansèd stand beside Thee,
> White and shining stand beside Thee, Lord,
> Among Thy blessed children (33)

In this way Hodge quietly demonstrates the damage done to a young black child as she encounters the negative or zero image of herself, taught to see "white as the symbol of goodness and purity; black as the symbol of evil and impurity" (Gerald 131).

Still, despite these onslaughts, Tee manages to retain a positive sense of self. She manifests this the next time "The Bitch" enters her life. Accompanied by a policewoman, Beatrice brandishes a court order as she carries off the children. Now it is the law that legitimates the children's capture, enforcing their migration to Auntie Beatrice's home, where Beatrice's oldest daughter objects to Toddan's nose, "calling him Flat-Nose" (37). But Tee beats up her cousins at every opportunity and urges Toddan to be naughty so that they might be sent back to Tantie. When Beatrice insists on calling her Cynthia, "as if I were in school," and Toddan "Codrington," Tee takes "personal offence": "'He name Toddan,' I informed her sharply. 'Is I who name him'" (40). Here Tee unabashedly uses Creole as she claims her own power of naming. And she is "distraught with joy" when Tantie arrives with a court order of her own. "*Look* mih girl!," Tantie exclaims when she sweeps the children up. "Tee! Dou-dou!," she calls, restoring to the narrator the name she feels is hers (42).

Yet, colonial education, as it progresses, separates Tee from her Afro-

Caribbean reality and identity, from her name and her power to name. She learns to value the world she finds in books, the world of "real Girls and Boys who went a-sleighing and built snowmen," and "called things by their proper names, never saying 'washicong' for plimsoll or 'crapaud' when they meant a frog" (67). By the time she reaches Third Standard, she has invented an imaginary friend named Helen, an English girl who spends summers by the sea with "her aunt and uncle who had a delightful orchard with apple trees and pear trees" (67). Helen's fancied orchard with apple trees replaces the very real breadfruit tree at Pointe d'Espoir; even more significantly, the Helen whose identity is derived from books replaces "all the other characters" in the "unending serial" Tee had been "spinning" for her brother and neighbors "from time immemorial" (67). In this way, Hodge dramatizes the replacement of a vivid oral tradition with the alienating—but "proper"—literary world.

Around this time Tee begins to wear shoes from "the moment I woke up on mornings" (67). Her action causes "hilarity" in the household, and Mikey, another one of Tantie's wards, mocks her, calling her "Ma-Davis." When she starts to wear socks every day, Tantie is not amused: "Look, Madam, when yu start to wash yu own clothes then yu could start to play the monkey" (68). But Tee is lost in her fantasy world now, longing for the identity that comes to her from books. Looking back, she comments on the "doubleness" she had come to take for granted: "Why, the whole of life was like a piece of cloth, with a rightside and a wrongside. Just as there was a way you spoke and a way you wrote, so there was the daily existence which you led, which of course amounted only to marking time and makeshift, for there was the Proper daily round . . . which encompassed things like warming yourself before a fire and having tea at four o'clock" (68). While books might occasionally portray "Natives" and "Red Indians," these are only "for chuckles and for beating back" (68).

In effect, then, Tee has already migrated, in her imagination, to the European Mother Country, where "Right prevaileth" (68), abandoning both African Motherland and Caribbean mother('s)land. Her mental colonization is complete, and the next time Auntie Beatrice shows up, she goes willingly to live with her, abandoning Tantie. Just before Tee's departure, Tantie had suffered another loss—the migration of her ward Mikey to New York, where he had obtained a job. "It ain' have no blasted Heaven here," Tantie exclaims as she tries to persuade him to say, "but it ain' have that no-whe" (70). Once Mikey leaves, she goes about "looking dazed and absent-minded" (72), and she does not protest when Beatrice arrives to take Tee. For Tee has won a government scholarship and Beatrice promises to get her into "the very best" secondary school (75). But Tantie rouses herself when Beatrice promises to buy Tee's uniforms: "Well thank you Madam, but we will see about that," Tantie counters, demonstrating her mastery of Standard English when she wants to use it.

Sadly, Tee's voluntary migration to Beatrice's shows her how far she is from her colonial, European ideal. While living with Tantie, she could "play the monkey." But at Aunt Beatrice's she is reminded every day of her distance from the values, behaviors, and skin color of the world into which she seeks admittance. "Uhm . . . what's your name again?," her cousins cruelly ask, "I can't remember—Agatha or Emmalina?" (77). Beatrice "suppress[es]" the clothes Tee has brought with her, calling them "niggery-looking" and inappropriate for "nice people" (85). She disapproves of the food Tee likes and rages when Tee makes the mistake of serving herself rice in a bowl and eating it with a spoon. "Don't bring your ordryness here!" Beatrice exclaims (105). Because of the darkness of her skin, Tee is turned down for participating in exclusive dancing schools, and she cringes when she overhears her cousin describing her to friends: "Oh, that's some lil relative Mommer found up in the country" (89).

Even more devastating than the violence inflicted upon Tee by her relatives is the violence she inflicts on herself. The deciding moment comes when she acquiesces to Auntie's wish that she not go to her East Indian neighbor Moonie's wedding, what Beatrice cruelly calls that "coolie affair," that "simmy-dimmy" (86). Humiliated, Tee hides her disappointment. While living with Tantie, Tee had been on intimate terms with her Indian neighbors. Doolarie, the daughter of "Neighb' Ramlaal" (11), was her constant companion, and she had attended many Indian festivals. East Indians form 40 percent of Trinidad's population, and their culture is an important part of the unique heritage of the island. But Aunt Beatrice wants to distance herself not only from dark-skinned blacks, but also from "coolies," descendants of the people brought over in the nineteenth century as indentured servants to work the sugarcane plantations against which the newly liberated slaves had understandably turned their backs.

In abandoning her intimacy with Moonie—a "coolie—Tee abandons a central part of her self. When Carnival time arrives, she discovers that she does not want to go home. Instead, she joins her cousins and goes to "the Stands," where she sits "primly" in the company of tourists to watch the bands. With shame, she remembers how she used to ride in "Ramlaal's inelegant truck" with a "herd of neighbours and neighbours' children" (94), determined now to distance herself from "all those common raucous niggery people and all those coolies" (95). A few months later, when Tantie comes to visit along with Toddan and Doolarie, Tee is mortified: "The worst moment of all was when they drew forth a series of greasy paper bags, announcing that they contained polorie, anchar, roti from Neighb' Ramlaal-Wife, and accra and fry-bake and zaboca from Tantie, with a few other things I had almost forgotten existed, in short, all manner of ordinary nastiness" (118). Tee fears that her cousins will find out about Ma, "who was a market-woman," and tries to erase all evidence of her former life. Still, her memories persist, as she longs for the unselfconscious freedom she once knew. She imagines making her way back to Pointe d'Espoir, envisioning Ma's delight at her arrival: "And then we would sit down facing each other; and the picture stubbornly snuffed itself out" (120).

Back when Tee *had* been able to face Ma and find in her a positive reflection, she had learned about her great-great-grandmother, "a tall straight proud woman who lived to an old old age and her eyes were still bright like water and her back straight like bamboo, for all the heavy-load she had carried on her head all her life" (21). Characterized by Ma in vividly figurative language that relies on natural images (eyes "bright like water," "back straight like bamboo") and Creole rhythms ("tall straight proud," "old old age"), this ancestress is indomitable; she "would come back and come back and come back," and, according to Ma, she has "come back again" in Tee (21).

This ancestor appears to be an African woman who survived the Middle Passage, or, at the very least, a daughter of such a woman, for she has retained her African name. "The People gave her the name Euphemia, or Euph-something," Ma tells Tee, "but when they called her that she used to toss her head like a horse and refuse to answer so they'd had to give up in the end and call her by her true-true name" (21). The European name imposed on the African ancestress, "Euphemia, or Euph-something," is brutally ironic, suggesting as it does the term "euphemism," the substitution of a "good" word for a purportedly "bad" reality. The imposed name represents the European masters' attempt to control the African woman. In her refusal to answer, she asserts her autonomy and integrity, despite her enslavement. What the colonial masters would identify as bad, she claims as good; in insisting that they use her "true-true" name, she demands that they honor her essence.

This great-great grandmother—along with Ma, who introduces her to Tee—is one of those "timeless people whose relationship to the characters are benevolent, instructive, and protective" that Toni Morrison sees as so vital to black identity (201). "If we don't keep in touch with the ancestor . . . we are . . . lost," Morrison asserts (202). Yet Tee's relationship with her ancestor is flawed. Maria Diedrich, Henry Louis Gates, and Carl Pederson write of the ancestors before the Middle Passage: "they had always known who they were. They had always known their parents' names and their parents' parents'" (5–20). But Ma has forgotten her grandmother's "true-true name"; try as she might, she cannot call it back. What the Middle Passage has failed to destroy, life in the New World has erased. As V. S. Naipaul observes, "Twenty million Africans made the middle passage, and scarcely an African name remains in the New World" (63).

For all Ma's preservation of African traditions, she has failed fully to "defend the 'I am' against the onslaught of definitions the 'masters' imposed upon the 'black other'" (Diedrich, Gates, and Pedersen 17). Tee may well be a new incarnation of her ancestor, but without her name her identification is incomplete. Thus, Hodge refuses to offer a "redemptive" narrative celebrating unproblematic unity with a traditional past; instead, like Paul Gilroy in *The Black Atlantic*, she emphasizes rupture as she foregrounds the losses wrought not only by the Middle Passage but also by the years of slavery and, most significantly, the colonialism that continued for over a hundred years after the abolition of slavery.

In contrast to the unnamed African ancestress, there is another ancestress in *Crick Crack, Monkey*, the ostentatiously named "White Ancestress," Elizabeth Helen Carter. Memorialized in Aunt Beatrice's home in the form of a faded photograph, this ancestress has not one but three names repeated among her descendants. The photograph, "reddish-brown with age" and surrounded by "a heavy frame of gilded foliage," forces itself "into the attention of all who entered the livingroom" (90). Tee's fair-skinned cousin Carol resembles this ancestress, and so her middle name is Elizabeth, as was the narrator's "poor mother" (90). When Tee invents her imaginary British friend, it is no accident that she calls her "Helen." Yet while we learn again and again of the White Ancestress's names—and Tee sees her "indistinguishable" looks—we learn little of her spirit, nothing of her essence (91). The nameless African ancestress is all essence, a living presence; the White Ancestress is an empty name, a faded textual remnant. Still, she manages to make Tee "thoroughly ashamed" of herself: "it seemed to me that my person must represent the rock-bottom of the family's fall from grace" (91).

The opposition between the (black) unnamed African and the white named (European) ancestresses vividly dramatizes the conflict that rends the narrator's life. Emilia Ippolito argues with respect to Caribbean women's writing in general—and to this text in particular—that such a conflict may be understood using the terms of Lacanian psychoanalytic theory. If the unnamed African ancestress suggests "the real but erased mother tongue (representing the Real to which access is denied)" and the White Ancestress is identified with the "British mother tongue (representing the Law of the Father or the Symbolic Order)," then it is only in the realm of the Imaginary, "the space of the literary text" (92), that a reconciliation can be achieved.

Language enables the "diasporic imaginings of a self which needs to be reconstructed" (93), and it is only "in a continuous exchange between the symbolic and the imaginary" that the "post-colonial subject" can "resolve its past history of colonization . . . and begin again, as a hybrid form" (92). Tee uses the "Imaginary"—the text she narrates—to fight "the Symbolic," associated with Aunt Beatrice, which "denies the ancestral part of her identity" (125) and "which suffocates her" (126).

Yet while it is tempting to employ such a psychoanalytic model to understand *Crick Crack, Monkey* and other Caribbean texts, Dominick LaCapra offers an important caveat in his *Writing History, Writing Trauma*. Arguing that his is not a simple binary opposition, LaCapra distinguishes between "historical" and "structural" trauma, asserting that structural trauma appears in "different ways in all societies and all lives" (77). Structural trauma encompasses "the separation from the (m)other, the passage from nature to culture, the eruption of the pre-oedipal or presymbolic in the symbolic, the entry into language, the encounter with the 'real,' the alienation from species-being, the anxiety-ridden throwness of *Dasein*, the inevitable generation of the aporia, the constitutive nature of originary melancholic loss in relation to subjectivity, and so forth" (77). By contrast, historical trauma is generated by specific historical events that devastate a specific person or a specific people—events such as the Middle Passage, slavery, colonialism, and, in the twentieth century, the Holocaust. It is vital, LaCapra argues, "not to hypostatize particular historical losses," not to "present them as mere instantiations of some inevitable absence or constitutive feature of existence" (65). In other words, while the psychoanalytic model may provide a convenient paradigm for understanding the works of contemporary Caribbean women writers, such a model may gloss over the all too *real* historical suffering of the African ancestors and their descendants. To use LaCapra's terms, by conflating a universal human "absence" with a specific African diasporic "loss," the psychoanalytic model short-circuits the work of mourning, suggesting that the historical trauma of the African diaspora is as inevitable as the psychological trauma of the separation from the mother. "Historical losses call for mourning—and possibly for critique and transformative sociopolitical practice," LaCapra writes (68).

In *Crick Crack, Monkey*, Hodge uses another strategy to forestall the easy psychoanalytic formulas that might tempt the critic: for in this text the White Ancestress is on the mother's side, the African ancestress on the father's. Thus Hodge complicates the binarism that has become a critical commonplace in the study of works by women of color: mother is to father as black is to white, native to colonial, authenticity to alienation, etc. For Tee, identification with her light-skinned mother leads towards her European heritage. But because her darker father has migrated to the Mother Country, identification with him also leads to Europe. There is no "pure" identity Tee can claim, no "Sameness," only "Diversion."

Thus, when Tantie realizes how self-divided Tee has become through her schooling and her association with Auntie, she arranges for Tee's father to send the children tickets to England. The first time Tee had been captured by Beatrice, Tantie had sent her to Ma's—in effect, to the Motherland. Now she sends her to the Mother Country—perhaps the only place from which Tee can finally make a decision about her actual mother('s)land.

On a final trip back to Tantie's before she is to leave for England, Tee learns to her dismay that Ma has died just the week before. Tantie tells her that Ma had asked for her, but Tantie had said Tee had no time to visit. "In the last days Ma had suddenly remembered her grandmother's name and wanted it to be added to my names," Tantie tells Tee, but she "hadn't even bothered to remember it" (122). The true-true name of the ancestor is thus lost, and the reader, along with Tee, must mourn. There is, for Tee, no going back, no return to the ancestral past nor even to her own former unified identity. "Everything was changing, unrecognizable, pushing me out," she writes (122) as she records her longing to be "lift[ed] off the ground" by the plane taking her to England (123). On her final night in Trinidad, Tantie is "mirthlessly drunk," and one of the compès urges Tee to "come and dance for the last." Calling her "Cyntie," he reminds her that "they don' do much o' that whe' allyu goin, yu know, come dance, man!" (123).

Crick Crack, Monkey, then, concludes with no fully formed identity for its narrator, no resolution of the conflicts that tear her apart. The plot offers no redemption for the colonial subject, no restoration of wholeness. Indeed, it is on a note of loss and mourning that the novel ends—with no hopeful vision for the future, no promise of self-integration. Yet the use of the name "Cyntie" on the last page of the novel suggests the possibility of melding of the two identities, "Cynthia" and "Tee," as does the narrator's blending of Creole and Standard English throughout the text. Migration to the Motherland or to the Mother Country—in imagination or in fact—are equally illusive options. It is only by standing still—or by dancing—on the mother('s)land to which she belongs that the narrator can claim the modern Caribbean identity that *includes* Africa and England (and India) in a unique, as yet unnamable hybridity. "You see, when I wrote this novel I was in England," Hodge recalls, "and one of the things I was aware of . . . was that whole business of all these Caribbean and African people going to European countries and discovering *there* that all they'd been told about their own countries was a lot of hogwash, and that their own culture was valid" (Balutansky 654). The reader can only hope that Cyntie has made the same discovery—that she returns to the mother('s)land with a renewed sense of self-acceptance, and a commitment to "cultural sovereignty" ("Challenges" 203). Her narrative suggests that this is so—as does Hodge's choice, unique among contemporary Caribbean women writers, to live and work in the land of her birth.

[CHAPTER 8]

Place and Displacement in Djanet Sears's *Harlem Duet* and *The Adventures of a Black Girl in Search of God*

Elizabeth Brown-Guillory

A frican Canadian woman playwright Djanet Sears rose to international prominence with the productions and subsequent publications of *Harlem Duet* (2000) and *The Adventures of a Black Girl in Search of God* (2003), two plays that offer complex explorations of the lives of women who struggle daily to cope with issues of displacement and who search for healing in a world characterized by fragmentation. Sears's plays reveal the nuances of the struggle that black Canadian women endure as they attempt to negotiate destabilizing terrain. Her writings offer insights about the cultural practices that both inhibit and advance the transformation of women's lives in Canada as well as across the African diaspora. Sears's heroines live with contradictions as they navigate societies that view them simultaneously as valuable and valueless. These bold female characters are able to reconcile contradictions, adapt to ambivalence, and become community builders in an increasingly individualistic, modern society. The degree to which these women warriors are able to live productive, full lives in a supportive community depends, in large part, upon their ability to negotiate the tensions that come with spiritual, physical, psychological, or social movement. Sears's emphasis on healing serves as an augury of a movement toward repairing the psychic damages heaped upon descendants of Africans in Canada.

While Sears's plays only recently reached North American audiences, she has maneuvered center stage in Canadian arts and letters since 1989 with the production of her first theater piece, *Afrika Solo*. First released in 1990 by Sister Vision Press, *Afrika Solo* is Canada's first publication of a stage play written by a person of African descent. A one-woman show, *Afrika Solo* chronicles a young black woman's quest for self-discovery. The plot of *Afrika Solo* begins with a reenactment of the Middle Passage, a powerful rendition of the forced movement that led to the enslavement of blacks throughout the African diaspora. Sears's theater piece reminds audiences that Canada sanctioned slavery in its provinces until around 1800, a fact that may be surprising to those unfamiliar with Canadian history. Noted African Canadian scholar and poet George Elliot Clarke writes, "A 1995 poll conducted by the Canadian Civil Liberties Association found that 83 percent of Canadian adults did not know that slavery was practiced in pre-Confederation Canada until 1834, when Britain abolished the institution throughout its empire" (103). *Afrika Solo* debunks the myth that Canada always served as a safe haven for blacks. Historian Joseph Mensah argues that the secret has been so well hidden that even many Canadians deny slavery existed in Canada. Mensah challenges the displacement of black history in his observation that "[t]he exploitation of Black labour through slavery was such an essential element in the foundation of Canada that the neglect of Black history can hardly be accidental" (44). Sears also indicts the former slave-holding Canada in *Afrika Solo*, wherein she critiques North American media for its portrayal of blacks as servants and man-eating savage tribesmen worthy of enslavement. An excellent blend of pathos and comedy, *Afrika Solo* tells the story of a black woman's response to her best friend's challenge to go back from whence she came. This dare propels the heroine to question her place of origin and her relationship to blacks in the media, in Africa, and throughout the African diaspora. Sears's one-woman performance piece bolsters Arlene Keizer's assertion in *Black Subjects* that contemporary black writers "have seized hold of slavery as an existential condition through which to articulate the difficult coming-into-being of the black subject in the New World" (165).

Afrika Solo exposes a history of demoralization of blacks in Canada. The play supports what Mensah views as white Canada's attempt to "black out Black history" (57). Mensah posits that Canada's black population (662,215—approximately 2 percent of the entire Canadian population—of which many are situated in Toronto, Montreal, Ottawa, Vancouver, and Halifax) is highly heterogeneous and continues to struggle with rampant racism (3). Sears's *Afrika Solo* reinforces Mensah's assessment that Canada "includes Canadian-born descendants of those who came through the slave trade; the descendants of those who migrated from the United States during and after the Civil War; and Blacks who have immigrated from Caribbean, African, and other countries in recent decades" (3).

Sears's interest in identity issues and the impact of forced migration stems from her resentment of the otherization of blacks in Canada. Lisbeth Goodman, in *Contemporary Feminist Theatres*, cites a quote from Sears's *Afrika Solo* in which the heroine comments, "You know, nothing exists until a white man finds it!" (148). In *Afrika Solo,* according to Goodman, Sears describes "her experience of multiple marginalization from a white male norm, as an English-born woman living in Canada, whose mother is Jamaican and whose father is Guyanese" (178). Sears was born in London and moved with her parents at age fifteen to Saskatoon, Saskatchewan, Canada. Her name change, from Janet to Djanet after a visit to a West African town of the same name, signals Sears's longing to connect with a distant past and an African heritage. In an interview with Robert Breon, Sears acknowledges her connection to Africa: "It seemed like I had discovered a little part of myself [in Djanet] so I made it mine" (Breon).

In a March 2004 interview with Mat Buntin, Sears notes, "Apart from Aboriginal people, we come from a bunch of other places, and I have many of those traits in me. . . . [A] lot of my work is about questioning home, and looking at this idea of what home means, whether it's in terms of literature or whether it's in terms of culture or cultural voice" (Buntin). Sears relates to home in the way that editor of *Voices: Canadian Writers of African Descent* Ayanna Deck describes African Canadian identity and its link to place:

> We come from Jamaica, Trinidad, Barbados, Ghana, Haiti, Guyana, Nigeria, Canada, the United States and South Africa. As writers, we push the limits of literature and redefine images of representation. In the process, we create our realities. We are a new generation of griots—town criers, or spiritual messengers—whose stories have been transferred to the printed page. Despite the diversity of cultural backgrounds, we write out of a collective African consciousness—a consciousness embodied in the fabric of oral traditions, woven from one generation to the next, through rhythms, storytelling, fables, proverbs, rituals, worksongs and sermons meshed with Western literary forms. (xi)

Sears avers that her work and that of other African Canadians deals with "claiming home and . . . navigating this territory between where you've come from, and where you are" (Buntin). Rinaldo Walcott, in *Black Like Who? Writing Black Canada*, echoes Sears's sentiments about displacement theory, noting that "writing blackness is a scary scenario: we are an absented presence always under erasure" (27).

The issues of migration, alienation, and dejection loom large in her work as Sears attempts to cast a wide net around the polyvalent experiences of African Canadians. An adjunct professor at the University of Toronto who has served as writer-in-residence in a number of North American cities, Djanet Sears includes in her work a nuanced African Canadian context. Rinaldo Walcott echoes Sears's focus on the discriminatory practices against blacks in Canada when he observes that "Diaspora conditions work to produce black peoples in the contradictory space of belonging and not. . . . Black people in Canada continue to exist in precarious relations to older versions of citizenship and older versions of belonging" (22–23). Evangelia Tastsoglou, like Walcott, underscores Sears's assessment of life for black women in Canada: "In Canada as elsewhere, ethnic and racial minority women (hereafter 'racialized women') encounter structural, institutional, and systemic racism, at work and in the media, as producers, consumers, and individuals with unequal access to social services and political representation" (93). While *Afrika Solo* catapulted Sears into prominence within Canada, *Harlem Duet* and *The Adventures of a Black Girl in Search of God* attracted an international audience. Both plays deserve serious critical treatment because of the engaging explorations of displacement and healing of blacks in Canada and throughout the African diaspora.

Sears's *Harlem Duet* garnered a series of awards, including four Dora Mavor Moore Awards, the Floyd S. Chalmers Canadian Play Award, Phenomenal Woman of the Arts Award, and the coveted Governor General's Award for Drama. Before its premier in Toronto in 1997, Sears workshopped *Harlem Duet* under the tutelage of George C. Wolf (author of the hugely successful *The Colored Museum*) in 1996 during Sears's writer-in-residency stint at the Joseph Papp Public Theater in New York City. A complexly woven tale of identity, place, and race, *Harlem Duet* is a riff on Shakespeare's *Othello*. *Harlem Duet* responds to and revises the oft-told tale of the Moor and his passion for the white Desdemona. In Sears's play, Othello was married to a black woman, Billie, before he chooses (Desde)Mona, his white colleague at Columbia. The play stages displacement in its themes, structure, and sound design, all of which work together to emphasize loss, alienation, disenfranchisement, and the ultimate determination to survive the challenges that beset blacks in a racist society.

Even a cursory reading of *Harlem Duet* reveals that it is much more than a play about jealousy; it is an exploration of a black woman attempting to cope with oppressive racist conditions exacerbated by Othello's abandonment of Billie for Mona. The central theme is survival in a world that encourages white privilege and essentializes black women's relationships with their male counterparts. Othello, who is battling to extricate himself from blackness, explains to Billie why he no longer gravitates toward black women: "You . . . the Black feminist position as I experience it in this relationship, leaves me feeling unrecognized as a man. The message is, Black men are poor fathers, poor partners, or both. Black women wear the pants that Black men were prevented from wearing" (601). While Othello blames Billie for his emasculation, the audience experiences outrage, or a sense of detachment at the very least, because it was Billie's inheritance (life insurance from her mother's death) that Othello happily exhausted to support his doctoral studies at "Harlumbia—those 10 square blocks of Whitedom, owned by Columbia University, set smack dab in the middle of Harlem" (599). It is ironic that Othello lives among blacks in Harlem but sees no connection between Harlem residents and himself.

Sears levels an indictment, through Othello, against a society that rewards blacks monetarily for disengaging from their black families and communities. Caricatured as disembodied and displaced, Othello brashly explains why he prefers white women:

> Yes, I prefer white women. They are easier—before and after sex. They wanted me and I wanted them. They weren't filled with hostility about the unequal treatment they were getting at their jobs. We'd make love and I'd fall asleep not having to be aware of someone's inattentive father. I'd explain that I wasn't interested in a committed relationship right now, and not be confused with every lousy lover, or husband that had ever left them lying in a gutter of unresolved emotions. . . . The white women I loved saw me—could see me. (602)

In truth, Othello is misguided, even delusional as is evident when he quips, "I am not a minority. I mean my culture is not my mother's culture—the culture of my ancestors. My culture is Wordsworth, Shaw, *Leave it to Beaver, Dirty Harry*" (603). Sears portrays him as the penultimate example of invisibility. Othello struts upon the stage as a vapid, pseudointellectual who is enamored of white privilege and disdainful of the black struggle proliferating around him in Harlem. African Canadian actress Alison Sealy-Smith, who originated the role of Billie, characterizes Othello as someone who feels that "he's not limited by his skin color and can move into white society, but Billie counters that she's defined by the continuity of experience—that she's trapped in history just as history is trapped inside of her" (Kaplan 39).

Sears further mirrors Othello's brokenness in his choice of Mona, a white woman who never appears wholly on stage. The audience hears her voice and sees a glimpse of her white arm. Sears suggests that Othello is destined to hang, like a trophy, from Mona's white arm. Instead of gravitating toward a whole person who might serve as a solid anchor for Othello, he chooses an ethereal arm. Though Mona is portrayed as incomplete, which reinforces Othello's fragmentation, he delights in what Katerina Deliovsky refers to as "hypervisibility" (238), an opportunity to experience a high profile, interracial relationship. Othello is the embodiment of dislocation and displacement, due to his internalization of the dominant group's view of blacks. When Othello attempts to navigate between Billie and Mona, displacement and longing collide in his ambivalent feelings for Billie. His longing for Billie, who represents home, security, familiarity, community, shared oppression, etc., is not fully extinguished by his desire for white privilege. During Othello's visit to collect his belongings from their apartment, they reminisce until they work their way into bed. Billie still loves Othello, but she recognizes that she is responsible for changing the circumstances of her life. Her lapse in judgment becomes the catalyst for her journey to wholeness. She stares reality in the face when Othello rushes from her bed to the white arm that beckons him.

Sears links Billie's story of love, sacrifice, abandonment, and race oppression to the extensive history of displacement of blacks in the African diaspora. She stages displacement by creating in her play textual disjuncture. She structures *Harlem Duet* around three parallel stories that repeatedly move forward and circle backward throughout the course of the play. This lack of linearity of plot and the individual stories that echo and extend each other serve to create dissonance in the play as well as in the viewer who is experiencing the theater piece. The competing stories—tantamount to textual displacement—function to create a sense of alienation and loss in the characters whose history spans from slavery to present. Each story nuances the struggles of blacks associated with race prejudice.

In one story, set on a plantation in 1860, characters named Him and Her are making plans to escape to Canada via the Underground Railroad. Sears takes an opportunity in the story of Him and Her to link slavery to atrocities foisted upon blacks in the African diaspora. Him commiserates over the lynching and mutilation of the body of a slave named Cleotis while Her references the mutilation of blacks in France, where Saartjie Baartman, the Hottentot Venus, was "paraded naked on a pay-per-view basis. Her derrière was amply endowed. People paid to see how big her butt was, and when she died, how big her pussy was" (573). Sears's reference to Baartman (1789–1816), the South African woman who was exploited first in England and then in France, foregrounds mutilation of black bodies as an insidious tradition among Western hegemony. Sears postulates in *Harlem Duet* that the degradation and defilement of Baartman's body is but one case of the dominant group's obsession with and repulsion of the black body, an unmitigated insignia of man's inhumanity to man. Within twenty-four hours of Baartman's death, her body was dissected and her skeleton articulated. Her genitalia and brain were pickled and displayed publicly, albeit ironically, at the Musée de l'Homme (Museum of Mankind) until 1974. Resulting from the pleas of scores of South African people, including Nelson Mandela, Baartman's remains were returned to South Africa in 1994 for burial in sacred grounds. Sears's inclusion of Saartjie Baartman's story in the narrative of *Harlem Duet* aligns her with Pulitzer Prize winner Suzan-Lori Parks whose play about Baartman, entitled *Venus* (1996), was circulating while Sears was workshopping *Harlem* Duet in 1996 at New York's Public Theater. In addition to the reference to Baartman, Sears also conjures up the spirit of Emmett Till. Her refers to Emmett's lynching, although the scene is set in 1860 and predates the 1955 murder of the fourteen-year-old black boy for whistling at a white woman. Her bemoans the fact that there "must be a lot of us there walking around in purgatory without genitals" (573). Sears joggles the audience—thereby disrupting a sense of complacency and stability—by merging distant past, present, and future in this dramatic beat, while at the same time prefiguring the destruction that can happen when blacks cross the line into acculturation. Later, when Him betrays Her by choosing to remain with his white mistress whom he feels is helpless and is in need of his protection, destruction reigns supreme. In Him's refusal to become a transplant, Sears disrupts the notion of Canada as a haven in the literary imagination.

Abandonment is also the theme of the 1928 storyline in which He, a Harlem vaudeville actor forced to accept minstrel roles, convinces She that they must escape to Canada to a "white house, on an emerald hill" where he will be free to live up to his full potential as an actor (575). He expresses humiliation at having to perform in blackface and laments that he is of "Ira Aldridge stock" (619) and longs "to play the Scottish King, The Prince of Denmark" (619). He is heartsick that his extensive experience has not secured for him the recognition he deserves. Sears accomplishes an important disruption in the second storyline, namely that she dislodges the myth that acculturation leads to full acceptance of blacks by whites. Sears further establishes that He is misguided when he reveals to She that his white director, Mona, "sees my gift. She's cast me as the Prince of Tyre. She breathed new life into my barren dream" (619). The language He uses suggests victimization or objectification. Like his "barren" dreams, He is an empty shell, and he anticipates that Mona can make him whole. Later, when He confesses that he loves director Mona because she sees him for his true value, we understand that he is articulating that she makes him feel like a man. The scenario concludes with She stabbing He to death. Sears writes in the stage instructions, "his neck appears to devour the blade" (620), a description that conjures up disembodiment.

The third plotline is set in contemporary Harlem, where Billie has migrated from Canada to do graduate work. Sears joins a long line of black women writers, such as Jamaica Kincaid, Paule Marshall, Buchi Emecheta, Tess Onwueme, Winsome Pinnock, Ama Ata Aidoo, and Merle Hodge, to name but a few, whose characters participate in border crossings—movement in search of a better place to enjoy life. This reverse migration, from an idealized historical place, demystifies Canada as an inviting place to blacks in the distant past or present. Instead of finding freedom in the United States, Billie collides with obstacles similar to those she left behind in Canada. In Canada, her father, whose name is also Canada, had taken a white wife after Billie's mother died, a choice which initiated the heroine's feelings of abandonment. Traumatized by what she perceives as betrayal and emotional disconnection from her father, Othello's abandonment of Billie for Mona the professor sends Billie to a psychiatric ward. Turning to herbal medicines and Caribbean potions, Billie plots to place poison on a white handkerchief—a key plot device for Shakespeare—given to Othello by his grandmother. Jon Kaplan draws parallels between the two plays by asserting, "Shakespeare talks about the 'magic of the web' of the handkerchief, a conceit that *Harlem Duet* also manipulates—except that in this case the spider spins a web of toxic racism. Billie plays with this venom to reach Othello, but she finds herself systemically poisoned by its virulence, which she has internalized" (39). Though she allows the anger to consume her for a time, Billie ultimately chooses family and friends as her support group. Sears's creation of textual displacement with the parallel stories telescopes the upheavals and the scars that mar the lives of black men and women who lust after white privilege.

The sense of dislocation—or living between worlds—created by the play's structure is bolstered by Sears's strategic use of sound design. Sears examines the lives of blacks who are forced to live in the space in between, an idea voiced in Homi K. Bhabha's *The Location of Culture* and Paul Gilroy's *The Black Atlantic*. She interweaves music and voice-overs among the three parallel storylines. In her stage instructions, Sears writes, "the cello and the bass call and respond to a heaving melancholic blues" (563). Musicians sat in a corner of the stage playing a blues/jazz duet in the original production. Peter Dickinson reads Sears's use of the cello and the bass as a means of contextualizing the friction between the dominant group and its Other: "This tension between European and African-Americana forms of cultural expression, between Billie's feminist and postcolonial resistance to dominant forces of acculturation and Othello's apparent patriarchal and self-abnegating acquiescence to those forces, evoked on stage through music and sound is . . . simultaneously accompanied by a more expressly (inter)textual form of call and response" (192). Dickinson explains that Sears's use of the cello and bass functions as a "kind of chorus to her own re-writing of Shakespeare" (192). Sears eloquently offers her own explanation of her implementation of the cello and bass:

> When I was looking at how to approach *Harlem* as a director, the first question—"What kind of play is this? Is it comedy, is it tragedy?"—I came up

with this phrase that this was a "rhapsodic blues tragedy." There's a wonderful book called *The Blues Aesthetic and African Americans,* and Amiri Baraka wrote a book called *Blues People* that talks about how blues music can be deconstructed and applied to any art form. So you say, "What is the construct of the blues?" You have call-and-response. You have fragmentation. You have polyrhythmic solos. You have a whole list of different parts of that idiom that you apply to theatre. Syncopation. . . . In *Harlem Duet* I wanted a tension between European culture and African American culture. I used blues music . . . to create blues music for a cello and a double bass. But double bass and cello says chamber music. So the blues creates that tension, it's beautiful and it has that drama implicit in it. (Sears and Sealy-Smith 28–29)

While the music, the blues/jazz duet, serves to underscore the struggles of displaced blacks, the voice-overs are equally, if not more, powerful.

Sears uniquely and strategically places audio clips of great orators and black leaders—Marcus Garvey, Paul Robeson, Booker T. Washington, W. E. B. Du Bois, Martin Luther King Jr., Malcolm X, Jessie Jackson, Louis Farrakhan—who themselves lived at the intersections of slavery and freedom, Jim Crow and civil rights. One effective case in point of Sears merging music with voice-overs simultaneously to stage displacement and call for healing is in her stage instructions regarding Malcolm X: "The strings thump out an urban melody blues/jazz riff, accompanied by the voice of Malcolm X, speaking about the nightmare of race in America and the need to build strong black communities" (565). In another voice-over, "Malcolm X speaks about the need for Blacks to turn their gaze away from Whiteness so that they can see each other with new eyes" (592). The voice-overs are especially powerful when we recognize that Billie and Othello's apartment is located at the intersection of Malcolm X and Martin Luther King Boulevards, a physical location that serves to disrupt the notion of "the black community as a homogenous group" and demonstrates in the voices of two political leaders the "range of strategies for surviving in a hostile world" (Kaplan 39). Sears gives us a glimpse into the lives of black men who often held, if not opposing views, then certainly opposing strategies for black freedom, while at the same time interweaving their narratives among the three parallel stories of Billie and Othello, who are at their own crossroad and who have very different notions of what it means to be free.

Though nearly all of the voice-overs are of men, there is one powerful female that Billie conjures up: Sojourner Truth. In Act 1, Scene X, when Billie is at her lowest, she reaches back to her ancestor and says, "Ain't I a woman" (604). The referencing of Truth's speech signals Billie's identification with and need to belong to a community of women who are not afraid to do battle against the triple bind of race, gender, and class biases. The cello and bass as well as the voice-overs all participate in a call and response with Billie and Othello. Though Billie is challenged by the cacophony of voices—both the ones on audiotape and the ones in her head—with the inclusion of Sojourner Truth to the mix, Sears is underscoring a black feminist approach to survival in a hostile environment.

While Billie contemplates killing Othello because of his betrayal of her with Mona, it is women—her landlady, Magi, and her sister-in-law, Amah—to whom she turns for solace. Magi, who brings the healing balm of laughter, helps Billie to realize that she cannot take life too seriously. Billie brims with laughter at Magi's philosophy about love and marriage. Magi, who doesn't have a boyfriend, is so confident that she'll be married and pregnant within the year, that she has booked Convent Baptist Church a year in advance (565). Magi also assists Billie with her potions and tells her that to keep a man, "you rub his backside with margarine.... But you've got to be careful. He might be a fool. You don't want to be dragging no damn fool behind you the rest of your days" (568). Amah, like Magi, reaches out to comfort Billie after the final breakup and after the final love making. While the various flashbacks develop Billie as a confident graduate student supporting her husband of nine years, the advancing plotline portrays the unraveling of Billie as Othello moves on with his life with Mona. Sears makes use of the trope of madness to allow us to see the transformation that eventually occurs in Billie. She shields herself from the world under the cloak of insanity until she is able to process the chaos of her circumstances. Amah is a key figure in Billie's return to wellness, because it is Amah who grounds Billie with talk of Jenny, Amah's daughter, whom Billie cherishes. As Amah sits oiling and twisting Billie's hair, an act associated black female bonding, Amah functions as a healing balm.

The most interesting twist in the play occurs when Billie's father, named Canada, shows up unexpectedly in Harlem. Billie has been estranged for some years from her recovering alcoholic father who "hauled us all the way back to Nova Scotia from the Bronx, to be near Granma, when Mama died" (581). When Billie questions Canada about coming to visit after many years of not being in touch with his family, he replies, "Nothing wrong with seeing family is there?" (607). Much of the interaction between Billie and her father centers on his past mistakes and his willingness to beg forgiveness for abandoning Billie as a child. To Billie's response that her father's return is too little too late, Amah tells Billie, "Forgiveness is a virtue" (581). Later, Amah offers Billie additional advice about dealing with her father and Othello: "If I don't forgive my enemy, if I don't forgive him, he might just set up house, inside me" (631). With Canada's return to New York, his crossing of emotional and physical boundaries, Sears is, again, addressing the issue of place and displacement. Canada, who was born in Dartmouth and moved to the Bronx and then back to Nova Scotia, represents the displaced black. His need to find Billie facilitates his own healing as well as hers. When he reconciles with Billie, we see the beginnings of transformation in both characters. To help Billie move forward, Canada offers to clean her apartment. The symbolism of the cleaning speaks volumes about their beginning afresh. There is hope for Billie because in forgiving her father, Canada, she is also reconciled with Canada as a locale. The absence of a black presence or sense of erasure Billie associates with Canada—both her father and her country—dissipates. In reclaiming his displaced family now living in Harlem, Canada serves as a symbol for healing all blacks in the African diaspora. Canada—as patriarch and place—is transformed, a metamorphosis that suggests healing and rebirth. Finally, with the strength of her family buoying her up, Billie is able to forgive Othello and move on. Alison Sealy-Smith supports the notion that the black family has a special resonance in Sears's *Harlem Duet*: "Throughout our history, in Africa and North America, families have been ripped apart. To reestablish a family after centuries of division means you've succeeded, no matter what shape the family takes" (Kaplan 39). That Sears ends *Harlem Duet* as the family is reconciling and begins *The Adventures of a Black Girl in Search of God* in the midst of a crisis of family and faith suggests continuity of concerns and Sears's deep need to explore dislocation and the healing places of black history.

The Adventures of a Black Girl in Search of God (2002) borrows its title from George Bernard Shaw's 1933 fable "The Adventures of Black Girl in Her Search of God." The frightening dramatization of loss is the common denominator linking these two works, but beyond this parallel, the play explores displacement issues among blacks in Canada. Sears's play is a fictional conflation of two events that made headlines in Canada (Sanders 487). The first event chronicles African Canadians in Holland Center, Ontario—approximately 140 kilometers from Toronto—who staged a protest when the local town council sought to change the name of Negro Creek Road because it seemed old fashioned and insulting to blacks. Instead, they voted to rename the street Moggie Road in honor of an early white settler. The local black community, whose ancestors date back to the days of the Underground Railroad, refused to let their heritage be erased and forced the council to reinstate the name. The second event that inspired Sears's play was the 1989 controversy over an exhibition of African artifacts entitled "Into the Heart of Africa" at the Royal Ontario Museum in Toronto. The black community accused the curator of misrepresenting the artifacts and glorifying the white missionaries of the colonial period.

In *The Adventures of a Black Girl in Search of God*, Sears entwines historical events, mourning, determination, and spirituality. Two plotlines run parallel, with crucial points of intersection: the heroine Rainey's mourning of the loss of her daughter and her search for spiritual healing interface with her father Abendigo's quest to ensure that his community's roots in Negro Creek remain intact. Rainey, an obstetrician, remains in the throes of mourning three years after her daughter's death from meningitis. She indicts herself doubly for not diagnosing her daughter's condition and for not being as attentive as she should have been to her dying father. Feeling powerless in the hands of an angry or, at the very least, apathetic God, Rainey has abandoned medicine to pursue a Ph.D. in religion and science in an attempt to make sense of the chaos engendered by her loss. Sears connects Rainey's crisis of faith and her abhorrence of racist practices in Canada to the African diaspora. She seamlessly ties Rainey's questioning of God to the lynching of Texan James Byrd: "God has allowed the most vicious atrocities. . . . When that man, Byrd, James Byrd, was dragged by a chain from the back of a pick-up truck, conscious to the last, feeling his limbs crumble, separate from his body, one by one—WHAT DO YOU SUSPECT GOD WAS THINKING" (521).

Paralleling Rainey's narrative of separation and loss is her father's struggle with his heart condition and his humorously executed acts of reclamation of black artifacts. Abendigo and his septuagenarian squad disguise themselves as Jehovah's Witnesses, janitors, chauffeurs, delivery men, industrial housekeeping staff, lawn care personnel, etc., as they work their way across the countryside "liberating," or stealing, stereotypic representations of blacks, such as lawn jockeys, cookie jars, figurines, plaques, piggy banks, and various garden gnomes. Abendigo and his team of senior rebels stash the offensive items in his basement and surreptitiously restore them to dignity by refashioning the buffoonish grins into real-life, human smiles. Their final mission, however, is to recover from the mainstream museum Abendigo's grandfather's uniform worn during the British War of 1812. His grandfather's service to the British Crown garnered the deed to land near Negro Creek, and recovering the uniform is a special, ultimate act of reclamation for Abendigo. In essence, Abendigo's final effort symbolically rescues him and his community from possible future invisibility, thereby reestablishing their roots; it also coincides with the reestablishment of the name Negro Creek Road, as the town council's effort to name the street Moggie Road is repealed. Abendigo's machinations serve as one of the catalysts for Rainey's act of self-reclamation.

Djanet Sears portrays displacement by foregrounding land and water as the controlling imagery. She links the stripping away of the history and land from blacks in Negro Creek—the action of the play takes place before the rescinding of the name Moggie Road—to forced migration and its concomitant displacement of blacks throughout the African diaspora. The heroine's name "Rain"ey—and the play's link to water, earth, and rain—suggests place and fertility and yearning for rebirth or renewal. Sears stages longing associated with separation and loss in her depiction of Rainey as an eater of dirt. Rainey associates this craving for dirt with a yearning to return to her former community of Negro Creek: "I've been trying to get out here all my life and now, now I just hunger for the soft sugary earth by Negro Creek. My Pa's family lived and died on this bush land—been ours since 1812. Maybe that's why it tastes so sweet" (507). The movement between urban and rural, modernity and tradition, and transition and stasis advances the plot and serves as the main frame of reference for Sears's characters; their present displacement is a reenactment of a larger, deeper, more pervasive dislocation originating in the Middle Passage and the slave experience that purposefully relocated blacks to break familial bonds. Sears provides us with another example of the soil as a symbol of rootedness in the conversation between Rainey and Michael, whom Rainey is divorcing. When Michael accuses her of eating dirt to fill the void of losing their child and to secure a strong foothold on reality, Rainey, quite ironically, tells him, "I just wanted someone to make the earth stop shaking" (553). We can read Rainey's "shaking earth" as signifier of destabilization—of the shifting physical, emotional, and spiritual movement that characterizes her life as an African Canadian female. Of interest is the evidence Sears provides for her preoccupation with land as a healing device—an epigram from Aned Kgositsile's *Part of Each Other; Part of the Earth:* "We, Africans in America, come from a people tied to the Earth, people of the drums which echo the Earth's heartbeat. . . . People tied to soil and wind and rain as to each other" (493). Rainey's identity is enmeshed in Negro Creek; it is her connection to who she is, her immediate present, and her distant past. Djanet Sears employs a Chorus that assumes the role of the waters of Negro Creek. Leslie Sanders, who in 2002 witnessed a production of *The Adventures of a Black Girl in Search of God* at the DuMaurier Theatre in Toronto, suggests that "as theme, emblem, and subject, water was everywhere in the production, extending the geography of Negro Creek, to the Atlantic itself and to Africa, the source" (489).

Sears gives birth to healing in her experimental use of space. Her Chorus of thirteen actors sings and dances throughout the play, signaling scene changes and abstracted expressions. Robin Breon argues, "When the Chorus moves into the downstage pit, they represent the creek that bears the community's name, and as source of life that they represent, their movement and sound is quietly penetrating" (Breon). The Chorus's framing of Rainey's father's impending death, as well as her preacher husband's trials with racism, particularly the desecration of his church, serve to initiate the healing process for the heroine. Rainey is finally able to release her feelings of guilt when she runs from the cemetery and jumps into the living water. Sears writes in the stage instructions, "The Chorus of souls envelops her and she disappears into the creek. By the time Michael reaches the water's edge, Rainey re-emerges, buoyed by the movement of water" (575). Her baptism in Negro Creek is also a rebirth. Later in the action, Rainey is able to release her daughter's black dolls into the creek, symbolic of her readiness to move forward. Michael, too, experiences healing, signaled by his joining Rainey in eating a morsel of dirt. Sanders argues eloquently that the living waters of Negro Creek "[evoke] the river-crossings that saved escaping slaves and the Middle Passage that brought them into slavery, the waters of baptism and waters of birth. Through voice, dance, and spectacle, as well as story, *The Adventures of a Black Girl in Search of God* situates the struggles of African Canadians within a national narrative, indeed, but also with the history and space of the African Diaspora, a larger imaginary and a deeper root" (489). *The Adventures of a Black Girl in Search of God*, with its multifarious evocations of an imagined African community, replicates the initial rupture that separated blacks from their African origins and performs healing as an act of resistance for modern-day African Canadians who continue to struggle and triumph over disenfranchisement and dislocation.

Sears's *Harlem Duet* and *The Adventures of a Black Girl in Search of God* valiantly explore acts of reclamation. *Harlem Duet* revises Shakespeare's *Othello* by interrogating Othello's life before his involvement with Desdemona. In retelling the story of Othello, Sears revisits history and inserts the concerns of contemporary blacks. In reimagining *Othello*, Sears is able to examine the lives of black women that escaped treatment in Shakespeare's version. Additionally, Sears's revisioning of Shakespeare's play recasts and foregrounds Othello as a symbol of displacement during the English Renaissance. In a sense, Sears carves a hole in the whole of Western history, thereby inscribing in the story of the Moor a black heritage that eclipses the story of his love for a white woman. Sears boldly reclaims Othello's story and retells it in a way that delineates his emptiness in both versions. Sears makes us want to revisit Shakespeare's version to explore other ghosts that need to be exorcised. In her "Notes of a 'Colored Girl': Thirty-two Short Reasons Why I Write for the Theatre," Sears explains her fascination with revising Othello's story: "As a veteran theatre practitioner of African Descent, Shakespeare's Othello had haunted me since I first was introduced to him. Sir Laurence

Olivier in blackface. Othello is the first African portrayal in the annals of western dramatic literature. In an effort to exorcise this ghost, I have written *Harlem Duet* [which] explores the effects of race and sex on the lives of people of African descent. It is a tale of love. A tale of Othello and his first wife, Billie" (Sears). In Sears's version of the story, Othello gravitates toward whiteness, but voice-overs from Malcolm X and other black leaders whisper in his ears that he has lost much by turning away from his black wife and his black community. A second act of reclamation involves Sears's use of the Chorus, which she views, in some respects, as an African tradition borrowed by Westerners:

> I had to fight to maintain the importance of the chorus. Using thirteen actors adds significantly to the budget, but the play needs the chorus. In a kind of Aristotelian way, I wanted to create a vehicle not to advance the narrative so much in any neo-classical sense, but to advance the unity of action within the play. It really comes more out of African story-telling techniques, which I observed there. Constant movement, gesture, dance, sound—reaching as many senses as possible, sometimes without audience even being consciously aware of it. (Breon)

Sears's Chorus in *The Adventures of a Black Girl in Search of God* is the single most powerful device in the play, because it allows her to link Rainey to her African ancestors and also serves as an efficient device for advancing the plot seamlessly from scene to scene. Both plays offer dynamic explorations of dislocation and strategies for healing the (w)hole of black history.

Djanet Sears's plays—treating a range of themes, including dispossession, displacement, slavery, racist exploitation, sexuality, sexual oppression, history, family, and healing—may someday be recognized as defining works of the African diaspora experience. Her work is a masterful conjunction of the lyrical with the visceral. Billie in *Harlem Duet* and Rainey in *The Adventures of a Black Girl in Search of God* struggle for mobility and violate the boundaries that confine them physically, spiritually, emotionally, and socially. Billie and Rainey's journeys resonate with what Angeletta Gourdine, in *The Difference Place Makes,* describes as "the relationship between present and past locations: the geographical spaces we occupy, the cultural borders with which we place ourselves, and the intellectual positions we take. . . . The dispersal of Africans from the continent resulted in African bodies in non-African places" (ix). Sears's heroines struggle to make sense of the chaos of their worlds; their sense of displacement almost obfuscates their dreams of freedom, but their ultimate reliance upon the strength of family and community transforms these heroines. Billie and Rainey chant, drum, sing, and dance, merging their liberating strategies with those of the souls of their ancestors that line the Atlantic Ocean. Sears's competing stories in *Harlem Duet* and the Chorus of voices in *The Adventures of a Black Girl in Search of God* demand a space where women are allowed freedom to live productive lives that include a connection to a community of men and women working together to support each other. Her plays, ultimately, offer hope to a displaced people. Sears's call for healing is the voice that connects with world literatures and seeks to inculcate in all humans a greater sense of communality.

[CHAPTER 9]

Recovering the Past
Transatlantic Migration, Hybrid Identities, and Healing in Tess Onwueme's *The Missing Face*

Juluette Bartlett-Pack

Nigerian playwright Tess Onwueme critiques in *The Missing Face* the aftermath or effects of the colonial experiences on Africans, Nigerians in particular, and the African diaspora. Much of the focus on migration of African Americans to Africa as a result of the involuntary crossings of Africans during the transatlantic slave trade has been done in the context of back-to-Africa movements in the nineteenth and early twentieth centuries. Onwueme utilizes the trope of migration to portray the voluntary crossings of African Americans to Africa in the late twentieth century. Onwueme's *The Missing Face* tells the story of an African American woman who immigrates to Africa to find her historical, psychological, and genealogical past after being abandoned by a Nigerian man who had come to America for education and financial stability. Ida Bee immigrates to Nigeria to attempt to heal on an individual level what the Middle Passage induced: male familial apathy and abandonment, which on a larger scale is indicative of many black American families. Her journey to wholeness from feelings of alienation is fraught with conflicts, crises, and obstacles that are ultimately overcome as a new hybrid identity evolves simultaneously while family healing and reunification occur.

Onwueme dramatizes Ida Bee's journey to wholeness from alienation through a series of conflicts, crises, and obstacles. For example, the play opens with Ida Bee and her son Amaechi's arrival in the village of Idu where they are met with curiosity and skepticism. During a ritual procession, the elder of the village notices the strangers and immediately inquires, "Who are you? Where do you come from?" (Onwueme 8). While Ida Bee goes to Nigeria to escape alienation in America, she initially faces rejection and skepticism from people who cannot fathom her claim to being a descendant of one of their family members. In addition, when Ida Bee attempts to explain that she belongs to the lineage of Idu, Odozie, the village elder, impatiently corrects her: "If you say you are from Idu, you must belong to a particular lineage. . . . Everyone in Idu kingdom, even the poorest person, belongs to a clan, a lineage" (12). Ida Bee, as many black Americans do, naïvely claims the entire continent of Africa as home when she pronounces, "We are the children of Africa . . . born in the new world. . . . We do not have to claim any particular land or country because Africa was our nation" (10). As a result, Ida Bee's presence and comments bring conflict to the village, and her chances of dispelling feelings of alienation seem unlikely.

Ida Bee's sense of displacement in America compels her to leave to find distant family. Afam Ebeogu describes Ida Bee as a "strong willed African American woman for which Idu is a dream that must be given reality, a land of promise that holds real meaning in legacy" (106). Ida Bee's quest to find distant family recognizes a void felt by some blacks in the diaspora, which causes them to envision a more fulfilling life in Africa. For instance, in *The Empire Writes Back,* Bill Ashcroft, Gareth Griffiths, and Helen Tiffin argue that some people in the diaspora experience physical and cultural displacement, resulting in feelings of alienation (8–9). Consequently, Ida Bee's impetuous decision to go to Nigeria without assessing the situation does not quickly alleviate her feelings of cultural alienation; rather, she generates conflict and anger.

In particular, Ida Bee's action causes conflict with Nebe, the village elder's wife who is also her son's grandmother. To illustrate, when Ida Bee reveals that Nebe's son, Momah, is Ida Bee's husband and the father of their child, Nebe angrily tells her to leave. "Be gone! Evil! Day and night never meet! Who gave you birth? Even a chick knows when its own mother cackles. What have you come for? To ruin our world with your knowledge? What do you want from us?" (Onwueme 17). Nebe is not only angry about the sudden revelation of a wife and grandson, but she also thinks this situation will influence Momah to leave the village for the city. Simultaneously, as she expresses this fear, "Momah has packed his bag ready to run back to the city" (17). Rather than face his responsibilities, Momah prepares to abandon his wife and son again. In many ways, his erratic behavior demonstrates a postcolonial mentality that demeans women, particularly women who are perceived as inferior, which in his mind describes Ida Bee. Therefore, since Momah does not accept Ida Bee, he feels no responsibility for their son.

Ida Bee's sudden appearance in Idu angers and shames Momah to the extent that the old conflicts they experienced are renewed with vengeance and hatred. For example, after Odozie calls the village together to hear Ida Bee's explanation of her relationship with Momah, and the truth is revealed, Momah threatens Ida Bee. He screams, "I've heard enough. Woman! You will do no further damage. With the powers borne in me as the son of Idu, I cast you to the bush of demons where you will become food for the gods!" (38). Onwueme's use of Nigerians' belief in a forest of demons demonstrates what Elleke Boehmer argues is an "adaptation of indigenous myth [that] represented another mode of retrieval" for the postcolonial writer seeking identity and constructing stability (202). Additionally, Boehmer suggests that "writers came to recognize that the gods, daemons, half-children, warriors, and strange beasts of local legend and oral epic still had explanatory power, despite the efforts of missions and schools to eradicate them" (202). In Western rationale, a forest of demons would not exist. Onwueme utilizes the indigenous myth of the existence of supernatural forests as a place to stage Momah's nefarious behavior. Momah hopes that Ida Bee's abandonment in the supernatural forest will destroy her mentally and physically, thereby resolving their conflict.

In a flashback scene in Movement Three, the initial meeting and conflict between Ida Bee and Momah are recounted. Ida Bee tells the village that Momah, a student, came to her door selling raffle tickets for trips to Africa. Because of Ida Bee's attraction to African men, whom she refers to as "fine, young robust men with a strong sense of who they were" (Onwueme 28), she gives Momah an opportunity to pursue a relationship that proves disastrous for her. His subsequent abandonment of Ida Bee and their son, whom Momah initially wanted aborted, serves as a catalyst in her transformation from a young, naïve woman to an older, wiser woman.

In addition to disagreement over aborting their son, Ida Bee and Momah differ over Africa's position in the world. Momah exhibits characteristics of a psychologically damaged colonized subject. An example of this damage is his view of ancestors and family as antiquated ideas (29). On the other hand, Onwueme portrays Ida Bee as the complete opposite. Ida Bee privileges family, including extended family. She does not view Africa as culturally and technologically inferior; however, Momah criticizes African culture and technology, and he is "determined to transfer American, European, and Russian technology to Africa" (29). Ida Bee is not like the colonized man Frantz Fanon describes who breathed the "appeal of Europe like pure air" (Boehmer 115). Nor is she like Momah and other elitist academics who think that Africa is hindered by a lack of technological advances. Thus, from the very beginning of their relationship, Ida Bee and Momah have different worldviews about a variety of subjects, which dooms them to strife and conflict.

The tensions that become a great part of Ida Bee and Momah's relationship are also symptomatic of their self-identify. Ida Bee is proud to be a descendant of her African great-grandfather, from whom she has inherited an Ikenga, a wooden staff signifying manhood, and great personal achievement. Even though her name could be considered a common American name, she challenges Momah about adopting a common name, Jack. In her view, since he has an African name that has a meaning, calling himself Jack is illogical. She tells him, "It matters! It does! To me . . . to us . . . who are here, without. . . . It has to do with the true African identity" (Onwueme 27). In *Black Skin, White Masks,* Frantz Fanon argues that subjects who adopt the mother country's culture become distant and alienated from their own culture while privileging that of the colonizer (18). Similarly, Boehmer describes the double vision of the colonial nationalist and in particular the colonized native: "From the moment of their geneses . . . national elites were caught in a situation of split perception or double vision. Bilingual and bicultural, having Janus-like access to both metropolitan and local cultures, yet alienated from both" (115). Boehmer's theory of double vision echoes W. E. B. Du Bois's theory of black double consciousness, in which the subaltern is forever aware of contemptuous looks from America's white majority. Du Bois writes, "[O]ne ever feels his twoness—an American, a Negro, two souls, two unreconciled strivings; two warring ideals in one dark body" (45). Thus, both Ida Bee and Momah suffer from identity crises that manifest in different ways. Ida Bee seeks to embrace her African heritage, while Momah resolutely attempts to discard his African heritage.

In seeking to know her African heritage, Ida Bee wants to recover family history and claim a homeland. Her desire to find a homeland is similar to yearnings documented by writers such as Maria Harris. In "Not Black and/or White: Reading Difference in Heliodorus' *Ethiopica,* and Pauline Hopkins' *Of One Blood,*" Harris writes, "For Hopkins, it is the American experience of slavery that has dispossessed characters, robbing them of their homeland and their family history, bestowing upon them aliases that effectively prevent them from recognizing each other or fully knowing themselves" (377). Onwueme creates a character who laments the loss of African familial connections, and she seeks to know her family history. For this reason, "she [Ida Bee] dares," as Ebeogu writes, "to reject her American present and embarks on a search for a past and future in Africa" (107). To Ida Bee, "the homeland of black people is Africa, not Milwaukee" (Onwueme 3). Ida Bee is also representative of black Americans who believe that returning to ancestral lands and reuniting with distant family forges a stronger identity.

Since there are many types of identities such as cultural, ethnic, or national, Ida Bee wants to establish her genealogical identity and confirm her visible resemblance to family members living in Africa. She searches for, as Homi Bhabha writes, "a measure of the me, which emerges from an acknowledgement of my inwardness, the depth of my character, the profundity of my person, to mention only a few of those qualities through which we commonly articulate our self-consciousness" and identity (*The Location of Culture* 48). Living in America and hearing from her father what he knew about their African ancestor, Meme, Ida Bee increases in her thirst to find out more about her African family. Upon first meeting Momah, she is amazed that he is from the same region as her great-grandfather. Furthermore, she is enthralled with Momah because he resembles her father. Ida Bee shares with Momah, "Yes, my great-grandfather is from that region [Idu]. They say I look just like him. . . . And here you are, Jack, standing in my home like the living image of my own father" (Onwueme 28). All of these coincidences serve to encourage her to welcome Momah, seeing him not only as a distant African brother, but also as an acceptable mate who can link her to a genealogical tree.

Momah's subsequent abandonment of Ida Bee and their son puts in jeopardy her genealogical search, and it exacerbates Ida Bee's double identity Du Bois identifies. Her irreconciled double consciousness or split identity causes her to feel out of place in America even though it is the only home she has ever known. She has been displaced through ancestral enslavement in America, causing the "alienation of vision and the crisis in self-image which this displacement produces" (Ashcroft, Griffiths, and Tiffin, *The Empire Writes Back,* 8–9). Subsequently, Ida Bee suffers from a crisis of self-identity and self-image.

In America, Ida Bee experienced numerous crises that conflated to demean her self-image. To demonstrate, she suffered a crisis when "fire raged on North Avenue, Milwaukee. A fire set by angry white men that swept through my home, trapping my mother inside the flames. Nothing was left of her besides her charred body amidst the debris" (Onwueme 24). Demoralized and hopeless because of no work and the death of his wife, her father abandons his family after the fire, never to be seen again. Thus, Ida Bee's sense of identity and security is fractured. The Ikenga, which her father presented to her on her twenty-first birthday, becomes a genealogical symbol to Africa, although other crises await her in her pursuit to find descendants of the original owner of the Ikenga.

The racial crisis resulting in her mother's death and father's abandonment has other family ramifications. As is typical of many families including African American families, family dysfunction is not unusual. Ida Bee enumerates for her son, Amaechi, a litany of problems that afflict their family to dissuade him from wanting to remain in America: "All we got in Milwaukee is a bunch of fractured lives. Uncle Henry is an alcoholic. . . . His wife and children livin' up in Kenosha with Uncle Ron, whose little Oshkosh job can hardly feed himself, let alone some extra mouths. And Uncle Charlie? Well, you know Uncle Charlie. So slick he can't keep himself out of jail. And Aunt Gloria is alone. She's got seven children and she's alone and don't even know it" (4). Ida Bee further explains that her youngest brother completed college and obtained a good job but abandoned his family to live in New York, leaving them in a financial crisis.

Another crisis that confronts Ida Bee is that of being a single mother raising an adolescent son. Without financial assistance from Momah, Ida Bee works menial jobs to provide basic necessities and some luxuries for her son. In exasperation about Amaechi's unappreciative attitude, she asks him, "What do you know about gettin' anywhere? I'm the one who works from paycheck to paycheck in an empty job goin' nowhere" (3). Furthermore, Ida Bee explains that the Nike shoes and video games she purchases for Amaechi come from her hard work and sacrifice. She fits the type of mother Estelle Freedman discusses in *No Turning Back: The History of Feminism and the Future of Women:* "The model of male breadwinner and female caregiver has never fit well the experiences of working-class and minority families, nor does it describe most families in developing nations" (171). Onwueme, in bringing attention to the problems of fatherless children, seems to suggest that a father's involvement is crucial in helping to prevent delinquent behavior and other negative social pathologies. Absent fathers have become epidemic in America, especially in the African American community, where "55 percent of African American children live with single parents compared to 23 percent of whites and 31 percent of Hispanics" (United States Department of Health and Human Services 2). Furthermore, according to Jerry Adler in a *Newsweek* article, more than half of all American children born in the 1970s and 1980s are expected to spend part of their childhood with just their mothers. He further reports, "A Census Bureau study found that 16.3 million were living with just a mother in 1994—and 40% of those hadn't seen their father in a year" (qtd. in *Perspectives in Argument* 460). The preceding statistics apply to Ida Bee, and to her the solution to Amaechi's juvenile delinquency is finding the father who deserted him ten years earlier in hopes that Momah can teach Amaechi how to be a man. A hopeful Ida Bee tells Amaechi: "He [Momah] can teach you that an African man carries the power of the gun in his heart, then walks boldly through the forest of demons with a steady stride, his feet planted firmly on the ground like an elephant trampling vipers and scorpions that threaten his progress toward the light of the sun" (Onwueme 6). Recognizing that fathers can provide benefits to children that mothers cannot, Ida Bee has another important reason to go to Africa to resolve this crisis with Amaechi.

The final crisis that Ida Bee faces comes when Momah in anger and hatred pushes her into the forest to die. He tells her, "Away with you woman. Out of my sight! Into the bush where you will be fed down the gullet of the gods. As Osu you came, as Osu will you return" (39). An Osu in Nigeria is someone who is an outcast and normally does not marry non-Osus. If Ida Bee is an Osu, her acceptance into the village would be complicated even though generations have passed. Nevertheless, Ida Bee perseveres in the onslaught of Momah's sexist and misogynist behavior that is similar to what Albert Memmi describes as that of a racist and xenophobic colonizer. According to Memmi, "[A]ll racism and xenophobia consist of delusions about oneself, including absurd and unjust aggressions towards others" (130). In spite of Momah's reprehensible behavior towards Ida Bee, she comes through the crisis and brings healing to herself and to her distant family.

Not only does Ida Bee contend with various crises; she also has obstacles to achieving her goal of family acceptance that must be surmounted. The primary obstacle is village traditional beliefs about the West and foreigners. Even though Ida Bee is black, she is an American who is not to be trusted. Demonstrating the village's esteem felt for identifiable family and distrust of outsiders, Nebe entreats Ida Bee to "be gone [. . .] because her son has no relationship with the white man" (Onwueme 17). Interestingly, Nebe identifies Ida Bee as white in black skin because she is from a Western country, and Nebe implies that Ida Bee's acculturation is foreign or oyibo, not African. Nebe echoes Fanon's description of blacks who are culturally Western in black skin. Similarly, Reginald McKnight describes his experience in a Senegalese village: "The children there would be fascinated with this "otherness" that they perceived, and they called me *toubob*. And I said but *toubob* means white man, doesn't it? A white person. And they [adults] said well, it really means foreigner. Either way suggests a certain kind of foreignness that really suggests, to many Africans, whiteness" (qtd. in Ashe 432). To Nebe, Ida Bee is a foreign threat, someone who can potentially take her son away again from the village. Therefore, Nebe will do all in her power to obstruct Ida Bee's quest to be recognized as a distant family member.

Nebe, on a personal level, serves as an obstacle to Ida Bee's goal of family acceptance because of Nebe's interest in whom Momah chooses as a mate. As a traditionalist, Nebe wants input into Momah's choice of a wife. Nebe represents those associated with a movement from tradition to modernity in Nigeria. Daniel Jordan Smith addresses the conflict involved in a transitional time in his "These Girls Today Na War-O: Premarital Sexuality and Modern Identity in Southeastern Nigeria." Smith discusses the conflict between older and younger generation Igbos regarding choosing spouses, dating, and premarital sexual relationships, a commentary that has relevance to Nebe's rejection of Ida Bee. Smith makes the following observations: "In Nigeria, access to employment, urban migration, higher education, business deals, and government services are all determined, to a large extent, by the strength of one's social networks, especially one's kinship networks. . . . Children create and cement the kinship networks and affinal ties that Igbos depend upon so heavily. Biological reproduction is about social reproduction, and extended families and communities take great interest in a couple's fertility" (101). Although modern Igbos are challenging the older generation's attempt to dictate who can marry whom, which is perceived as "bush, backward, and uncivilized" (Smith 100), some younger Igbos have internalized their parents' sense of importance of kinship—a value reinforced as they observe how one achieves success in Nigeria" (Smith 101). As a result of this tradition, if Momah had returned to Nigeria with Ida Bee, then he and she might have been treated unfavorably by the elders, causing conflict along with placing obstacles in the couple's smooth integration into the family.

Momah's antipathy toward Ida Bee is a monumental obstacle that she must confront. Momah has no intention of or interest in rekindling their relationship, and he is determined to stand in the way of any effort on Ida Bee's part to be accepted as his wife. To accomplish his goals, he uses verbal and physical intimidation tactics to remove Ida Bee. During their heated conversations, Ida Bee refuses to be subdued. Previous years of providing a home for her son and providing the financial resources to enable Momah to complete his college education have given her a sense of empowerment and self-respect. Consequently, since Momah has no control or power over her, Ida Bee defiantly stands her ground against him. Confident in her identity as a "child of this land" (Onwueme 39), Ida Bee tells Momah that "no matter what you do to smash the shadow of me in the past, my image shines to reflect the face of tomorrow through my son whose umbilical cord is planted deep in the earth of this homestead, where now I am condemned to be a stranger" (39). In turn, Momah responds to Ida Bee's independence and self-confidence by physically assaulting her, "pouncing on Ida Bee, pushing her to the forest of the demons, while she resists and fights back. The struggle intensifies, but in the end, Momah subdues her and pushes her into the forest" (39). Ida Bee is left to wander in the forest until Nebe searches for her and finds her near the end of the play.

The physical assault and wandering in the forest of demons are traumatic experiences for Ida Bee that commence another obstacle: Ida Bee's mental condition. According to studies that research the subject of trauma and Post-Traumatic Stress Disorder, emotional trauma has three elements: it is unexpected, the person is unprepared, and there is nothing the person can do to prevent the act (Carlson 116). All three of these elements are present in Ida Bee's confrontation with Momah. Unfortunately, Ida Bee's time in the forest and, perhaps, her encounter with horrors render her mind hysterical and delirious. By the time Nebe locates Ida Bee, and they emerge from the forest, Ida Bee is nonsensical and focused on death, which is one of the consequences of emotional trauma. Ida Bee exemplifies this behavior according to stage directions when she appears with a bundle of wood "with a far-away smile . . . (acting crazy, she scoops sand with her hand, letting it drop slowly with relish. She begins singing a dirge)" (56). To counter this behavior, Nebe explains to Ida Bee that carrying bundles of wood in dreams signifies death. Wood is the symbol of a casket. She implores Ida Bee to sing a song of life (56). Finally, Ida Bee returns to her right mind after Amaechi, with the help of Odozie, spews a traditional medicinal potion into her eyes. Amaechi uses the mgbidimgbi plant, which "heals all wounds, especially the tormented soul, . . . soothing the nerves for good mental health" (55). Ida Bee's healing from emotional trauma removes the final impediment to her goal of mending her individual family rift and the larger chasm caused by African enslavement centuries before.

Ida Bee's journey to heal an individual rift mends another critical family rupture caused by ancestral enslavement. Even though she has had many positive experiences in her life, Ida Bee suffers from some of the negative socioeconomic consequences that are illustrated in the play. For example, Onwueme enumerates a number of social pathologies that afflict black Americans: dangerous inner-city neighborhoods and black men increasingly being incarcerated in prisons that are often fed by crime and violence; unemployment; and race, gender, and class prejudices (Onwueme 1). Ida Bee's family portrays many of these debilitating circumstances. Her family lives in a culture that is conducive to fostering dysfunctional individuals. In his critique of *Legacies,* the title Onwueme first gave *The Missing Face,* Chris Dunton explains: "Mimi's, [Ida Bee], expression of alienation in the U.S. has echoes of a familiar, patronizing, externalized insistence that Afro-American culture is somehow less real and substantial than authentic African culture, rather than having generated its own, but different reality" (105). All of the negative experiences combine to put Ida Bee in a tenuous position, driving her to want to find "[her] place in the world" (Onwueme 3). She feels displaced in America, causing an identity crisis that fuels the need to find stability through locating ancestral roots. Ida Bee embarks on a bold cross-Atlantic journey to return to her origins in Nigeria, taking with her the Ikenga, the physical object that can link her to distant family members.

Onwume uses the Ikenga as an object to validate Ida Bee's identity and symbolize healing among family members. Ida Bee's great-grandfather brought with him from Africa one half of an Ikenga, which is passed along with ancestral stories from generation to generation. The villagers' acceptance of Ida Bee and Amaechi as family is a result of revelations about a common, distant ancestor, Meme. Bhabha, in *The Location of Culture,* analyzes the process of identification in the "perverse palimpsest of colonial identity" (44). He cites three conditions that underlie an understanding of the colonial native's desire to merge body with soul to mitigate the native's identity as "Other." Of the three conditions, the last—"identification . . . is always the return of an image of identity that bears the mark of splitting in the Other place from which it comes" (45)—has particular relevance to Ida Bee's search for ancestral identity, her missing face. After experiencing conflict and facing crises, Ida Bee is allowed to tell her story that establishes her identity, resulting in healing and reunification with distant family.

Allowing Ida Bee to tell her story, which could be the story of many black Americans, is the first step in the reconciliation process. Unlike most black Americans whose knowledge about their African ancestors is scant, if any knowledge exists at all, Ida Bee does have a few facts to relate, including the name of the region, Idu. In addition, she has the most important object, the Ikenga that serves as evidence of her ancestry. Ida Bee knows the part of her great-grandfather's story that begins in America after the Middle Passage and that he was captured from an African village in Idu. The villagers know Meme's story before he was kidnapped and taken away. Unfortunately, Meme "was returning from the grotto after the rites of manhood. Then came the foreigners who swooped like hawks on the village and devoured Meme" (Onwueme 53). During the last movement of the play, all of the pieces fall into place. Emerging crazed and delirious from the forest of demons, Ida Bee brandishes the Ikenga saying, "I am wood . . . carved with a half a face . . . lost in the bush. Did anyone find my face carved in wood? Did anyone find it? The missing face? The missing face? Deep in the bush . . . black with night? My daddy's face, all buried in the sand? Buried in this sand. Where is my face? Missing? Where is my face?" (57). In this scene, the past and the present meet to establish identity and to explain mistaken assumptions about what happened to Meme in the distant past. As Gaurav Desai states in reviewing "Literary Theory and African Literature," "[colonial writers] draw from cultural memory, invoke revertants, dig up forgotten history, [and] quest for roots. . . . The writers reclaim history, tradition, and language in their yearning for home" (6, 7). Onwueme appropriates this theme in Ida Bee's search for her past, her family's story, and her identity on a genealogical tree. Her strong family resemblance affirms that hers is the missing face.

The second step in the process of healing and reunification of Ida Bee's distant family is not only seeing strong family resemblance, but the parents' acceptance of the truth that a family member who disappeared years before lived and produced descendants who are now standing in the village. For example, Nebe, Momah's mother, initially is very hostile towards Ida Bee and wants her to leave the village as is indicated when she tells Odozie, "[F]or the sake of all that binds us together, for the sake of his (Momah's) father Meme, discharge the strangers" (Onwueme 18). However, during the course of the play, she, along with Odozie, begins to recognize Momah's culpability and lack of character. They confront Momah about his dastardly act of pushing Ida Bee into the bush: "Enough! When will you ever know yourself, Momah? When will you ever learn that the present must see a reflection of self in the contorted face of the past! Momah, you will not grow. You can not desert your land that weeps for your soothing hands to heal her burning face, her wounded heart. No. Momah, you cannot run away from the responsibility we now share" (43). Consequently, Nebe plays a vital role in that her acceptance of Ida Bee signals the possibility of healing as she exhorts Momah to acknowledge Ida Bee: "If she's your wife, then she is my own wife, and daughter, too" (37). Nebe's proclamation brings Ida Bee one step closer to final acceptance.

Bhabha argues that "to see a missing person, or look at invisibleness, is to emphasize the subject's transitive demand for a direct object of self-reflection . . . or a demand that identity be acknowledged and embraced" (*The Location of Culture* 47). When Ida Bee presents the Ikenga with the image of her great-grandfather carved into it, Nebe in amazement asks Ida Bee to explain. At this point, Ida Bee relates what she knows of her African ancestor: "Meme, my own great father. Kidnapped. Snatched. Robbed of manhood. In the struggle that ensued, the great father's symbol was split—one half lost. But the other, he carried with him. And he handed to me as a Le-ga-cy" (58). Subsequently, "Momah is ordered to fetch the legendary half of the face of the 'Ikenga' in the grotto" (58). When the two halves are joined, the missing face becomes whole, the legacy confirmed. The two halves, now joined, have a scar or seam down the middle, which symbolizes that two cultures have developed over the years and have developed differently, as hybrids, all over the diaspora. Nevertheless, they are authentic in their own respects. When Ida Bee and Amaechi's identity is confirmed, final acceptance is accomplished. Reunification and healing among distant family members transpire in the last rite of passage ritual.

Through crossing the Atlantic, migrating back to Africa, Ida Bee and Amaechi authenticate their Nigerian Igbo identity, essentially recovering the past and promoting symbolically healing for people of African descent in the diaspora. In contrast to the first forced Atlantic crossing of her great-grandfather, Ida Bee's crossing is voluntary and serves to establish identity and to reconnect family members. Her new identity is as a daughter of the village; no longer is she just a black American woman of distant Nigerian ancestry. Onwueme's therapeutic use of migration to treat feelings of alienation and instability that alter identity in black Americans and Africans is timely and correlates with other postcolonial writers' treatment of migration.

Finally, Onwueme in *The Missing Face* illustrates that identity is often compromised even years after migration has occurred, especially if the migration is initially forced. She demonstrates the psychological problems resulting from colonial and postcolonial experiences. Significantly, Onwueme underscores the parallel healing that can occur in one family and in all African descendants in the diaspora. Along with healing of scars in family members, split identities are mended, forming hybrid identities. *The Missing Face* offers a different perspective on the effects of the Middle Passage on the African diaspora while providing hope for healing and reconciliation of distant family.

[NOTES]

Notes to Chapter 2

1. A very brief summary on doollee.com, a Web site dedicated to contemporary playwrights, describes Pinnock's *Talking in Tongues* as a play about social miscegenation. http://www.doollee.com/PlaywrightsP/PinnockWinsome.htm.

2. See Spike Lee, *Jungle Fever*, directed by Spike Lee (New York: 40 Acres and a Mule Productions, 1991). Spike Lee's film explores the complexities of an interracial romance between an African American man (Snipes) and an Italian American woman (Sciorra). The film is set in contemporary New York City from the vantage point of both white and black communities.

3. See 1 Corinthians 14:2–4. This St. Paul chapter is dedicated to the gifts of the spirit, one of which is the gift of speaking in unknown tongues. "For he that speaketh in an unknown tongue speaketh not unto men, but unto God: for no man understandeth him; howbeit in the spirit he speaketh mysteries. . . . He that speaketh in an unknown tongue edifieth himself."

4. See Gayl Jones, *The Healing*. When describing the chanting customs of the Masai peoples, Norvelle the medical anthropologist married to the protagonist Harlan, says that chant fills the space between speaking and song.

5. For further analyses, see Shyllon 202–24. Shyllon also examines the literature, particularly protest pieces that emerged in and around Britain that directly affected black life.

6. See Zora Neale Hurston, *Their Eyes Were Watching God* (New York: HarperCollins, 1937). In this bildungsroman, Janie's grandmother claims that black women are the mules of the world: "Honey, de white man is de ruler of everything as fur as Ah been able tuh find out. Maybe it's some place off in de ocean where de black man is in power, but we don't know nothin' but what we see. So de white man throw down de load and tell de nigger man tuh pick it up. He pick it up. He pick it up because he have to, but he don't tote it. He hand it to his womenfolks. De nigger woman is de mule uh de world so fur as Ah can see. Ah been prayin' fuh it tuh be different wid you. Lawd, Lawd, Lawd!" (14). In a similar vein, Ama Ata Aidoo insists that the African woman is the most ignored in all concerns, the most invisible of all visibles, and the most debased of all humanity. See Aidoo, "To Be an African Woman Writer—An Overview and a Detail."

Notes to Chapter 3

1. Internal migration (i.e., migration from rural to urban areas within the country) is not an uncommon phenomenon and is seen to feature prominently in some of Buchi

Emecheta's novels, particularly *The Joys of Motherhood*. Our concentration, however, will be on international migration—the subject of the two works in our selection: *In the Ditch* and *Kehinde*. Both novels deal with migration from Africa to the United Kingdom.

2. Immigration causes disruptions that change the individual's sense of identity, and "consequently the individual struggles with reorganizing and reintegrating identity within the new context" (Espin 448). One's identity is molded and remolded within a socioeconomic and environmental context. Once this is disrupted through migration, which of course truncates a whole network of friends and extended family, the resultant possibilities are loneliness, unbelonging, feelings of rejection from the new society, alienation, and the loss of self-esteem (Rogler 704).

[WORKS CITED]

Achebe, Chinua. *No Longer at Ease.* London: Heinemann, 1958.
Adell, Sandra. *Double-Consciousness/Double Bind: Theoretical Issues in Twentieth-Century Black Literature.* Urbana: University of Illinois Press, 1994.
Adler, Jerry. "Building a Better Dad." In *Perspectives in Argument,* edited by Nancy V. Wood, 460–62. Upper Saddle River, NJ: Prentice-Hall, 2004.
Agbese, Aji-Ori. "Maintaining Power in the Face of Political, Economic and Social Discrimination: The Tale of Nigerian Women." *Women and Language* 35.1 (2003): 1–10.
Aidoo, Ama Ata. *Anowa.* London: Longman, 1970.
———. *Changes: A Love Story.* UK: Women's Press, Ltd., 1992. New York: Feminist Press of CUNY, 1993.
———. *The Dilemma of a Ghost.* Accra: Longman, 1965; New York: Collier, 1971.
———. *No Sweetness Here: A Collection of Short Stories.* London: Longman, 1970.
———. *Our Sister Killjoy, or Reflections from a Black-eyed Squint.* New York: Longman USA, 1977.
———. "To Be an African Woman Writer—An Overview and a Detail." In *Criticism and Ideology,* edited by Kirsten Holst Peterson, 155–72. Uppsala, Sweden: Scandinavian Institute of African Studies, 1988.
Alexander, Simone A. James. *Mother Imagery in the Novels of Afro-Caribbean Women.* Columbia: University of Missouri Press, 2001.
Allan, Tuzyline Jita. Afterword to *Changes: A Love Story,* by Ama Ata Aidoo. New York: Feminist Press at CUNY, 1993.
Andermahr, Sonya, Terry Lovell, and Carol Wolkowitz. *A Glossary of Feminist Theory.* New York: Oxford University Press, 2000.
Anzaldua, Gloria. *Borderlands/La Frontera. The New Mestiza.* San Francisco: Spinsters, Aunt Lute, 1990.
Ashcroft, Bill, Gareth Griffiths, and Helen Tiffin. *The Empire Writes Back.* New York: Routledge, 1989.
———, eds. *The Post-Colonial Studies Reader.* London: Routledge, 1995.
Ashe, Bertran D. "Under the Umbrella of Black Civilization: A Conversation with Reginald McKnight." *African American Review* 35.3 (2001): 427–38.
Azodo, Ada Uaoamaka, and Gay Wilentz, eds. *Emerging Perspectives on Ama Ata Aidoo.* Trenton, NJ: Africa World Press, 1999.
Bakhtin, Mikhail. *The Dialogic Imagination.* Translated by Michael Holquist. Austin: University of Texas Press, 1983.
Balutansky, Kathleen M. "We Are All Activists: An Interview with Merle Hodge." *Callaloo: A Journal of African-American and African Arts and Letters* 12.4 (Fall 1989): 651–62.

Bernard, Louise. "Countermemory and Return: Reclamation of the (Postmodern) Self in Jamaica Kincaid's *The Autobiography of My Mother* and *My Brother.*" *Modern Fiction Studies* 48.1 (Spring 2002): 113–38.

Berrian, Brenda F. "Her Ancestor's Voice: The Ibieje Tanscendence of Duality in Buchi Emecheta's *Kehinde.*" In *Emerging Perspectives on Buchi Emecheta,* edited by Marie Umeh, 169–84. Trenton, NJ: Africa World Press, 1996.

Bhabha, Homi K. "Cultural Diversity and Cultural Differences." In *The Post-Colonial Reader,* edited by Bill Ashcroft, Gareth Griffiths, and Helen Tiffin, 206–9. New York: Routledge, 1994.

———. "How Newness Enters the World: Postmodern Space, Postcolonial Times and the Trials of Cultural Translation." In *Writing Black Britain: 1948–1998,* edited by James Procter, 300–307. Manchester: Manchester University Press, 2000.

———. "Interrogating Identity: Frantz Fanon and the Postcolonial Prerogative." *The Location of Culture.* London: Routledge, 1994. 40–66.

———. *The Location of Culture.* New York: Routledge, 1994.

———. *Locations of Culture: Discussing Post-Colonial Culture.* London: Routledge, 1996.

Boehmer, Elleke. *Colonial & Postcolonial Literature.* Oxford: Oxford University Press, 1995.

Bone, Robert. "Merle Kinbona Was Part Saint, Part Revolutionary, Part Obeah-Woman." *The New York Times Book Review* (30 November 1969): 4, 54.

Bonetti, Kay. "An Interview with Jamaica Kincaid." *Missouri Review* 15.2 (1992): 124–42.

Brah, Avtar. *Cartographies of Diaspora: Contesting Identities.* London: Routledge, 1996.

Braithwaite, Edward. "West Indian History and Society in the Art of Paule Marshall's Novel." *Journal of Black Studies* 1.2 (December 1970): 225–38.

Breon, Robin. "Interview with Djanet Sears: A Black Girl in Search of God." *AISLE SAY* Toronto. http://www.aislesay.com/ONT-SEARS.html (accessed April 2006)

Brøndum, Lene. "'The Persistence of Tradition': The Retelling of Sea Islands Culture in Works by Julie Dash, Gloria Naylor, and Paule Marshall." In *Black Imagination and the Middle Passage,* edited by Maria Diedrich, Henry Louis Gates, Jr., and Carl Pedersen, 153–63. Oxford: Oxford University Press, 1999.

Buntin, Mat. "An Interview with Djanet Sears." Canadian Adaptations of Shakespeare, University of Guelph. http://www.Canadianshakespeares.ca/i_dsears.cfm (accessed April 2006)

Busia, Abena P. A. "What Is Your Nation? Reconnecting Africa and Her Diaspora through Paule Marshall's *Praisesong for the Widow.*" In *Changing Your Words: Essays on Criticism, Theory, and Writing by Black Women,* edited by Cheryl Wall, 196–211. New Brunswick, NJ: Rutgers University Press, 1989.

Byerman, Keith E. "Anger in a Small Place: Jamaica Kincaid's Cultural Critique of Antiqua." *College Literature* 22.1 (February 1994): 91–102.

Byrne, K. B. Conal. "Under English, Obeah English: Jamaica Kincaid's New Language." *CLA Journal* 43.3 (March 2000): 276–98.

Campbell, Elaine, and Pierrette Frickey, eds. Introduction to *The Whistling Bird: Women Writers of the Caribbean,* 1–8. Boulder, CO: Lynn Rienner Publishers, 1998.

Carlson, Bonnie E. "The Most Important Things Learned about Violence and Trauma in the Past 20 Years." *Journal of Interpersonal Violence* 20.1 (January 2005): 116–24.

Chancy, Myriam. "Natif-Natal." Prologue to *Searching for Safe Spaces: Afro-Caribbean Women Writers in Exile,* xi–xxiii. Philadelphia: Temple University Press, 1997.

Chapman, Karen C. Introduction to *Dilemma of a Ghost,* by Ama Ata Aidoo. New York:

Collier, 1971.
Chetin, Sara. "Reading from a Distance: Ama Ata Aidoo's *Our Sister Killjoy.*" In *Black Women's Writing*, edited by Gina Wisker, 146–59. New York: St. Martin's Press, 1993.
Chick, Nancy. "The Broken Clock: Time, Identity, and Autobiography in Jamaica Kincaid's *Lucy.*" *CLA Journal* 40.1 (September 1996): 90–103.
Chopin, Kate. *The Awakening*. New York: W. W. Norton, 1994.
Christian, Barbara. *Black Women Novelists: The Development of a Tradition, 1892–1976.* Westport, CT: Greenwood Press, 1980.
Christol, Hélène. "Reconstructing American History: Land and Geneaology in Gloria Naylor's *Mama Day.*" In *The Critical Response to Gloria Naylor*, edited by Sharon Felton and Michelle C. Loris, 159–65. Westport, CT: Greenwood, 1997.
Cixous, Hélène, and Mireille Calle-Gruber. *Hélène Cixous, Rootprints: Memory and Life Writing*. Translated by Eric Prenowitz. London: Routledge, 1997.
Clark, Vèvè. "Dangerous Admissions: Opening Stages to Violence, Anger, and Healing in African Diaspora Theatre." In *Violence, Silence, and Anger: Women's Writing as Transgression*, edited by Deirdre Lashgari, 247–63. Charlottesville: University Press of Virginia, 1995.
Clarke, George Elliott. "White Like Canada." *Transitions* 73 (1997): 98–109.
Cobham, Rhonda. Introduction to *Watchers and Seekers: Creative Writing by Black Women*, edited by Rhonda Cobham and Merle Collins, 3–11. New York: Peter Bedrick Books, 1988.

———. "Revisioning Our Kumblas: Transforming Feminist and Nationalist Agendas in Three Caribbean Women's Texts." *Callaloo: A Journal of African-American and African Arts and Letters* 16.1 (1993): 44–64.
Condé, Maryse. "*Créolité* without Creole Language?" In *Caribbean Creolization: Reflections on the Cultural Dynamics of Language, Literature, and Identity*, edited by Kathleen M. Balutansky and Marie-Agnès Sourieau, 101–9. Gainesville: University Press of Florida, 1998.

———. "The Tropical Breeze Hotel." In *Plays by Women: Book Two*, translated by Barbara Brewster Lewis and Catherine Temerson, 113–64. New York: Ubu Repertory Theater Publications, 1995.
Condè, Maryse, and Paule Marshall. "Interview." Translated by John Williams. *SAGE: A Scholarly Journal on Black Women* 3.2 (Fall 1986): 52–53.
Cousin, Geraldine. "Related Spaces, Related Lives." *Women in Dramatic Place and Time: Contemporary Female Characters on Stage*, 31–66. London: Routledge, 1996.
Croft, Susan. "Black Women Playwrights in Britain." In *British and Irish Women Dramatists Since 1958*, edited by Trevor R. Griffiths and Margaret Llewellyn-Jones, 84–98. Buckingham: Open University Press, 1993.
Cudjoe, Selwyn R. Introduction to *Caribbean Women Writers: Essays from the First International Conference*, edited by Selwyn R. Cudjoe, 5–48. Wellesley, MA: Calaloux, 1990.

———. "Jamaica Kincaid and the Modernist Project: An Interview." In *Caribbean Women Writers: Essays from the First International Conference*, edited by Selwyn R. Cudjoe, 215–42. Wellesley, MA: Calaloux, 1990.
Dance, Daryl C. "An Interview with Paule Marshall." *Southern Review* 28.1 (Winter 1992): 1–20.

———."Matriarchs, Doves, and Nymphos: Prevalent Images of Black, Indian, and White Women in Caribbean Literature." *Studies in the Literary Imagination* 26.2 (1993): 21–30.

Dash, Michael. "In Search of the Lost Body: Redefining the Subject in Caribbean Literature." In *The Post-Colonial Studies Reader*, edited by Bill Ashcroft, Gareth Griffins, and Helen Tiffin, 332–35. New York: Routledge, 1995.

Davies, Carole Boyce. *Black Women, Writing and Identity: Migrations of the Subject*. New York: Routledge, 1994.

———. "Black British Women Writing the Anti-Imperialist Critique." In *Writing New Identities: Gender, Nation, and Immigration in Contemporary Europe*, edited by Gisela Brinker-Gabler and Sidonie Smith, 100–115. Minneapolis: University of Minnesota Press, 1997.

Davies, Carol Boyce, and Anne Adams Graves, eds. Introduction to *Ngambika: Studies of Women in African Literature*. Trenton, NJ: African World Press, 1986.

Deck, Ayanna, ed. Foreword to *Voices: Canadian Writers of African Descent*, xi–xiii. Toronto: HarperCollins Publishers Ltd., 1992.

Deliovsky, Katerina. "Transgressive Whiteness: The Social Construction of White Women Involved in Interracial Relationships with Black Men." In *Back to the Drawing Board: African-Canadian Feminisms*, edited by Njoki Nathani Wane, Katerina Deliovsky, and Erica Lawson, 234–61. Toronto: Sumach Press, 2002.

Desai, Gaurav. "Postcolonial Criticism in an African(ist) Frame." *Research in African Literatures* 29.1 (1998): 211–18.

Dickinson, Peter. "Duets, Duologues, and Black Diasporic Theatre: Djanet Sears, William Shakespeare, and Others." *Modern Drama* 45.2 (Summer 2002): 188–208.

Diedrich, Maria, Henry Louis Gates Jr., and Carl Pedersen, eds. Introduction to *Black Imagination and the Middle Passage*, 5–20. New York: Oxford University Press, 1999.

Donlon, Jocelyn Hazelwood. "Hearing Is Believing: Southern Racial Communities and Strategies of Story-Listening in Gloria Naylor and Lee Smith." *Twentieth Century Literature* 41 (1995): 16–35.

Du Bois, W. E. B. *The Souls of Black Folk*. New York: Penguin, 1969.

Dunton, Chris. *Make Man Talk True: Nigerian Drama in English Since 1970*. London: Hans Zell, 1992.

Ebeogu, Afam. "Feminism and Mediation of the Mythic in *Three Plays By Tess Onwueme*." *The Literary Griot* 3.1 (1991): 97–111.

Eckard, Paula Gallant. "The Prismatic Past in *Oral History* and *Mama Day*." *MELUS* 20.3 (1995): 121–35.

Edwards, Paul. "The Early African Presence in the British Isles." In *Essays on the History of Blacks in Britain: From Roman Times to the Mid-Twentieth Century*, edited by Jagdish Gundara and Ian Duffield, 9–29. Avebury: Aldershot, 1992.

Eke, Maureen N. "Diasporic Ruptures and (Re)membering History: Africa as Home and Exile in *Anowa* and *The Dilemma of a Ghost*." In *Emerging Perspectives on Ama Ata Aidoo*, edited by Marie Umeh, 61–78. Trenton, NJ: Africa World Press, 1996.

Eko, Ebele O. "Oral Tradition: The Bridge to Africa in Paule Marshall's *Praisesong for the Widow*." *The Western Journal of Black Studies* 10.3 (Fall 1986): 143–47.

Elia, Nadia. *Trances, Dances and Vociferations: Agency and Resistance in Africana Women's Narratives*. London: Routledge, 2001.

Eliot, T. S. *The Complete Poems and Plays 1909–1950*. New York: Harcourt, Brace and World, 1971.

Emecheta, Buchi. *The Bride Price*. London: Allison & Busby, 1976.

———. "Feminism with a small 'f.'" In *Criticism and Ideology*, edited by Kirsten Petersen, 173–85. Stockholm: Scandinavian Institute of African Studies, 1988.

———. *Head above Water.* Ibadan: Heinemann, 1986.
———. *In the Ditch.* Ibadan: Heinemann, 1979.
———. *Kehinde.* Ibadan: Heinemann, 1994.
———. *The Family.* New York: George Braziller, 1990.
———. *The Joys of Motherhood.* London: Allison & Busby, 1979.
———. *Second Class Citizen.* London: Fontana, 1977.
Erickson, E. H. *Life History and the Historical Movement.* New York: Norton, 1975.
Ervin, Hazel Arnett, ed. *African American Literary Criticism, 1773 to 2000.* New York: Twayne, 1999.
Espin, Olivia. "The Role of Gender and Emotion and Women's Experience of Migration." *Innovation: The European Journal of Social Sciences* 10.4 (December 1997): 445–61.
Fanon, Frantz. *Black Skin, White Masks.* Translated by Charles Lam Markmann. New York: Grove, [1952] 1967.
———. *The Wretched of the Earth.* Translated by Constance Farrington. New York: Penguin, 1967.
Felski, Rita. *Beyond Feminist Aesthetics.* London: Hutchinson Radius, 1989.
Felton, Sharon, and Michelle C. Loris, eds. *The Critical Response to Gloria Naylor.* Westport, CT: Greenwood, 1997.
Ferguson, Moira. "A Lot of Memory: An Interview with Jamaica Kincaid." *Kenyon Review* 16.1 (Winter 1994): 163–86.
———.*Colonialism and Gender Relations from Mary Wollstonecraft to Jamaica Kincaid: East Caribbean Connections.* New York: Columbia University Press, 1994.
———. *Jamaica Kincaid: Where the Land Meets the Body.* Charlottesville: University Press of Virginia, 1994.
———. "Of Bears & Bearings: Paule Marshall's Diverse *Daughters. MELUS* 24.1 (Spring 1999): 177–96.
Fishburn, Katherine. *Reading Buchi Emecheta.* Westport, CT: Greenwood Press, 1995.
Flanagan, Joseph. "The Seduction of History: Trauma, Re-Memory, and the Ethics of the Real." *Clio* 31.4 (2002): 387–402.
Forbes, Curdella. "Writing the Autobiography of My Father." *Small Axe: A Caribbean Journal of Criticism* 13 (March 2003): 172–76.
France, Anna Kay, and P. J. Corso, eds. "Changing Domestic and Family Roles." In *International Women Playwrights: Voices of Identity and Transformation,* 105–120. Lanham, MD: Scarecrow Press, 1993..
———. "Pioneer and First Generation Women Playwrights." *International Women Playwrights: Voices of Identity and Transformation,* 15–25. Lanham, MD: Scarecrow Press, 1993.
Freedman, Estelle B. *No Turning Back: The History of Feminism and the Future of Women.* New York: Ballentine, 2002.
Frye, Karla Y. E. "'An Article of Faith': Obeah and Hybrid Identities in Elizabeth Nunez-Harrell's *When Rocks Dance.*" In *Sacred Possessions: Vodou, Santeria, Obeah, and the Caribbean,* edited by Margarite Fernandez Olmos and Lizabeth Paravisini-Gebert, 195–215. New Brunswick, NJ: Rutgers University Press, 1997.
Garvey, Johanna X. K. "Passages to Identity: Re-Membering the Diaspora in Marshall, Phillips, and Cliff." In *Black Imagination and the Middle Passage,* edited by Maria Diedrich, Henry Louis Gates Jr., and Carl Pedersen, 255–70. Oxford: Oxford University Press, 1999.
Gaspar, David Barry. "From 'The Sense of Their Slavery': Slave Women and Resistance in

Antigua, 1632–1763." In *More than Chattel: Black Women and Slavery in the Americas*, edited by David Barry Gaspar and Darlene Clark Hine, 218–38. Bloomington: Indiana University Press, 1996.

Gennari, John. "Jazz Criticism: Its Development and Ideologies." *Black American Forum* 25.3 (Fall 1991): 449–523.

A Genuine Narrative of the Intended Conspiracy of the Negroes at Antigua. New York: Arno, 1972.

George, Kadija. Introduction to *Six Plays by Black and Asian Writers*, edited by Kadija George, 5–7. London: Aurora Metro Press, 1993.

Gerald, Carolyn F. "The Black Writer and His Role." In *African American Literary Criticism, 1773 to 2000*, edited by Hazel Arnett Ervin, 206–222. New York: Twayne, 1999.

Gikandi, Simon. "Narration in the Post-Colonial Moment: Merle Hodge's *Crick Crack, Monkey*." In *Past the Last Post: Theorizing Post-Colonialism and Post-Modernism*, edited by Ian Adam and Helen Tiffin, 13–22. New York: Harvester Wheatsheaf, 1993.

Gilroy, Paul. *The Black Atlantic: Modernity and Double Consciousness*. Cambridge, MA: Harvard University Press, 1993.

Glissant, Edouard. *Caribbean Discourse: Selected Essays*. Translated by J. Michael Dash. Charlottesville: University Press of Virginia, Caraf Books, 1989.

Goodman, Lisbeth. *Contemporary Feminist Theatres: To Each Her Own*. New York: Routledge, 1993.

Gourdine, Angeletta K. M. *The Difference Place Makes: Gender, Sexuality, and Diaspora Identity*. Columbus: The Ohio State University Press, 2003.

———. "Slavery in the Diaspora Consciousness: Ama Ata Aidoo's Conversations." In *Emerging Perspectives on Ama Ata Aidoo*, edited by Mari3 Umeh, 27–44. Trenton, NJ: Africa World Press, 1996.

Grier, William, and Price Cobbs. "Marriage and Love." Chap. 5 in *Black Rage* New York: Basic Books, Inc., 1968.

Griffin, Farah Jasmine. *"Who Set You Flowin'?" The African-American Migration Narrative*. Oxford: Oxford University Press, 1995.

Griffin, Gabriele. "Constitutive Subjectivities." *The European Journal of Women's Studies* 10.4 (2003): 377–94.

Hall, R. Mark. "Serving the Second Sun: The Men in Gloria Naylor's *Mama Day*." In *Gloria Naylor: Strategy and Technique, Magic and Myth*, edited by Shirley A. Stave, 77–95. London: Associated University Press, 2001.

Hall, Stuart. "New Ethnicities." In *Writing Black Britain: 1948–1998*, edited by James Procter, 265–75. Manchester: Manchester University Press, 2000.

Harris, Maria. "Not Black and/or White: Reading Racial Difference in Heliodorus' *Ethiopica* and Pauline Hopkins' *Of One Blood*." *African American Review* 35.3 (2001): 375–89.

Harris, Trudier. "Shaping a Narrator to an Audience, an Audience to a Tale." In *The Power of the Porch: The Storyteller's Craft in Zora Neale Hurston, Gloria Naylor, and Randall Kenan*, 53–104. Athens: University of Georgia Press, 1996.

Hawley, John C. "Coming to Terms: Buchi Emecheta's *Kehinde* and *The Birth of A 'Nation.'*" In *Emerging Perspectives on Buchi Emecheta*, edited by Marie Umeh, 333–48. Trenton, NJ: Africa World Press, 1996.

Hesse, Barnor. "Diasporicity: Black Britain's Post-Colonial Formations." In *Un/Settled Multiculturalisms: Diasporas, Entanglements, Transruptions*, edited by Barnor Hesse, 96–120. London: Zed Books, 2000.

Hill-Lubin, Mildred A. "'Tell Me, Nana': The Image of the Grandmother in the Works of

Ama Ata Aidoo." *SAGE* 5.1 (Summer 1988): 37–42.
Hodge, Merle. "Challenges of the Struggle for Sovereignty: Changing the World versus Writing Stories." In *Caribbean Women Writers: Essays from the First International Conference,* edited by Selwyn R. Cudjoe, 202–8. Wellesley, MA: Calaloux, 1990.
———. *Crick Crack, Monkey.* 1970; Oxford: Heinemann, 2000.
———. *For the Life of Laetitia.* New York: Farrar Straus, 1993.
Hogan, Patrick Colm. *Colonialism and Cultural Identity: Crises of Tradition in the Anglophone Literatures of India, Africa, and the Caribbean.* New York: State University of New York Press, 2000.
Hogg, J. A., and M. L. Frank. "Toward an Interpersonal Model of Codependence and Contradependence." *Journal of Counseling and Development* 70.3 (January/February 1992): 371–76.
Holmes, Julie. "Interview." *The Voice,* 9 July, 1999.
hooks, bell. *Talking Back: Thinking Feminist, Thinking Black.* Boston: South End Press, 1989.
Horne, Naana Banyiwa. "The Politics of Mothering: Multiple Subjectivity and Gendered Discourse in Aidoo's Plays." In *Emerging Perspectives on Ama Ata Aidoo,* edited by Marie Umeh, 505–32. Trenton, NJ: Africa World Press, 1996.
Houston, M. F., R. G. Kramer, and J. M. Barrett. "Female Predominance of Immigration to the United States since 1930: A First Look." *International Migration Review* 18 (1984): 908–63.
Hoving, Isabel. *In Praise of New Travelers: Reading Caribbean Women Writers.* Stanford, CA: Stanford University Press, 2001.
Hudson-Weems, Clenora. *Africana Womanism: Reclaiming Ourselves.* Troy: Bedford, 1998.
Hurston, Zora Neale. *Their Eyes Were Watching God.* New York: HarperCollins, 1937.
Ibsen, Henrik. *A Doll's House.* Translated by Frank McGuinness. London: Faber, 1996.
Ippolito, Emilia. *Caribbean Women Writers: Identity and Gender.* Rochester, NY: Camden House, 2000.
Ivory, James M. "Self-Colonization, Loneliness, and Racial Identity in Ama Ata Aidoo's *Our Sister Killjoy or Reflections from a Black-eyed Squint.*" In *Postcolonial Perspectives on Women Writers from Africa, the Caribbean, and the U.S.,* edited by Martin Japtok, 249–73. Trenton, NJ: Africa World Press, 2003.
JanMohamed, Abdul R. "The Economy of Manichean Allegory." In *The Post-Colonial Studies Reader,* edited by Bill Ashcroft, Gareth Griffiths, and Helen Tiffin, 18–23. New York: Routledge, 1994.
Johnson, Beverly A. "Revolutionary Solutions: Challenging Colonialist Attitudes in the Works of Paule Marshall." *CLA Journal* 45.4 (June 2002): 460–76.
Jonas, Joyce. *Anancy in the Great House: Ways of Reading West Indian Fiction.* New York: Greenwood, 1990.
Jones, Gayl. *The Healing.* Boston: Beacon Press, 1998.
Joseph, May. "Bodies outside the State: Black British Women Playwrights and the Limits of Citizenship." In *The Ends of Performance,* edited by Peggy Phelan and Jill Lowe, 197–213. New York: New York University Press, 1998.
Juhasz, Suzanne. "The Magic Circle: Fictions of the Good Mother in Gloria Naylor's *Mama Day.*" In *The Critical Response to Gloria Naylor,* edited by Sharon Felton and Michelle C. Loris, 129–42. Westport, CT: Greenwood, 1997.
Juneja, Renu, and James Kingsland. "The Caribbean-American Connection: A Paradox of Success and Subversion." *Journal of American Culture* 21.3 (Fall 1998): 63–67.

Jungle Fever. Directed by Spike Lee. New York: 40 Acres and a Mule Productions, 1991.
Kaplan, Jon. "Alison Sealy-Smith Bursts Bard's Bubble." *Now* (24–30 April 1997): 39.
Keizer, Arlene R. *Black Subjects: Identity Formation in the Contemporary Narrative of Slavery.* Ithaca, NY: Cornell University Press, 2004.
Kemp, Yakini. "Woman and Womanchild: Bonding and Selfhood in Three West Indian Novels." *Sage* 2.1 (Spring 1985): 24–27.
Kenyon, Olga. *The Writer's Imagination: Interviews with Major International Women Novelists.* Bradford, U.K.: Bradford University Print Unit, 1992.
Kincaid, Jamaica. *Annie John.* New York: Farrar, Straus and Giroux, 1985.
———. "Antigua Crossing." *Rolling Stone* (29 June 1978): 48–50.
———. *At the Bottom of the River.* New York: Farrar, Straus and Giroux, 1983.
———. *The Autobiography of My Mother.* New York: Plume, 1996.
———. *Lucy.* New York: Plume, 1990.
———. *My Brother.* New York: Farrar, Straus and Giroux, 1997.
———. *Mr. Potter.* New York: Farrar, Straus and Giroux, 2002.
———. *A Small Place.* New York: Farrar, Straus, and Giroux, 1988.
Knox, A. D. Foreword to *West Indian Migrants,* by R. B. Davison, v–vii. London: Oxford University Press, 1962.
Kolawole, Mary E. Modupe. *Womanism and African Consciousness.* Trenton, NJ: Africa World Press, 1997.
Kreilkamp, Ivan. "Jamaica Kincaid: Daring to Discomfort." *Publishers Weekly* (1 January 1996): 54–55.
LaCapra, Dominick. *Writing History, Writing Trauma.* Baltimore: Johns Hopkins University Press, 2001.
Larrier, Renee. The Poetics of Ex-ile: Simone Schwarz-Bart's Ton Beau Capitaine." *World Literature Today* 64.1 (Winter 1990): 57–59.
Lattin, Patricia Hopkins. "Naylor's Engaged and Empowered Narratee." *CLA Journal* 41.4 (1998): 452–69.
Lawrence, Leota S. "Three West Indian Heroines: An Analysis." *College Language Association Journal* 21 (1977): 238–50.
Leseur, Geta. "The Monster Machine and the White Mausoleum: Paule Marshall's Metaphors for Western Materialism." *CLA Journal* 39 (September 1995): 48–61.
———. "'Read Your History, Man': Bridging Racism, Paternalism, and Privilege in Paule Marshall's *The Chosen Place, The Timeless People.*" *CLA Journal* 44.1 (September 2000): 88–110.
Loomba, Ania. *Colonialism, Postcolonialism.* New York: Routledge, 1998.
Lynch, Joy M. "'Beyond Recognition': Heritage and Identity in Paule Marshall's *The Chosen Place, The Timeless People.*" In *Postcolonial Perspectives on Women Writers from Africa, the Caribbean, and the U.S.,* edited by Martin Japtok, 173–91. Trenton, NJ: Africa World Press, 2003.
MacDonald-Smythe, Antonia. *Making Homes in the West/Indies: Constructions of Subjectivity in the Writings of Michelle Cliff and Jamaica Kincaid.* New York: Garland, 2001.
Maes-Jelinek, Hena, and Bénédicte Ledent. "The Novel since 1970." In *A History of Literature in the Caribbean,* vol. 2, edited by A. James Arnold, 149–98. Amsterdam: John Benjamins, 2001.
Marshall, Paule. *The Chosen Place, The Timeless People.* New York: Random House, 1969.
———. *Daughters.* New York: Atheneum, 1991.

———. *The Fisher King.* New York: Scribner, 2000.
———. "From Poets in the Kitchen." *Callaloo* 18 (Spring/Summer 1983): 22–30.
———. *Praisesong for the Widow.* New York: Plume, 1983.
———. "Shaping the World of My Art." *New Letters* 40 (1973): 97–112.
McAdams, D. "Unity and Purpose in Human Lives: The Emergence of Identity as a Life Story." In *Studying Persons and Lives,* edited by A. Rabin et al. New York: Springer, 1990.
McClennen, Sophia A. *The Dialectics of Exile.* West Lafayette, IN: Purdue University Press, 2004.
Meisenhelder, Susan. "False Gods and Black Goddesses in Naylor's *Mama Day* and Hurston's *Their Eyes Were Watching God.*" *Callaloo* 23.4 (2000): 1440–48.
———. "The 'Whole Picture' in Gloria Naylor's *Mama Day.*" *African American Review* 27.3 (1993): 405–419.
Memmi, Albert. *The Colonizer and the Colonized.* Translated by Howard Greenfeld. Boston: Beacon Press, 1965.
Mensah, Joseph. *Black Canadians: History, Experiences, Social Conditions.* Halifax: Fernwood Publishing, 2002.
Metting, Fred. "The Possibilities of Flight: The Celebration of Our Wings in *Song of Solomon, Praisesong for the Widow,* and *Mama Day.*" *Southern Folklore* 55.2 (1998): 145–68.
Meyer, Adam. "Memory and Identity for Black, White, and Jew in Paule Marshall's *The Chosen Place, The Timeless People.*" *MELUS* 20.3 (Fall 1995): 9–120.
Miller, Adam David. "Women and Power, The Confounding of Gender, Race and Class." *The Black Scholar* 22.4 (Fall 1992): 48–51.
Minh-ha, Trinh T. "No Master Territories." In *The Post-Colonial Studies Reader,* edited by Bill Ashcroft, Gareth Griffiths, and Helen Tiffin, 215–18. London and New York: Routledge, 1995.
Moch, Leslie Page. Introduction to *European Migrants: Global and Local Perspectives,* edited by Dirk Hoerder and Leslie Moch. Boston: Northeastern University Press, 1996.
Mordecai, Pamela, and Betty Wilson, eds. *Her True-True Name: An Anthology of Women's Writing from the Caribbean.* Oxford: Heinemann, 1989.
Morris, Mervyn. *Is English We Speaking and Other Essays.* Kingston: Ian Randle, 1999.
Morrison, Toni. "Rootedness: The Ancestor as Foundation." In *African American Literary Criticism, 1773 to 2000,* edited by Hazel Arnett Ervin, 198–202. New York: Twayne, 1999.
Mühleisen, Susanne. "Encoding the Voice: Caribbean Women's Writing and Creole." In *Framing the Word: Gender and Genre in Caribbean Women's Writing,* 169–81. London: Whiting and Birch, 1996.
Mullard, Chris. *On being Black in Britain.* Washington, DC: Inscape Publishers, 1975.
Naipaul, V. S. *The Middle Passage: Impressions of Five Colonial Societies.* 1962; London: Picador, 2002.
Nazareth, Peter. "Paule Marshall's Timeless People." *New Letters* 40.1 (October 1973): 113–31.
Naylor, Gloria. *Mama Day.* New York: Random House, 1993.
Ngcobo, Lauretta. Introduction to *Let It Be Told: Essays by Black Women in Britain,* edited by Lauretta Ngcobo, 3–34. London: Virago, 1988.
Niesen de Abruna, Laura. "Jamaica Kincaid's Writing and the Maternal-Colonial Matrix." In *Caribbean Women Writers: Fiction in English,* edited by Maryse Condè and Thorunn

Lonsdale, 172–83. New York: St. Martin's, 1999.

———. "Twentieth Century Women Writers from the English-Speaking Caribbean." In *Caribbean Women Writers: Essays from the First International Conference*, edited by Selwyn R. Cudjoe, 86–97. Wellesley: Calaloux Publications, 1990.

Nnaemeka, Obiomma. "Nego-Feminism: Theorizing, Practicing, and Pruning Africa's Way." *Signs* 29.2 (2004): 357–85.

Oczkowicz, Edyta. "Jamaica Kincaid's *Lucy:* Cultural 'Translation' As a Case of Creative Exploration of the Past." *MELUS* 21.3 (Fall 1996): 143–57.

Odamtten, Vincent O. *The Art of Ama Ata Aidoo: Polylectics and Reading against Neocolonialism*. Gainesville: University Press of Florida, 1994.

Ogundipe-Leslie, Molara. *Re-Creating Ourselves: African Women & Critical Transformations*. Trenton, NJ: Africa World Press, 1994.

Olmstead, Jane. "The Pull of Memory and the Language of Place in Paule Marshall's *The Chosen Place, The Timeless People* and *Praisesong for the Widow*." *African American Review* 31.2 (Summer 1997): 249–67.

Onwueme, Tess. *The Missing Face*. New York: Africana Legacy, 1997.

Opoku, Kofi Asara. *West African Traditional Religion*. Accra: FEP International, 1978.

Opoku-Agyemang, N. Jane. "A Reading of Ama Ata Aidoo's *Anowa*." In *Nwanyibu: Womanbeing and African Literature*, edited by Phanuel A. Egejuru and Katu H. Katrak-Asmaa, 21–31. Trenton, NJ: Africa World Press, 1997.

Pannill, Linda. "From the 'Wordshop': The Fiction of Paule Marshall." *MELUS* 12.2 (Summer 1985): 63–73.

Paravisini-Gebert, Lizabeth. *Jamaica Kincaid: A Critical Companion*. Westport, CT: Greenwood, 1999.

Parmar, Pratibha. "Black Feminism: The Politics of Articulation." In *Writing Black Britain 1948–1998: An Interdisciplinary Anthology*, edited by James Procter, 293–99. Manchester: Manchester University Press, 2000.

Patterson, Orlando. *Slavery and Social Death: A Comparative Study*. Cambridge, MA: Harvard University Press, 1982.

Pedraza, Sylvia. "Women and Migration: The Social Consequences of Gender." *Annual Review of Sociology* 17 (1991): 303–325.

Perry, Donna. "Initiation in Jamaica Kincaid's *Annie John*." In *Caribbean Women Writers: Essays from the First International Conference*, edited by Selwyn R. Cudjoe, 245–53. Wellesley, MA: Calaloux, 1990.

Petersen, Kirstern Holst. Interview in *African Voices: Interviews with Thirteen African Writers*, edited by Raoul Granqvist and John Stotesbury, 17–20. Mundelstrup, Denmark: Dangaroo Press, 1989.

Pettis, Joyce. "Legacies of Community and History in Paule Marshall's *Daughters*." *Studies in Literary Imagination* 26.2 (Fall 1993): 89–100.

———. "A *MELUS* Interview: Paule Marshall." *MELUS* 17.4 (Winter 1991/1992): 117–29.

———. "'Talk' as Defensive Artifice: Merle Kinbona in *The Chosen Place, The Timeless People*." *African American Review* 26.1 (Spring 1992): 109–117.

Phillips, Maggi. "Engaging Dreams: Alternative Perspectives on Flora Nwapa, Buchi Emecheta, Ama Ata Aidoo, Bessie Head, and Tsitsi Dangarembga's Writing." *Research in African Literatures* 25.4 (1994): 89–103.

Pinckney, David. "Roots." *New York Times Review of Books* (28 April 1983): 26–30.

Pinnock, Winsome. *A Hero's Welcome*. In *Six Plays by Black and Asian Writers*, edited by

Kadija George, 21–54. Aurora: Metro Press, 1993.

———. *Leave Taking*. In *First Run: New Plays by New Writers,* edited by Kate Harwood, 139–89. London: Nick Hern Books, 1989.

———. *Talking in Tongues*. In *Black Plays: Three,* edited by Yvonne Brewster, 171–228. Great Britain: Methuen Drama, 1995.

Polkinghorne, D. E. *Narrative Knowing and the Human Sciences.* Albany: State University of New York Press, 1988.

Ponnuswami, Meenakshi. "Small Island People: Black British Women Playwrights." *The Cambridge Companion to Modern British Women Playwrights,* edited by Elaine Aston and Janelle Reinelt, 217–34. Cambridge: Cambridge University Press, 2000.

Procter, James, ed. Introduction to *Writing Black Britain 1948–1998: An Interdisciplinary Anthology,* 1–12. Manchester: Manchester University Press, 2000.

———. "Part Three: Mid-1980s to Late 1990s." In *Writing Black Britain 1948–1998: An Interdisciplinary Anthology,* 193–96. Manchester: Manchester University Press, 2000.

Ramchand, Kenneth. *The West Indian Novel and Its Background.* London: Heinemann Press, 1983.

Reyes, Angelita. *Mothering across Cultures: Postcolonial Representations.* Minneapolis: University of Minnesota Press, 2002.

Richardson, Alan. "Romantic Voodoo: Obeah and British Culture, 1797–1807." In *Sacred Possessions: Vodou, Santeria, Obeah, and the Caribbean,* edited by Margarite Fernandez Olmos and Lizabeth Paravisini-Gebert, 171–94. New Brunswick, NJ: Rutgers University Press, 1997.

Rody, Caroline. *The Daughter's Return: African-American and Caribbean Women's Fictions of History.* Oxford: Oxford University Press, 2001.

Rogers, Susan. "Embodying Cultural Memory in Paule Marshall's *Praisesong for the Widow.*" *African American Review* 34.1 (Spring 2000): 77–93.

Rogler, L. H. "International Migrations: A Framework for Directing Research." *American Psychologist* 49 (1994): 701–8.

Said, Edward W. *Culture and Imperialism.* New York: Vintage Books, 1993.

———. *Representations of the Intellectual: The 1993 Reith Lectures.* London: Vintage, 1994.

———. *The World, the Text, and the Critic.* Cambridge, MA: Harvard University Press, 1983.

Sanders, Leslie. "History at Negro Creek; Djanet Sears' *The Adventures of a Black Girl in Search of God.*" In *Testifyin': Contemporary African Canadian Drama: Vol. II,* edited by Djanet Sears, 487–89. Toronto: Playwrights Canada Press, 2003.

Sayyid, S. "Beyond Westphalia: Nations and Diasporas." In *Un/Settled Multiculturalisms: Diasporas, Entanglements, Transruptions,* edited by Barnor Hesse, 33–51. London: Zed Books, 2000.

Schmidt-Grozinger, Dagmar. "Problems of the Immigrant in Commonwealth Literature: Kamala Markandaya, *The Nowhere Man,* Buchi Emecheta, *Adah's Story.*" In *Tensions between North and South: Studies in Modern Commonwealth Literature and Culture,* edited by Edith Merke. Wurzburg: Konigshausen and Neumann, 1990.

Schulte, Bernd. "Cultural Transfer and Cultural Transformation: Attempts at Exploring Dimensions of 'Interculturalism' in the New Literatures in English." In *Mediating Cultures Probleme des Kulturtransfers: Perspektiven fur Forschung und Lehre,* edited by Norbert H. Platz, 29–39. Essen: Die Blaue Eule, 1991.

Sears, Djanet. *The Adventures of a Black Girl in Search of God.* In *Testifyin': Contemporary African Canadian Drama: Vol. II,* edited by Djanet Sears, 491–604. Toronto: Playwrights Canada Press, 2003.

———. *Afrika Solo.* Toronto: Sister Vision Press, 1991.

———. *Harlem Duet.* In *Testifyin': Contemporary African Canadian Drama: Vol. I*, edited by Djanet Sears, 560–631. Toronto: Playwrights Canada Press, 2000.

———. "Notes of a 'Colored Girl': Thirty-two Short Reasons Why I Write for the Theatre." http://www.fb10.uni-bremen.de/anglistik/kerkoff/blackcanadian/searsreasons.html

Sears, Djanet, and Alison Sealy-Smith. "The Nike Method." Interview with Ric Knowles. *Canadian Theatre Review* 97 (1998): 24–30.

Sesay, Kadija. Introduction to *IC3: The Penguin Book of New Black Writing in Britain*, edited by Courttia Newland and Kadija Sesay, xii–xiv. London: Penguin Books, 2000.

Shyllon, Folarin. "The Black Presence and Experience in Britain." In *Essays on the History of Blacks in Britain: From Roman Times to the Mid-Twentieth Century*, edited by Jagdish Gundara and Ian Duffield, 202–224. Aldershot: Avebury Publishers, 1992.

Simmel, Georg. "The Metropolis and Mental Life." In *Art in Theory*, edited by Charles Harrison and Paul Wood, 130–35. Oxford, UK: Blackwell, 1992.

Simmons, Diane. *Jamaica Kincaid.* New York: Twayne, 1994.

Small, Valerie. "The Importance of Oral Tradition to Black Theatre." In *Six Plays by Black and Asian Women*, edited by Kadija George, 8–11. London: Aurora Metro Press, 1993.

Smith, Daniel Jordan. "These Girls Na War-O: Premarital Sexuality and Modern Identity in Southeastern Nigeria." *Africa Today* 47.3 (2000): 99–120.

Soyinka, Wole. *Myth, Literature and the African World.* Cambridge: Cambridge University Press, 1976.

Stander, Bella. "A Conversation with Paule Marshall." *Albermarle* (February/March 2001). http://www.bellastander.com/writer/Paule.htm (accessed April 2006).

Steady, Filomina Chioma. "African Feminism: A Worldwide Perspective." In *Women in Africa and the African Diaspora*, edited by Rosalyn Terborg-Penn and Andrea Benton Rushing, 3–21. Washington, DC: Howard University Press, 1996.

Talib, Ismail S. *The Language of Postcolonial Literatures: An Introduction.* New York: Routledge, 2002.

Tastsoglou, Evangelia. "Race and the Politics of Personal Relationships: Focus on Black Canadian Women." *Affilia: Journal of Women and Social Work* 17:1 (Spring 2002): 93–111.

Thomas, Ena V. "*Crick Crack, Monkey*: A Picaresque Perspective." In *Caribbean Women Writers: Essays from the First International Conference*, edited by Selwyn R. Cudjoe, 209–214. Wellesley, MA: Calaloux, 1990.

Thorpe, Marjorie. "The Problem of Cultural Identification in *Crick Crack, Monkey*." *Savacou* 13 (1977): 31–38.

Tiffin, Helen. "The Institution of Literature." In *A History of Literature in the Caribbean*, vol. 2, edited by A. James Arnold, 42–66. Amsterdam: John Benjamins, 2001.

Timothy, Helen Pyne. "Adolescent Rebellion and Gender Relations in *At the Bottom of the River* and *Annie John*." In *Caribbean Women Writers: Essays from the First International Conference*, edited by Selwyn R. Cudjoe, 233–42. Wellesley, MA: Calaloux, 1990.

Timothy, Helen Pyne. "Language as Subversion in Postcolonial Literature: The Case of Two Caribbean Women Writers." *MaComère: Journal of the Association of Caribbean Women Writers* 1 (1998): 101–114.

Torres-Saillant, Silvio. *Caribbean Poetics: Toward an Aesthetic of West Indian Literature.* Cambridge: Cambridge University Press, 1997.

Tucker, Lindsey. "Recovering the Conjure Woman: Texts and Contexts in Gloria Naylor's

Mama Day." *African American Review* 28.2 (1994): 173–88.
United States Department of Health and Human Services. "Why Marriage Matters." African American Healthy Marriage Initiative: Roundtable Summary Report. Washington, DC: GPO, 2003. http://www.acf.dhhs.gov/healthymarriage/pdf/AAHMI_RT.pdf (accessed April 2006).
Utudjian, Elaine Saint-Andre. "Two Nigerian Dramatists." *Commonwealth Essays and Studies* 15.1 (Autumn 1992): 96–101.
Walcott, Rinaldo. *Black Like Who: Writing Black Canada.* Toronto: Insomniac Press, 2003.
Walker, Alice. "A Writer Because of, Not In Spite of, Her Children." In *In Search of Our Mothers' Gardens: Womanist Prose,* 66–70. San Diego: Harcourt Brace, Jovanovich, 1983.
Wall, Cheryl. "Extending the Line: From *Sula* to *Mama Day.*" *Callaloo* 23.4 (2000): 1449–63.
Williams, Martin T. *The Jazz Tradition.* New York: Oxford University Press, 1983.
Williamson, George. *A Reader's Guide to T. S. Eliot.* London: Thames and Hudson, 1955.
Wisker, Gina. *Post-Colonial and African American Women's Writing: A Critical Introduction.* New York: St. Martin's Press, 2000.
Woolf, Virginia. *Three Guineas.* London: Hogarth Press, 1943.
Wordsworth, William. "Michael." In *English Romantic Writers,* edited by David Perkins, 271–76. New York: Harcourt Brace Jovanovich, 1967.
Young, Lola. "What Is Black British Feminism." *Women: A Cultural Review* 11.1/2 (2000): 45–60.

[INDEX]

Abiku spirit, 17
Achebe, Chinua, 74
acts of reclamation, 11, 12, 166, 168–69
African oral traditions, 11
Aidoo, Ama Ata, 5–6, 15–16, 19–20, 23–30, 49, 56, 161, 183
ancestors, 10, 17–19, 22, 30, 76–77, 88–92, 107, 121, 128, 130–31, 134–35, 137, 140, 150–53, 159, 163, 169, 173, 175, 179–81
Angelou, Maya, 95
Anzaldua, Gloria, 15

"been-to," 16, 27, 30
Berrian, Brenda, 66–67
Bhabha, Homi, 7, 8, 22, 35–36, 42–43, 49, 64, 83, 162, 175, 180–81
The Black Atlantic (Gilroy), 151, 162
Black Imagination and the Middle Passage (Diedrich, Gates, and Pedersen), 91
Black Like Who? Writing Black Canada (Walcott), 157
Black Skin, White Masks (Fanon), 35, 143, 174
Black Subjects (Keizer), 2, 156
Black Women, Writing and Identity (Davies), 2, 15, 20, 36, 58, 76
Brah, Avtar, 34, 37, 43, 45–48, 50–51
Busia, Abena, 9, 106

Carib Indians, 10, 124
Caribbean Poetics: Toward an Aesthetic of West Indian Literature (Torres-Saillant), 140
Cartographies of Diaspora (Brah), 37
Cesaire, Aime, 61

Chancy, Myriam, 42, 47, 49
Cixous, Hélène, 37, 47, 49
Clark, Vèvè, 40
Clarke, George Elliott, 11
The Colonizer and the Colonized (Memmi), 35
communitas, 40, 50
Condè, Maryse, 140, 143
conflicting modernities, 8, 95
Cousin, Geraldine, 48, 50
Culture and Imperialism (Said), 55, 64

Dance, Daryl Cumber, 108, 111
Dash, Michael, 61, 76, 83, 103
Davies, Carol Boyce, 9, 21, 34, 36, 38, 58, 76
diaspora consciousness, 2
The Difference Place Makes (Gourdine), 2, 169
dilemma tale, 16, 24, 26
double-consciousness, 84, 174
Du Bois, W. E. B., 49, 174
Dunton, Chris, 179

El Saadawi, Nawal, 56
Emecheta, Buchi, 4, 5, 7, 52–54, 56, 61–66, 68–74, 161, 183–84
The Empire Writes Back (Ashcroft, Griffith, and Tiffin), 61–62, 172

Fanon, Frantz, 8, 12, 35, 38, 49, 61, 119, 124–25, 143, 173–74, 177
Felski, Rita, 60
Fishburn, Katherine, 61–62, 72

Gerald, Carolyn F., 129–31, 147

Gilroy, Paul, 151, 162
Glissant, Edouard, 11, 140, 144–45
Gourdine, Angeletta, 19, 27, 31, 169
Griffin, Farah Jasmine, 79, 95
Griffin, Gabriele, 37, 47

Hall, Stuart, 7, 32, 34–36, 43
Harris, Trudier, 77, 80
Head, Bessie, 56
The Healing (Jones), 183
hegemonic codes, 7, 34
Hodge, Merle, 5, 10, 139–40, 142–48, 151–53, 161
hooks, bell, 41
Hoving, Isabel, 41, 49
Hurston, Zora Neale, 49, 183

identity: black female identity formation, 3, 36, 52, 127, 137; black identity, 32–34, 38, 78, 84; collective identity, 16, 60, 150; competing identities, 3, 6, 141; conflicting identities, 15–16; cultural identities, 34, 83, 174; divergent identities, 19; *entredeux*, 34, 37, 47–50; hybrid(ity), 3,7, 8, 22, 35, 42–43, 50, 64, 83–84, 123, 128, 130, 135, 137, 140, 143, 152–53, 171, 182; identity crisis, 2, 98, 174, 179; identity dilemmas, 5; identity formation, 1, 2, 11, 52, 55, 70; inbetweenesss/living in the interstices, 8, 35, 42–43, 47–48, 63, 140, 162; language and identity, 141; migration and identity, 36; ruptured identity, 7, 50; shifting identities, 9; tropological site of identity disintegration, 5

Jones, Gayl, 42, 183

Kalawole, Mary Modupe, 71–72
Keizer, Arlene, 2, 156
Kincaid, Jamaica, 5, 10, 32, 117–21, 128, 130–34, 140, 161

LaCapra, Dominick, 152
The Location of Culture (Bhabha), 64, 162, 175, 180–81
Locations of Culture (Bhabha), 83

Marshall, Paule, 4, 5, 9, 96–98, 100, 102–3, 107–8, 110–12, 115–16, 140, 161
Meisenhelder, Susan, 77, 80, 85, 91
Memmi, Albert, 12, 35, 177
Mensah, James, 11, 156
Middle Passage(s), 2–6, 8–9, 19, 32, 76, 78, 89, 91, 95, 108, 119, 125, 130–31, 133, 140, 144, 150–52, 155, 167–68, 171, 180, 182
migration, 1–2, 6, 8, 12, 15, 19, 23, 28, 30, 32–35, 37, 39, 43–50, 52–54, 62–64, 72, 74, 78, 94–97, 103–5, 112–13, 115–16, 118, 130, 133, 137–38, 140–41, 145, 147–49, 153, 156, 161, 171, 178, 182–84; female migration, 53–54; The Great Migration, 79; migration and identity, 2, 3, 139; migration narratives, 2, 4, 95; migratory narratives, 2; narratives of separation and loss, 3, 5; reverse migration, 5, 101, 161; reversion, 11, 140; ritual migration, 7, 35; trope of exile, 49; transoceanic migration, 54
Moorings and Metaphors (Holloway), 2
Morrison, Toni, 76–77, 95, 135, 150
Mothering across Cultures (Reyes), 134
Mullard, Chris, 33, 46

Naipaul, V. S., 143, 146, 151
Naylor, Gloria, 5, 8, 9, 76–78, 80–81, 84–86, 89–95
Nkrumah, Kwame, 6, 15, 20, 30
Nwapa, Flora, 16, 56

Obeah(s), 10, 49–50, 103, 122–23, 134, 136
On being Black in Britain (Mullard), 33
Onwueme, Tess, 4, 5, 12, 161, 171–82

Parmar, Pratibha, 34
performance(s) of diaspora, 7, 34, 37, 41, 48, 50
Phillips, Caryl, 33
Phillips, Maggi, 6, 23
Pinnock, Winsome, 5, 7, 33–35, 37, 39, 41–44, 46, 48–51, 161, 183

Ponnuswami, Meenakshi, 33, 39
Postcolonial Perspectives on Women Writers from Africa, the Caribbean, and the U. S. (Japtok), 2
Procter, James, 7

racism, 9–10, 19, 33, 49, 53, 57–58, 61–62, 95, 110, 146, 158, 165, 168–69, 177
Ramchand, Kenneth, 36
Reading Buchi Emecheta (Fishburn), 72
Reconstruction era, 11
Representations of the Intellectual (Said), 63
Reyes, Angelita, 118, 122–23, 134–35
Rootprints (Cixous), 37

Said, Edward, 55, 59, 63–64
Sanders, Leslie Catherine, 11, 165, 167–68
Searching for Safe Spaces (Chancy), 42
Sears, Djanet, 4, 5, 11, 12, 155–70
sexism, 9, 10, 49
slavery, 2, 1, 16, 19–20, 22–23, 125, 128, 130–31, 140, 151–52, 155–56, 160, 163, 168–69, 174; transatlantic slave trade, 53, 171; triangular slave trade, 5; slave trade, 16, 19, 22–23, 30, 125
Slavery and Social Death (Patterson), 125
Soyinka, Wole, 33, 62
Sutherland, Efua, 15

Talking Back (hooks), 41
Their Eyes Were Watching God (Hurston), 49, 183
Their Place on the Stage (Brown-Guillory), 3
themes in black women's texts: alienation/displacement/dislocation/disruptions/loss/separation, 3–9, 12, 30, 32–35, 38–39, 48–51, 55, 62, 64, 107, 132, 141, 143, 148, 152, 155, 157–60, 162–63, 165–69, 171–72, 179, 182, 184; ambivalence, 3, 7, 10; ancestral memory/ancestry, 30, 77, 97, 108, 118, 123–24, 128, 180; betrayal, 63, 122, 127, 129, 162, 164; border crossings, 4–5, 72, 161; economic exploitation, 63, 117; erasure, 11; estrangement, 37; female bonds, 39, 165; female subjugation, 68; freedom, 10, 71, 117–18, 123, 125, 132–34; historical dissonance, 19–20, 31; heal/healers/healing/healing rituals, 3–6, 9–10, 12, 18, 24, 39–42, 46, 99–101, 107–8, 112, 118, 122–23, 131, 134, 155, 163–69, 171, 179–82; liberation strategies, 8, 170; longing for home/mother(land), 3, 37, 46, 51, 54, 63, 69, 140–41, 148, 153–54, 180; marginalization 8, 10, 38, 54, 61, 69, 119–20, 124; maternal subjectivity, 6, 17; motherhood, 16–17, 19, 112; polygamy, 67–68; reconfiguration, 96–97, 100–101, 103–5, 107, 109, 115–16; resistance, 128, 168; rites of passage, 9, 40, 50, 180–81; self-actualization, 56, 84; self-determination, 10, 118; self-empowerment, 117; self-exile, 7, 15–16, 30; self-exploration, 15; self-invention, 135–36; self-reconstruction, 7, 71; self-redemption, 62; self-rehabilitation, 8, 74; self-renewal, 103; spirituality, 64, 107, 122–23, 135, 166; tradition and modernity, 4, 8, 59, 70, 73–74, 177; transformation, 40–41, 52–54, 58–62, 64, 68, 70, 82, 92–93, 97, 103, 106–8, 111–12, 116, 165, 173; unbelonging, 51, 58, 67, 158, 184; woman's identity, 16; women on their way to becoming whole, 3,12; social spaces of survivability, 3; trope of moisture, 41

Walcott, Derek, 33
Walcott, Renaldo, 11, 157
Walker, Alice, 71, 95
Wilentz, Gay, 107–8
Women in Dramatic Place and Time (Cousin), 48
The World, the Text, and the Critic (Said), 59
The Wretched of the Earth (Fanon), 65
Writing History, Writing Trauma (LaCapra), 152

www.ingramcontent.com/pod-product-compliance
Lightning Source LLC
Chambersburg PA
CBHW020947230426
43666CB00005B/204